Big Data and the Welfar

A core principle of the welfare state is that everyone pays taxes or contributions in exchange for universal insurance against social risks such as sickness, old age, unemployment, and plain bad luck. This solidarity principle assumes that everyone is a member of a single national insurance pool, and it is commonly explained by poor and asymmetric information, which undermines markets and creates the perception that we are all in the same boat. Living in the midst of an information revolution, this is no longer a satisfactory approach. This book explores, theoretically and empirically, the consequences of "big data" for the politics of social protection. Torben Iversen and Philipp Rehm argue that more and better data polarize preferences over public insurance and often segment social insurance into smaller, more homogenous, and less redistributive pools, using cases studies of health and unemployment insurance and statistical analyses of life insurance, credit markets, and public opinion.

Torben Iversen is Harold Hitchings Burbank Professor of Political Economy at Harvard University. His most recent book (co-authored with David Soskice) is *Democracy and Prosperity: Reinventing Capitalism through a Turbulent Century* (2019).

Philipp Rehm is Associate Professor of Political Science at the Ohio State University. His research interests are located at the intersection of Political Economy and Political Behavior.

CAMBRIDGE STUDIES IN COMPARATIVE POLITICS

OTHER BOOKS IN THE SERIES

Christopher Adolph, *Bankers, Bureaucrats, and Central Bank Politics: The Myth of Neutrality*
Michael Albertus, *Autocracy and Redistribution: The Politics of Land Reform*
Michael Albertus, *Property without Rights: Origins and Consequences of the Property Rights Gap*
Santiago Anria, *When Movements Become Parties: The Bolivian MAS in Comparative Perspective*
Ben W. Ansell, *From the Ballot to the Blackboard: The Redistributive Political Economy of Education*
Ben W. Ansell and Johannes Lindvall, *Inward Conquest: The Political Origins of Modern Public Services*
Ben W. Ansell and David J. Samuels, *Inequality and Democratization: An Elite-Competition Approach*
Adam Michael Auerbach, *Demanding Development: The Politics of Public Goods Provision in India's Urban Slums*
Ana Arjona, *Rebelocracy: Social Order in the Colombian Civil War*
Leonardo R. Arriola, *Multi-Ethnic Coalitions in Africa: Business Financing of Opposition Election Campaigns*

Continued after the index

Big Data and the Welfare State

How the Information Revolution Threatens Social Solidarity

TORBEN IVERSEN

Harvard University

PHILIPP REHM

Ohio State University

CAMBRIDGE
UNIVERSITY PRESS

CAMBRIDGE
UNIVERSITY PRESS

University Printing House, Cambridge CB2 8BS, United Kingdom

One Liberty Plaza, 20th Floor, New York, NY 10006, USA

477 Williamstown Road, Port Melbourne, VIC 3207, Australia

314–321, 3rd Floor, Plot 3, Splendor Forum, Jasola District Centre,
New Delhi – 110025, India

103 Penang Road, #05–06/07, Visioncrest Commercial, Singapore 238467

Cambridge University Press is part of the University of Cambridge.

It furthers the University's mission by disseminating knowledge in the pursuit of
education, learning, and research at the highest international levels of excellence.

www.cambridge.org
Information on this title: www.cambridge.org/9781009151368
DOI: 10.1017/9781009151405

First published 2022

A catalogue record for this publication is available from the British Library.

Library of Congress Cataloging-in-Publication Data
Names: Iversen, Torben, author. | Rehm, Philipp Benjamin, 1977– author.
Title: Big data and the welfare state : how the information revolution threatens social
solidarity / Torben Iversen, Harvard University, Massachusetts, Philipp Rehm, Ohio
State University.
Description: Cambridge, United Kingdom ; New York, NY : Cambridge University
Press, 2022. | Series: Cambridge studies in comparative politics | Includes
bibliographical references and index.
Identifiers: LCCN 2021058391 (print) | LCCN 2021058392 (ebook) | ISBN
9781009151368 (hardback) | ISBN 9781009151399 (paperback) | ISBN
9781009151405 (ebook)
Subjects: LCSH: Social security – Political aspects. | Big data – Social aspects. | Big data –
Political aspects. | Risk – Sociological aspects. | Public welfare. | Welfare state. | BISAC:
POLITICAL SCIENCE / General
Classification: LCC HD7091 .I94 2022 (print) | LCC HD7091 (ebook) | DDC 368.4–
dc23/20211215
LC record available at https://lccn.loc.gov/2021058391
LC ebook record available at https://lccn.loc.gov/2021058392

ISBN 978-1-009-15136-8 Hardback
ISBN 978-1-009-15139-9 Paperback

To Lea.
To Isabelle and Esben.

Contents

List of Figures	*page* viii
List of Tables	x
Acknowledgments	xii
1 Introduction	1
2 Theoretical Framework	15
3 A Brief Analytical History of Social Protection	44
4 Private Markets for Life and Health Insurance	70
5 Credit Markets	105
6 Labor Market Risks	159
7 Conclusion	188
References	204
Index	219

Figures

2.1 Equilibria in the private insurance network game
 with private information   *page* 24
2.2 Equilibria in the private insurance network game
 with shared information   28
2A.1 Example of a pooled equilibrium with three risk groups   41
3.1 Summary of our historical–analytical argument   55
3.2 Information and the actual and perceived distribution
 of risks   57
4.1 Measures of medical information over time   85
4.2 Predicted life insurance penetration   88
4.3 Support for private health insurance plan versus
 government insurance plan (USA)   98
5.1 Household debt as a percentage of disposable income   106
5.2 Financialization of advanced economies, 1970–2020   107
5.3 Interest rate spread over time (year–month level)   122
5.4 FICO scores in sample, over time   123
5.5 Interest rate spread over time (year–month-FICO-2d level)   125
5.6 Interest rate spread over time (year–month-FICO-2d level),
 at FICO-2d   129
5.7 RD estimate at FICO-2d levels, different polynomials   130
5.8 Distribution of default risk before and after the 2005
 Hartz IV reforms   133
5A.1 The effect of public spending on the location of the
 distribution of income in the bad state relative to T_i 145

5A.2 The relationship between income in the bad state and
      the probability of repayment   145
5A.3 The relationship between income and being in arrears   147
 6.1 Total information and private information over time   168
 6.2 Total information and private information over time
      (Shapley decomposition)   170
 6.3 Total information and attitude polarization   173
 6.4 Political discussion and political preferences   175
 6.5 Membership fees for UIFs with highest and lowest fees   178
 6.6 Average fees and UIF membership in Sweden, 2004–2020   181

Tables

2.1 Time inconsistency and public versus private provision
(examples) *page* 34
2.2 Information and social insurance 39
4.1 Private spending on health as a percentage of GDP
and total health spending 90
4A.1 Life insurance penetration, information, and partisanship
(ECM) 104
5.1 Regression discontinuity estimates 127
5.2 Homeownership (EVS) 135
5.3 Homeownership (GSOEP) 136
5.4 Homeownership (GSOEP), conditional on being
homeowner pre-reform 137
5.5 Homeownership (GSOEP), rich versus poor employed 137
5.6 Cross-national correlation matrix 139
5A.1 Different bandwidth selection procedures 149
5A.2 Different kernel functions 151
5A.3 Covariate adjusted estimates 152
5A.4 Different specification of the running variable I 153
5A.5 Different specification of the running variable II 154
5A.6 Sensitivity to observations near the cutoff (donut hole
approach) 155
5A.7 Placebo outcomes 156
5A.8 Placebo cutoffs 157
5A.9 Mass points 158

6A.1 Total information and attitude polarization
        (OLS regression)   185
6A.2 Total information and attitude polarization (robust
        regression)   186
6A.3 Political discussion and political preferences (European
        Social Survey)   186

Acknowledgments

This book has been a long time in the making, and we are grateful for all the encouragement, comments, criticisms, and suggestions we have received over the years. We had the opportunity to present parts of the book to various audiences, and in all instances, we were impressed by the enthusiasm, thoughtfulness, and sometimes controversy that the topic evoked. From being a dull matter only of interest to computer nerds, Big Data has evidently become a topic of immense concern to many and one that arouses considerable passion across the social sciences and beyond!

We gratefully acknowledge the feedback we received at the following events and venues: the 26th International Conference of Europeanists (2019), the APSA Annual Meeting (2016, 2018), Aarhus University (2016, 2019), Duke University (2016), Hanse-Wissenschaftskolleg (2019), London School of Economics (2019), McGill University (2017), Nuffield College at University of Oxford (2019), Radcliffe Institute Fellowship Program (2020), SciencesPo (2019), the UB Law School at The State University of New York (2016), University of Amsterdam (2019), University of Bremen (2019), University of Duisburg-Essen (2019), University of Konstanz (2020), University of Pittsburgh (2017), Vienna University of Economics (2016), Wissenschaftszentrum Berlin (2016), and Yale University (2017).

We are indebted to too many colleagues who have supported this project one way or another to list them all. Nevertheless, we would like to specifically thank Jim Alt, Pablo Beramendi, Brian Burgoon, Marius Busemeyer, Jane Gingrich, Jacob Hacker, Peter Hall, Agnar Helgason, Herbert Kitschelt, Philip Manow, Vittorio Merola, Bruno Palier, Jonas

Pontusson, David Rueda, David Soskice, Kathy Thelen, and Kees van Kesbergen.

Carla Welch spent many hours copyediting the manuscript, and we are grateful for her meticulous work. We are much indebted to the two anonymous reviewers from Cambridge University Press who wrote detailed reports and provided insightful comments that greatly contributed to our revisions. Thank you! Finally, we are very grateful to Sara Doskow (then senior editor at Cambridge University Press), who expertly and efficiently guided our manuscript through the review process.

Philipp would like to express his sincere gratitude to the Department of Politics at Princeton University for hosting him during a sabbatical and the Hanse-Wissenschaftskolleg in Delmenhorst for hosting him as a EURIAS fellow (co-funded by Marie Skłodowska-Curie Actions, under the 7th Framework Programme) while he was working on the manuscript. Both stays were extremely satisfying and informative – special thanks to Nolan McCarty, Susanne Fuchs, Wolfgang Stenzel, and Kerstin Schill. He would also like to thank his colleagues in the Department of Political Science as well as the Ohio State University for their support throughout the project. Finally, he would like to thank his wife, Inés, for her patience and love.

Torben would like to express his profound gratitude to the Radcliffe Institute for Advanced Study at Harvard University, where he spent an invaluable year as a fellow working on this book. The in-person experience was upended by COVID, but Claudia Rizzini and Rebecca Haley worked tirelessly to create a vibrant and supportive virtual community. Thanks to the lockdown, Torben's wife, Charla, probably heard more about this project than she would have cared to, but her questions and feedback made it better.

Our children – Lea on Philipp's side and Esben and Isabelle on Torben's – and their generation will have to navigate dramatic social and economic change caused by the information revolution and climate change (among other factors) that will rival the upheavals of past revolutions. We are immensely proud of them and know they have the grit and empathy to face the challenges ahead. We dedicate this book to them.

Introduction

While we were writing this book, one of the authors fell ill. The diagnosis required two CAT scans, two MRIs, consultation with an otoneurologist, an otolaryngologist, and an audiologist, while the treatment required a week in the hospital, a total of fifteen hours of surgery carried out by a team of highly skilled neurosurgeons and an anesthesiologist, with several nurses on hand. Another six weeks of recovery involved physical therapy and multiple checkups. A back-of-the-envelope calculation suggests that the whole episode cost in excess of US$250,000, all of which was paid by a private insurance company, Blue Cross Blue Shield, via a standard employer-sponsored insurance plan. Nothing presaged this ordeal: no family history, no risky behavior – it was a bolt from the blue.

An episode like this would have cost many uninsured American workers their lifesavings, their house, and perhaps their job. But, while the cost to an uninsured individual of an adverse event such as this is potentially catastrophic, the cost to others in the insurance pool is very small: less than one cent, assuming the cost is spread evenly across all policyholders. That's the point of insurance: the lucky subsidize the unlucky. While private health insurance in America is not cheap, the payout, when it is needed, can be huge and sometimes literally lifesaving. For the same reason, insurers have a strong incentive to shun bad risks, and so do people who believe they are at low risk.

The previously mentioned event would have been impossible to predict ex ante, but information often allows those in bad health to buy good plans, which drives up prices and pushes out good risks and that, in turn, increases prices even further in a spiraling logic. In the insurance litera-ture, this is called adverse selection. Adverse selection is not the only reason insurance markets break down, but it is an important one and it helps explain why, inter alia, medical insurance in most rich democracies is public. Even in the USA, the elderly are covered by a public plan, Medicare, which would be exceedingly expensive if offered as a private plan. Private health insurance mostly covers non-extreme risks among the nonpoor and non-elderly population. Provided that people and insurers are not well-informed about risks, further segmentation is less likely. Yet, for much of the past three decades, we have seen growing risk segmentation, constrained by regulations that limit discrimination. More information about risks tends to cause fragmentation and political polarization between those at low and those at high risk.

This book is about the political tug-of-war between segmentation and integration, with more and better information favoring risk differentiation and segmentation, and democratic politics historically driving risk pooling and integration. We seek to deepen our understanding of the forces that integrate versus those that segregate and how this balance has shifted over time.

All forms of insurance are affected by incomplete information, and changes in the quantity, quality, or shareability of information can transform insurance. We want to understand how the information revolution influences social insurance. With this in mind, our book asks what happens to the politics of social protection, and to inequality, when information about risks to health, employment, credit, life, and so on becomes more widely available, more accurate, and more shareable. We find that more information tends to result in the fragmentation of insurance pools, increases inequality of access to and coverage of social insurance and credit, and intensifies polarization of welfare state preferences.

To appreciate the powerful impact that more, better, and increasingly shareable information has on insurance, we only need to look at the automobile insurance industry. Since its introduction about a century ago, car insurance has suffered from a widely acknowledged (asymmetric) information problem. To be able to charge actuarially fair prices, insurance companies need to tie premiums to driving behavior, yet driving behavior cannot be directly observed.[1] Therefore, companies traditionally

---

[1] When an insurance company cannot distinguish between good and bad risks, it must charge similar premiums for everyone. But these premiums are "too high" for good risks, and this leads to adverse selection: with these relatively high premiums, insurance is only attractive to bad drivers, leaving the company with only high-risk customers. For insurance markets to survive, however, good and bad risks have to be pooled. In car insurance

rely on static, auxiliary information to assess a customer's probability of causing an accident. Traditional risk classification in the car industry groups customers into broad risk classes, based on their age, gender, driving history, occupation, place of residency, car model, and the like.

However, a few years ago, car insurance companies started to offer so-called pay-how-you-drive (PHYD) policies that directly link a customer's premium to their driving behavior. These insurance policies were rolled out once it became possible to cheaply observe and accurately report individual driving behavior through GPS-enabled devices (including apps on cell phones). These trackers can record and transmit – in real time – information that has actuarial relevance for the insurer. Examples include distance driven, time of day, absolute and relative speed (relative to speed limits), acceleration, braking events and their harshness, swerving, cornering forces, and so on.

The ability to objectively track behavior at the microlevel ("micro-tracking") alleviates the widely recognized problem of asymmetric information that hampers insurance markets. PHYD policies that tie insurance rates to individual driving behavior are attractive for insurance companies because they allow them to use fine-grained classifications of their customers' risks. PHYD products are actuarially more accurate, connecting a driver's probability of causing an accident more closely to the insurance premium they have to pay. This is why PHYD insurance appeals to safe drivers ("good risks") – the type of customer insurance companies are particularly keen to sign up.

Micro-tracking has sparked a major transformation of the automobile insurance industry. It does not take much imagination to predict that soon, most car insurance policies will be of the PHYD kind. Once in place, these policies attract safe drivers. This leaves traditional car insurance products with a worse risk pool, which, in turn, makes it necessary to increase premiums. This then incentivizes even more safe drivers to select PHYD insurance and so on. This spiral only ends once everybody is covered by a PHYD product. One result of micro-tracking, therefore, is that good risks pay less, while bad risks pay more. This seems only fair, and it may even lead to more careful driving!

But more, better, and more shareable information can fundamentally change personal insurance as well, and we, along with many other observers, are concerned about the potential consequences for equality and

markets, this is typically achieved by governments making car insurance mandatory for everybody.

coverage. Personal insurance includes life insurance and credit markets, but it also includes social policy programs – accident insurance, unemployment insurance, health insurance, long-term care insurance, and old-age insurance – which are mostly run by the government. Collectively, these programs are known as "social insurance," or "the welfare state."

Like all insurance, these programs are affected by asymmetric information problems. Governments can avoid adverse selection by compelling (i.e., forcing) every citizen to be part of the insurance program. Moreover, premiums are tied to income (which governments can observe), not risk profiles (which governments traditionally cannot observe). This is then the basic structure of a typical social insurance program: all citizens are part of the risk pool, and contribution rates are based on income, either through general taxation or through social contributions. These programs are highly solidaristic because good risks subsidize bad risks and because high-income individuals pay more than those with low incomes for the same insurance. The lucky (often termed "socially strong") support the unlucky ("socially weak"): the healthy support the sick; the employed support the unemployed; the rich support the poor; the young support the old; and so on.

This solidaristic government solution, which dominated during the Golden Age of the first three post-WWII decades, is increasingly coming under pressure because of the information revolution. This is clearly illustrated by the car insurance case, but perhaps an even more instructive case is the life insurance market, where, much like in the car insurance industry, information and communication technology (ICT) is radically transforming the status quo. For example, John Hancock Life Insurance, a major player in the American market, has introduced a policy that calculates annual premiums partially based on data collected by an "activity tracker," which policyholders receive for free when they sign up. These types of devices can track and instantly share (via an app) things like steps and stairs taken, active minutes, calories burned, heart rate, sleep quality, and blood pressure. One of the company's sales pitches for this life insurance policy was that it would allow customers "to save money and earn valuable rewards by simply living a healthy life. In fact, the healthier you are, the more you can save."[2] It would be logical for health insurers to do the same – and when they can, they do (as is the case with many

[2] https://www.myadvisorschoice.com/sites/default/files/pdf-files/ProspectingLetterforLifeInsurance.pdf (last accessed June 3, 2021 [https://perma.cc/4V4M-LBCU]).

supplementary private insurance plans). Today, public plans and nondiscrimination clauses, not lack of information, are what stands between integration and segmentation.

It is not just private insurance companies getting in on the action. The leading technology companies – Apple, Alphabet, Amazon, Microsoft, and so on – are all committing huge resources to the development of a new data-based health industry, where, inter alia, doctors can interact with artificial intelligence (AI) enabled databases, and individuals can easily share their information with insurance companies. Similar efforts are underway in credit markets, where detailed information about credit history is linked to a trove of data on income, occupation, residence, and so on.

There is currently no integrated analytical framework we can use to examine the consequences of Big Data for social policy and inequality. This book offers such a framework and applies it to the history of social protection, with an emphasis on the rise of the knowledge economy and taking the role of partisanship and national political and regulatory institutions into account.

THE LOGIC: DIVISION OF INSURANCE POOLS

One of the most important drivers of redistribution and equality is large-scale risk pooling. When every worker pays into the same unemployment scheme and receives a benefit that is independent of their income, that scheme is highly redistributive provided that risks are not positively related to income. Typically, the opposite applies. The same is true for health insurance, life insurance, old-age insurance, and access to credit (when rates are not fully tied to underlying risks). Redistribution is usually thought of as politically contentious, but this need not be the case if people are uncertain how much risk they are exposed to. And even if risks are known, those with medium and high risks may force low-risk groups into a national pool under democratic rules. In this instance, social insurance *does* become politically contentious, with disagreement between low- and high-risk groups in terms of both the public character of insurance and the preferred level of insurance (albeit conditioned by the fact that insurance is usually a "normal good" – that is, demand increases with income).

Information and Social Insurance

Polarization is intensified when there are private alternatives to public provision, which can offer better insurance at lower prices for those at low risk. For private markets to be feasible, however, insurers need to be able to distinguish between good and bad risks. Otherwise, they will attract high-risk types, who drive up insurance premiums and push low-risk types out of the pool. The result of such "adverse selection" is the eventual breakdown of insurance markets, or the emergence of what Akerlof (1970) called a market for lemons (where the "lemons" are a metaphor, borrowed from the used car market, for bad risks). Such breakdowns can increase support for public insurance if people are also ignorant about their risks. On the other hand, they may in fact increase polarization over insurance spending if individuals are well-informed about their risks (while insurers are not).

Incomplete information is thus at the heart of the welfare state, and polarization will be a function of the level and distribution of information. Information is also at the heart of this book, although we will also engage with complementary arguments about political power and democratic institutions.

The early development of the welfare state took place during a time of franchise expansion, as (minor) insurance markets and mutual aid societies (MASs) retreated. Market failure itself did not bring about the welfare state, however; it emerged as the result of an expanding industrial working and middle class using the democratic state to force good risks into a national (and highly redistributive) insurance pool. Scholars of the early welfare state are right to emphasize the importance of power resources and partisanship in leveraging the coercive powers of the state (Bradley et al. 2003; Korpi 1983; Stephens 1979), but in the process, market failures were also overcome, which increased average welfare and often facilitated economic development (Iversen and Stephens 2008).

This logic has since been reversed. Because today's insurers have much better data enabling them to draw a distinction between good and bad risks, the middle class now has a new institutional incentive to exclude bad risks by privatizing those risks or by differentiating public insurance. This process, whereby large national insurance pools are parsed into smaller ones with more differentiation in contributions and benefits, is called segmentation.

Another early limitation of markets and MASs was their incapacity to solve time-inconsistency problems. These problems arose because industrialization and urbanization created immediate and urgent needs that could only be addressed by transferring resources from young, healthier, and more employable workers to older, sicker, and less employable ones. This required the institutional capacity to commit future generations to support current generations as they aged. Markets were unable to solve this distributive problem, but the democratic state managed to do so with the help of programmatic parties built on internal intergenerational bargains (Aldrich 1995; Soskice, Bates, and Epstein 1992). The result was credible commitment by governments to pay-as-you-go (PAYG) social policy expansion.

Over time, however, markets have gradually overcome this problem, at least in the areas of pensions and life insurance, by offering "funded" plans that avoid intergenerational transfers. Funded pension systems are part of broader financialization of modern economies where access to credit, and the terms of such access, has become an important determinant of welfare and inequality. People increasingly move between work and family and between work and education, and credit markets are used by more and more people to smooth these "nonlinear" career paths. This expansion of the welfare functions of credit markets once again puts information front and center because such information determines the capacity of lenders to estimate default risks and therefore who can borrow and at what cost.

That said, time-inconsistency problems do still persist in important areas of the welfare state, notably health insurance for the elderly. Because bad health is concentrated among the old, insurance against these risks requires contributions from the young and healthy. But private insurance is ill-equipped to solve this intergenerational transfer problem because insurers cannot credibly commit to future insurance for the young people who pay into the system to cover the current population in ill-health (mostly in old age). Health insurance for the old is therefore almost without exception provided by the state, even in a "liberal" welfare state like America's, where Medicare covers the elderly. Fully "funded" private healthcare accounts are not out of the question, and Germany has seen the emergence of individual health savings plans ("Alterungsrückstellungen" in the private primary health insurance market), but it has proven to be one of the hardest for markets to solve.

A closely related problem that markets never manage to solve is insurance against poverty. Much poverty is not transitory, and it thus requires continuous transfers from the nonpoor. To cover the risk of poverty by insurance, therefore, requires a credible commitment to the nonpoor that they too would be covered in the future, in the event they become poor. Private insurers generally cannot offer such a credible commitment, and it therefore falls to the government to create antipoverty programs with the political support of the nonpoor who themselves fear poverty. It is the capacity of the state to compel payments (through taxes) combined with long-standing political parties that open up the possibility of government transfers to the poor. Medicaid, to return to the US case of an otherwise large private health insurance system, is health insurance for the poor, which enjoys broad support among the nonpoor. Nonpoor requiring long-term care, for example, often have to spend down their savings.

Despite these important exceptions, increased information tends to fragment and polarize people's views on public insurance. At the birth of the modern welfare state, workers faced myriad risks – unemployment, illness, old-age insecurity, and so on – which were ill-understood and therefore a concern for most. In this low-information environment, risks were conducive to broad cross-class solidarity, as well as broad support for universal benefits. But by the same token, as information about risks has become more plentiful, public support for spending has diverged by class.

Simplifying greatly and ignoring many of the qualifications we discuss in subsequent chapters, the modern welfare state emerged in the first half of the previous century under democratic rules in a period of unprecedented upheaval and uncertainty. A majority wanted the state to assume responsibility where private alternatives (including MASs) had failed because of incomplete and asymmetric information. Higher-end groups, who knew they faced lower risks and could expect to assume a disproportionate share of the cost, opposed such welfare state expansion, but they were in a minority. Among the vast majority of the population, there was widespread consensus in support of the public system of social insurance.

With the ICT revolution, however, information has increasingly divided public opinion on many social insurance issues. Using Rawls's (1971) "veil of ignorance" metaphor, the data revolution has raised the veil and allowed people to see more clearly whether they are likely to lose or gain from public insurance. Many middle- and upper-middle-class constituencies have concluded that private insurance can be a superior option, at least as a supplement to public insurance (Busemeyer and Iversen 2020; Gingrich 2011). The result is the segmentation of social insurance with more choices within – and ways of opting out of – the public system and with private alternatives increasingly reducing the public system to a bare-bones insurance. In Denmark, a quintessential "social democratic" welfare state with a celebrated public healthcare system, nearly 2.2 million private-sector employees (in a country of 5.8 million people) are now covered by employer-provided private insurance, which complements the public system, especially for upscale professionals in areas where the public system is seen as inadequate (Hørkilde 2020). Another individual private top-up plan available in Denmark is based on documented good health, which is a common feature of upper tiers in many European countries. A parallel trend to the expanding use of supplementary private plans is a greater choice over providers and treatments in the public system. Such choice is strongly supported among the middle classes across Europe (Costa-Font and Zigante 2016).

One important qualification to the claim that information is having a polarizing effect is what is known in the welfare state literature as the "double-payment problem." Where private insurance is a substitute for insurance provided by the public system, people who opt into private alternatives must pay for their own insurance while still paying into the public system. This is an obvious deterrent against opting out, and if purchasing private insurance is not a feasible option, those who demand the best quality insurance – typically those with high incomes and education – may push for improvements in the public system. Although their "first-best" preference may be for a private system, or at least a public system that allows supplementary private insurance, their "constrained preference" may be to pour more resources into the public system. In other words, support for public insurance systems may be high even among the rich and healthy if they cannot opt out of the system. Of course, this means that the conditions for opting out – do you get a tax credit; can you still use the public system; and does the private insurance substitute or complement public offerings – become politically salient issues.

In general, when there is a double-payment issue, the individual choice to opt out of the public system depends on what others do, which can be modeled as a game of strategic complementarities, or a network game: as more opt out, the private option will become more attractive because the double-payment problem is attenuated (Busemeyer and Iversen 2014). Using this logic, we discuss in Chapter 2 how, for each (nonpoor) potential insurance holder, there is a critical threshold of participation in the private scheme that will make private insurance sufficiently attractive for the individual to opt out. In such a game, there can be multiple equilibria. Therefore, preferences can converge around, say, a predominantly public system even if, for some, the "first-best" option is a private system.

A second qualification is that information cannot solve all forms of market failure. As we noted previously, there is no private insurance against poverty, and private insurers struggle to insure against risks that are heavily concentrated at the end of life. Medicare (targeting those over the age of sixty-five) and Medicaid (targeting the poor) are popular in an otherwise predominantly private healthcare system. In addition, some risks are correlated across individuals, which violate actuarially sound insurance principles. Unemployment, which is subject to macroeconomic shocks, is an example. This does not rule out private providers, but it does require the state to be an "insurer of last resort," which itself leads to problems of moral hazard. For these reasons, the transition to a private system is by no means a foregone conclusion in a high-information environment. Yet privatization and public sector marketization enter the political debate in a way not seen in a low-information environment.

METHODS AND EVIDENCE

A study of the consequences of more and better information about individual risks faces the obvious problem that most of such information is private and protected by privacy policies. Even when information is shared with insurers and credit institutions, it is not available to researchers. The same is true of the algorithms used by private companies to analyze risks (with a few rare exceptions). For the most part, therefore, we have to rely on indirect evidence, and for this purpose, we mix analytical history, case studies, statistical analysis, and quasi-experimental methods. For example, while we cannot access the individual health records that private insurers use to determine eligibility and pricing for life insurance, we can obtain data on the availability of reliable diagnostic tests, which are rising exponentially, and we can acquire increasingly detailed data on life expectancy for each diagnosed disease. This should correlate with the data insurers are using and help explain market formation.

The historical analysis traces the shift from MASs to the rise of the solidaristic welfare state to the emergence of private markets and increasingly contested public programs. MASs were the private precursors of the welfare state, but they faced the same problems as private insurance companies because they could not effectively distinguish between good and bad risks, and any attempt to expand coverage and generosity caused many of the most prized members to leave. There is rich scholarship documenting the constraints on the scope, and ultimate demise, of MASs, which also helps us understand the conditions not only for public provision but also for the emergence of private markets. Our main focus is on the contemporary period, however, where we examine how technology, insurance, and financial companies are using data to enable and segment insurance and credit markets. Market-based insurers rather than MASs now dominate private insurance provision, but we will show how social networks have assumed an insurance role in the new economy that is not unlike the role played by MASs in the past, and we explain how these networks have become important when it comes to sharing information and forming policy preferences.

We also conduct several case studies of change. Since the mid-1970s, for example, statewide private health insurance in the USA has been broken up into smaller pools, usually based on large companies (called "self-insurance"). The result has been a sharp reduction in the cross-subsidization of risks (Hacker 2004). The Affordable Care Act (ACA) seeks to equalize access by switching more people to publicly subsidized plans, but the rest of the system continues to fragment. The American case clearly illustrates the political tug-of-war between the growing segmentation of private insurance and the centralizing force of state programs.

Another (unlikely) example of fragmentation is Swedish unemployment insurance. The system is organized around unemployment insurance funds (UIFs) run by unions. Because Swedish unions are sharply segregated by occupation and socioeconomic status and because unions serve as gatekeepers for entry into the UIFs based on detailed information about workers' employment backgrounds, differences in occupational unemployment rates can translate into uneven insurance rates. During the Conservative Bildt government in the early 1990s more funding was shifted to individual UIFs, as opposed to a common pool, and dispersion rose dramatically before being pared back again in 2014.

The Swedish case illustrates a broader trend in labor markets that intersects with our information story. Risks of unemployment and income losses are increasingly tied to occupation, education, and location. This is because the transition to the knowledge economy has strongly favored well-educated professionals in the expanding cities. Because this development is also a driver of growing neighborhood segregation, information is increasingly shared in narrow, socioeconomically homogenous groups. In more heterogeneous groups, people's views on risks and policies tend to converge to the mean of the national distribution, whereas in small homogenous groups, views tend to converge to the mean in each distinct group. This network effect is amplified by the rising housing prices in upscale neighborhoods with good schools and services because property prices are a barrier to entry for those with fewer resources and higher risks. Redlining – the discredited practice of discriminating against Black and minority zip codes in the USA – was outlawed in the Fair Housing Act of 1968, but "race-blind" location data can be plugged into algorithms along with hundreds or even thousands of other pieces of information to accurately pin down risks, and there are no laws against people forming differentiated risk perceptions and opinions based on class-divided social networks.

The main contribution of our book is to show how information is a long-term driver of welfare state development, inequality, and policy preferences – conditioned by institutions, partisanship, and past social protection – on par with other forces of change that existing literature has focused on, such as the rise and fall of unions, deindustrialization, skill-biased technological change, and globalization. Broadly speaking, we see the rise of a centralized and solidaristic welfare state as the solution to the problems of incomplete information and market failure (including the failure of MASs), combined with a democratic state that has the power to force good risks into a national pool with bad risks. Conversely, rising information and the capacity to share this information credibly have resulted in the fragmentation of insurance pools, growth of inequality in the coverage and level of social insurance and credit, and sometimes (under conditions that we specify) the polarization of public attitudes. Information played a pivotal role in the emergence of the modern redistributive welfare state; it plays an equally important one in its transformation.

ORGANIZATION OF THE BOOK

Chapter 2 develops our theoretical argument. The focus is on the relationship between information and social insurance. There is of course already a large literature on the welfare state as social insurance. Nicholas Barr's (2001) "piggy bank" metaphor for the welfare state – where people can tap into the piggy bank in times of need – succinctly captures the basic idea of social insurance. For Barr and other economists, the state takes over where markets fail, and starting with George A. Akerlof's work, robust economic models have been developed to show how incomplete information leads to market failure. But this can only be part of the story, since the rich usually have the option of self-insuring and have no interest in bankrolling an all-encompassing public risk pool. For the latter, coercive taxation is required. Even more critical for our understanding of the contemporary politics of social insurance are the consequences of ever more plentiful information that erodes the original cause of market failure. We develop a general model of this new reality in which risk segmentation is a key implication.

Chapter 3 provides a brief analytical history of the rise of the welfare state in a period of great uncertainty, and we illustrate the consequences of moving to a world of more abundant and shareable information. We begin by considering MASs as they represented the common private solution to the rising demand for both credit and social insurance, yet they failed everywhere. They clearly illustrate the difficulty of overcoming adverse selection problems, as well as the closely related problems of intergenerational transfers. Such transfers were required to address major issues of poverty and illness in the older generation at the beginning of the twentieth century, and while younger generations also wanted "insurance against old age," neither MASs nor private insurers could make credible commitments to such insurance. The welfare state replaced both markets and MASs through broad risk pooling that was beneficial to a majority of the lower and middle classes and sometimes even the upper middle classes when uncertainty was high. Big Data reduces uncertainty, and we outline the importance of this shift for three major policy domains – health and life insurance, consumer credit, and unemployment – that are examined in the rest of the book.

Chapter 4 explores the consequences of the information revolution for life and health insurance. In many advanced democracies, healthcare is among the largest, or the largest area of spending, even in a quasi-private system like the American one, and this is perhaps the single policy domain that has been most affected by the data revolution. Illness can be diagnosed and predicted with a degree of accuracy that was inconceivable in the first half of the previous century, and with independent labs as intermediaries, we are moving to a world of abundant and shareable information in healthcare. Although illnesses can still strike without warning – the pandemic is a stark reminder of that – the scope for differentiating by risk is much greater today than it was in the past. We see this both in the rise of supplementary private insurance, which is subject to the same adverse selection problems as other types of health insurance, and in the increased segmentation of both private and public provision. But the picture is more complex than that because of the network effects and double-payment problems noted previously; the extent and forms of change are very country-specific. From a methodological perspective, life insurance is a much simpler case because it is entirely in the private domain, even though it shares many of the same information-related dynamics as health insurance (notably the capacity of insurers to predict risks of illness and death). This enables us to conduct a quantitative analysis of the expansion of life insurance markets, which serves as a window into the relationship between information and markets in the healthcare domain.

Chapter 5 examines the role of information in credit markets. As noted, people are increasingly borrowing to smooth "nonlinear" careers, and this has brought an explosion of household debt in its wake. We explore the distributive consequences of lenders having access to better data in the context of such financialization. We also consider the closely related question of how regulatory changes affect lenders' incentives to acquire information. Following the financial crisis in the USA, quasi-public financial institutions in the mortgage market shifted more of the risk toward private lenders. These responded by investing more in information and carrying out more granular risk differentiation. Across countries, the dispersion in interest rates is also conditioned by the welfare state, which affects people's ability to service their debt even when they lose their regular income due to unemployment or illness. Reflecting this logic, when Germany tightened its eligibility requirements and cut replacement rates for unemployment benefits with the Hartz IV reforms, the inequality in homeownership rates increased.

Chapter 6 is a comparative analysis of the effect of information and private alternatives on labor markets and the formation of unemployment preferences. We use the Swedish case of unemployment benefit reforms to explore the consequences of a closer association between occupation and risk, which allows unions to police entry and enforce risk differentiation in UIFs. Solidaristic pooling of unemployment insurance is no longer the obvious choice for a majority of workers. Segmentation of labor markets is also colinear with more segmentation of social networks. In the new economy, the latter serve some insurance purposes themselves, but for individuals, they also function as an important source of information about their risks. We show that better information about unemployment risks leads to more polarized social policy preferences. There are thus two effects of growing socioeconomic differentiation of risk: one is a segmentation of insurance; the other is a decline in cross-class solidarity.

Lastly, Chapter 7 rounds off the book with a summary and conclusion. It also highlights some promising areas for future research.

2

Theoretical Framework

This chapter introduces the theoretical approach that informs our study of social insurance.[1] We make four related arguments. Our *first argument*, which informs the entire analysis, is that information about risks determines the economic and political scope for markets and welfare states. During the period of franchise expansion, low and asymmetric information limited the scope of insurance markets and undercut mutual aid societies (MASs). Yet market failure itself did not bring about the welfare state. Instead, it was the result of an expanding industrial middle class using the democratic state to force good risks into a national insurance pool. In this sense, the rise of social protection reflected a purely distributive battle: Those with lower risks or enough personal wealth to bypass collective insurance schemes were coerced, via taxation or contributions, to pay into the public system. A majority reasoned, correctly, that they would benefit from progressive taxation paying for all-encompassing insurance. In light of the fact that asymmetric information undercut insurance markets because the privileged opted out, the democratic state remedied the problem by forcing everyone into the public insurance pool. From this perspective, the modern welfare state is the result of majoritarian coercion.

At the same time, it is important to note that support for the public system was greatly enhanced by *uncertainty*. As argued by Harsanyi

---

[1] The chapter builds on a long intellectual history of mathematical and moral reasoning about social insurance, incisively analyzed by Friedman (2020); from Bernoulli's notion of "moral expectation" to the "frequentist" approaches developed by Cournot, Venn, Edgeworth and other prominent mathematicians of at the 19th century, to Rawls's Theory of Justice, and Harsanyi's "objectivist" interpretation of Bayesian probability theory.

(1953), when people are unsure about their position in the underlying risk distribution, their most reasonable response is to assume that they are like most people and to consequently use the average risk – which is simply the number of people who end up using the insurance relative to the size of the population – to assess their need for public insurance. This reduces the opposition to public schemes even further as fewer people see private alternatives as an opportunity to redistribute in their favor. Uncertainty creates a commonality of preferences, and the more uncertainty, the lower the variance in demand.

Better information has two effects that are of particular relevance to us. First, it reduces uncertainty and therefore tends to polarize preferences regarding the level of public insurance. A society in which there is more reliable information on the recipients and payers of benefits ex ante will be more polarized on questions of social protection. Second, if better information is available to insurers, they can differentiate good from bad risks, which makes markets easier to construct, with low-risk types being attracted to market insurance schemes, assuming information can be accessed by, or credibly shared with, insurance companies. Segmentation of insurance schemes by risk group is a profit-maximizing strategy, and it will expand the range of insurance policies that can, in principle, be provided through the market – but, of course, only at the expense of risk pooling and therefore equality.

Our *second argument* is that the feasibility of markets in insurance is affected not only by information but also by the capacity of insurers to redistribute from younger to older generations. We show that at the birth of the modern welfare state, markets and MASs were largely unable to solve time-inconsistency problems in intergenerational exchange, rendering them organizationally unfit to address mounting social demands as democracy took hold. Public pay-as-you-go (PAYG) systems addressed these problems by transferring resources from currently employed workers to workers who were unemployed, disabled, or old. But that, in turn, required the institutional capacity to commit to future benefits for current contributors. Private firms did not generally have this capacity, and MASs struggled mightily to acquire them.

Over time, however, markets have gradually made it possible for more and more workers to rely on "funded" retirement plans or life insurance products that are far less redistributive (if at all) than public systems. Related to this, as part of the broader financialization of modern economies, access to credit and the terms of such access have become important drivers of welfare and inequality. Workers increasingly move between work and family and between work and education, and credit is used to cushion the short-term loss of income this brings. This expansion of the welfare functions of credit markets once again puts information front and center because it determines the capacity of lenders to estimate default risks and therefore who can borrow and at what cost.

That said, funded health insurance systems remain underdeveloped, even though they would, in principle, not differ substantially from pension systems or life insurance, with individuals paying into a personal fund that triggers payments when certain objective criteria are met: not a certain age, or death – as in the case of pensions and life insurance – but certain medical conditions. In the USA, a small step in this direction, called health savings accounts (HSAs), was taken in 1993 under George W. Bush. Although annual maximum contributions are still low (US$3,600 per year for a single person in 2021), they appeal largely to young, healthy individuals who do not mind being covered under a high-deductible (but low-premium) health plan. It is still not possible to enroll in an HSA and Medicare at the same time, and the former cannot yet compete with the latter, but the potential is clearly there.

The other advanced industrialized country with a sizeable private primary health insurance market is Germany. The country covers about 11 percent of the population with primary health insurance based on medical underwriting (i.e., premiums are tied to health risk). In the private system, at least 10 percent of the premiums of those aged 22–60 are, by law, put into individual savings accounts managed by the health insurance company ("Alterungsrückstellung"). The savings and their returns are then used to offset higher expenses and premiums after age 65. Therefore, premiums are, in principle, constant across the life cycle, though, in practice, they typically increase because of medical inflation, new procedures being added to coverage, increasing societal life expectancy, or changing interest rates.[2] All told, premiums are actuarially fair, and the savings accounts just serve the purpose of smoothing premiums over time. Of course, some consumers end up paying more into the private system than they get out, while, for others, the opposite is true. This is the "risk redistribution" part of private insurance – where the lucky subsidize the unlucky – and with more information and hence better risk classification, this redistributive effect becomes smaller. But even today, there is no ex ante monetary subsidy in the private system. By contrast, in the public

---

[2] In some cases, premiums might actually go down: if any savings are left over when a customer reaches the age of 80, insurance companies have to lower their premium.

system, the books are balanced through a PAYG system where the young (healthy) subsidize the old (less healthy) and where premiums are charged based on income, not risk.

Information is still the key factor preventing the expansion of these funded systems. Predicting the age of death, or life expectancy, is fairly straightforward, and many health and labor market risks can be assessed fairly reliably in a time horizon of a few years or even a decade, but predicting this over half a century is nigh on impossible – at least with current technology. This suggests that effective private health insurance markets for the elderly will remain limited for now, but this could change in the future as medicine, and therefore, people and insurers become increasingly able to identify genes for longevity and good health. Indeed, genetic testing promises to be highly predictive in the long run but not very informative in the short run.

For "ordinary" risks, information and funded systems therefore have the potential to solve the market failure problem, but this is not synonymous with saying that they will induce majority support for marketization. The effects of moving to a market system are uncertain, even if risk data are plentiful. The US private health insurance system, while highly regulated, makes it harder to control costs because insurers lack the monopsony power of single-payer public systems and often face pervasive principal–agent problems (which are, of course, themselves rooted in incomplete information). The average voter is not able to discern all the pros and cons of market reforms, and they are therefore likely to adopt a cautious stance on such reforms.

Our *third argument* is that despite this, mass preferences for social protection should gradually shift with increased information about risks and with the growing feasibility of markets. At the birth of the modern welfare state, workers faced myriad risks – unemployment, health, old-age security, and so on – which were ill-understood and therefore feared by most. This low-information environment was conducive to broad cross-class solidarity and benefited universalism. But by the same token, as information about risks becomes more plentiful, it is reasonable to expect that public support for spending becomes more dispersed. The feasibility of markets also has profound consequences for class divisions because private insurance and pensions, unlike public systems, are graduated by income with little or no implied redistribution (in contrast to PAYG systems). In Chapter 6, we consider in much more detail how the availability of information about risks translates into perceptions of risks. Social networks, we argue, play a crucial role, and such networks are denser for people with an interest in greater segmentation of insurance.

While information is only one factor in shaping preferences, the effect is always to undercut support for solidaristic solutions.

Our *fourth argument* reiterates long-standing reasoning in the comparative welfare state literature: as left parties tend to represent low-wage, high-risk groups, we expect left-leaning governments to try to inhibit the development of private insurance markets and shore up support for the public system. This is done mainly through the regulation of markets and through the tax code, which determine the opportunities and costs of opting out.

The rise in inequality over the past four decades is usually attributed to "skill-biased technological change" and globalization. With this book, we would like to highlight another major source of inequality: increasing information about risks. The postwar welfare state was a major source of equality because it pooled risks across different classes and used taxation to provide relatively equal access to health insurance, pensions, and finance. Friedman (2020) succinctly summarizes the political and normative foundations of this outcome as a fusion of prudential calculations of self-interest and more collectivist notions of our responsibility to each other as members of a larger national community. But with risk being increasingly differentiated by group, the danger is that social insurance and many public goods are becoming differentiated, too. We believe that the breakup of solidaristic insurance pools may be one of the most important causes of rising inequality.

The rest of this chapter is organized into five sections: one devoted to each argument and one summarizing them. The first presents a simple model that informs most of the rest of the analysis. The model serves to highlight the effects of information. The second section focuses on time inconsistency in social policy and discusses the role of political parties in potentially solving the problem. The third turns to the consequences of increased information and private markets for social policy preferences, while the fourth deals with the role of partisanship. The final section provides a brief summary. The appendices at the end of this chapter provide some technical details.

FIRST ARGUMENT: INFORMATION, MARKET FAILURE, AND DEMOCRACY

This section presents a simple framework for our analysis, building on and extending the classic framework developed by Akerlof (1970), Rothschild and Stiglitz (1976), and Stiglitz (1982), with more recent extensions summarized in Barr (2001, 2012), Boadway and Keen (2000), and Przeworski (2003). It introduces some basic concepts and presents the logic using formal modeling. Readers who would prefer to skip the mathematical details can go straight to the "Nontechnical Summary" section.

We present the argument in three steps: (i) We begin by introducing the classic asymmetric information case and show that it leads to majority support for public provision under most realistic assumptions; (ii) we then turn to the symmetric information case and show that when information is plentiful and can be credibly shared with insurers, a majority may prefer market provision (or a public system that mimics markets); (iii) lastly, we show that when market solutions are blocked, whether for political or economic reasons, preferences over public provision will become polarized as information increases.

The model is developed from the perspective of individuals' demand for insurance, and it will be readily recognizable to readers familiar with canonical models of demand for public insurance in political science. For readers familiar with the standard economic model of private insurance markets, Appendix 2.1 shows the correspondence between that model and the one presented in the main text. For every result, Appendix 2.2 shows that the insurer's budget constraint is satisfied.

Basic Setup

We assume that people start out in a "good state" (healthy, employed, etc.) and, looking one period into the future, decide how much of their current income to spend on insurance against the risk of falling into a "bad state" (illness, unemployment, etc.) and hence of losing that income in the next period. The model uses log utility to capture risk aversion (RRA = 1) in a simple and tractable manner. Specifically, the expected utility (based on the von Neumann–Morgenstern theorem) of individual i is defined as follows:

$$U_i = \ln(y_i - c_i) \cdot (1 - p_i) + \ln(k_i + b_i) \cdot p_i, \qquad (1)$$

where $y_i > 1$ is income when in the good state, c_i is the cost of insurance, p_i is the risk of losing income, b_i is the insurance benefit in the bad state, and k_i is a pretransfer income from private sources when in the bad state. If the bad state is one in which the individual is unable to work, k_i can be understood as nonlabor income from savings or other assets ("self-insurance").

We initially assume that i knows everything there is to know: y_i, c_i, p_i, k_i, and b_i, and we define c_i as the share, π_i, of income that goes to pay for insurance so that $c_i = \pi_i \cdot y_i$. If insurers also have this information, they could offer insurance plans for each risk group, using premiums received from those in the good state to pay for the benefits of those in the bad state. Ignoring administrative costs, as well as any markups (which are irrelevant to our key results), the insurer breaks even when the benefit of the insured individual is:[3]

$$b_i = \frac{\pi_i \cdot (1 - p_i)}{p_i} \cdot y_i, \tag{2}$$

where $\pi_i \cdot (1 - p_i)/p_i$ is the income replacement rate and $- (1 - p_i)/p_i$ is the slope of the "fair bet" line in the standard economic model of insurance, as shown in Appendix 2.1.

Since i is risk-averse, he or she will purchase enough insurance to equalize expected income across the two states (good and bad), which is simply the value of π_i that maximizes Eq. (1):

$$\pi_i^* = p_i \cdot \left(1 - \frac{k_i}{y_i}\right) = p_i \cdot (1 - s_i), \tag{3}$$

where s_i is nonlabor income in the bad state as a share of labor income in the good state. Unsurprisingly, the higher the risk of losing income, the greater the share of income spent on insurance.[4] Higher labor income increases demand for insurance (as for any normal good), but higher nonlabor income reduces demand (because it provides self-insurance). If the latter comes from savings taken from the former, demand will depend on the savings rate, which tends to increase with income. Yet, since the relationship between income and savings is not important for our main purposes, we assume that the savings rate is constant: $s_i = s$. The

---

[3] To see this, note that for each insured, the expected payout by the insurer in each period is $p_i \cdot b_i$, while the expected premium received in each period is $(1 - p_i) \cdot \pi_i \cdot y_i$. Across a large insurance pool, expected payouts and premiums will be equal to actual payouts and premiums, and the insurer will break even when $p_i \cdot b_i = (1 - p_i) \cdot \pi_i \cdot y_i$, which yields Eq. (2).

[4] There is now an extensive literature on the determinants of redistribution preferences in general (Alesina and Giuliano 2011; Rueda and Stegmueller 2019) and on the relationship between risk exposure and attitudes toward social insurance and redistribution in particular (a few examples include Ahlquist, Hamman, and Jones 2017; Barber, Beramendi, and Wibbels 2013; Margalit 2013; O'Grady 2019; Rehm 2009; Rueda and Stegmueller 2019; Scheve and Slaughter 2004; Walter 2010). In this literature, risk exposure emerges as an important individual-level correlate of attitudes toward the welfare state, although there are some countervailing forces – such as religion (Scheve and Stasavage 2006a, 2006b; Stegmueller 2013; Stegmueller et al. 2012), fairness (Scheve and Stasavage 2010, 2012), other-regarding preferences (Dimick, Rueda, and Stegmueller 2016), or concerns about crime (Rueda and Stegmueller 2016) – and other correlates as well.

exception, which we will note, is for the very rich who save enough to be able to forgo paying the cost of insurance altogether ("self-insurance").

With these basic elements of the model in place, we now introduce variation in information about individual risks. We begin with the classic case of asymmetric information, where the buyer of insurance is informed, but the insurer is not. This is covered by the standard model of insurance. We then ask what happens when information is shared with insurers, and lastly, we consider the case where neither buyer nor insurer is informed. This latter scenario is rarely considered, but the second case of both the insurer and the insured being informed increasingly applies to today's Big Data world. The case where neither is informed was important in the early formation of the welfare state.

The Asymmetric Information Case

Insurance markets would not be problematic if insurers were aware of individual risks. But if insurers do not have information about those risks, they will only know the mean risk in the pool of insured, $\bar{p}$, which they can infer from the share of insured individuals who claim insurance. With asymmetric information, the benefit received by i now depends on $\bar{p}$ instead of p_i:[5]

$$b_i^{''} = \frac{\pi_i \cdot (1 - \bar{p})}{\bar{p}} \cdot y_i,$$ (4)

and the preferred level of insurance is a function of *both* individual risk *and* average risk:[6]

$$\pi_i^{**} = p_i - (1 - p_i) \cdot s \cdot \frac{\bar{p}}{1 - \bar{p}}.$$ (5)

[5] For each individual, the expected payout is now $\bar{p} \cdot b_i$ and the expected premium is $(1 - \bar{p}) \cdot \pi_i \cdot y_i$. In equilibrium, the two must be equal, which gives us Eq. (4). The process by which the equilibrium is reached is explained later.

[6] This is the value of π_i that maximizes Eq. (1) when the replacement rate is $\pi_i \cdot (1 - \bar{p})/\bar{p}$ instead of $\pi_i \cdot (1 - p_i)/p_i$. Note that for Eq. (5), we assume that insurers cannot infer an individual's risk from the amount of insurance purchased by each individual. We show in Appendix 2.1 that this assumption is satisfied if insurers do not know the total amount of insurance bought by each individual from all insurers and/or if they do not know that individual's income or degree of risk aversion, which will affect demand. In either case, it prevents an insurer from offering a "cheap" plan that will only be taken up by low-risk types.

Will individuals buy insurance at the price and replacement rate implied by Eqs. (4) and (5)? The answer depends on those individuals' own risk relative to the risk of others. Clearly, those with p_i above $\overline{p}$ will find the pooled insurance plan an unequivocally good deal; those with a p_i below $\overline{p}$ may or may not. This is because, for these individuals, there is an additional cost of insurance, which is the implied subsidy for those at higher risk. This cost is a function of the composition of risk in the pool of insured, so each individual's decision to buy insurance depends on the decision of others. It is therefore the outcome of a network game.

Specifically, an individual will buy insurance if and only if:

$$\pi_i^{**} > 0$$
$$\Downarrow$$
$$p_i > \frac{s}{1/\overline{p} - 1 + s}. \tag{6}$$

The equilibrium is found where the expected mean risk in the insured population, $\overline{p}^e$, is equal to the actual mean risk:

$$\overline{p}^{p_i > q} = \overline{p}^e,$$

where $\overline{p}^{p_i > q}$ is the mean risk in a pool of people who are above a critical threshold, q, which is given by Eq. (6). This is also the point at which the insurer breaks even – see Appendix 2.2 for proof.

The logic is illustrated in Figure 2.1, which uses an example of an even distribution of risk in the interval [0, 0.5], and $s = 0.5$. If everyone buys into the insurance plan so that coverage is 100 percent (recorded on the right y-axis), the expected $\overline{p}$ is 0.25. At this implied "price," only those with individual risks above 0.14 (given by Eq. (6)) would buy insurance, which here is equivalent to 71 percent of the population. As low-risk types leave, the insurer will no longer break even, and the average risk $\overline{p}$ in the insurance pool rises to $\overline{p} = .33$. This becomes the new expected risk, as indicated by the dotted arrow. The departure of good risks leaves behind a greater share of bad risks, which Akerlof (again, with reference to the used car market) called "lemons." In our example, this "lemons" logic continues until the line that maps expected risks onto actual risks intersects the 45-degree line (the dotted arrows). At this point, the equilibrium of the game is reached, which in our example implies a small majority (57 percent) buying private insurance. Incidentally, this is roughly the same as the share who bought insurance through MASs at their peak in the early twentieth century (de Swaan 1988, 144).

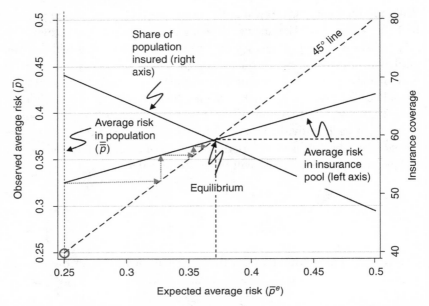

FIGURE 2.1 Equilibria in the private insurance network game with private information
Note: simulations assuming $s = 0.5$ and $p_i = [0, .5]$.

The example shows that Akerlof's (1970) market for "lemons only" is too pessimistic, since many people with medium risks might end up with at least some private insurance.[7] Yet the outcome is unequivocally inefficient, since we know that *someone* at low risk will always find it preferable to opt out of the private insurance plan even though they would buy insurance in a world with complete information.

The economic analysis ends here, and public provision is "explained" as a solution to the problem of private under-provision. Using Nicholas Barr's (2001) idiom, the welfare state is nothing more than a massive "piggy bank." Yet efficiency is *not* the decisive force behind the introduction of a public system, nor is demand from the completely uninsured. Instead, it results from a majority supporting a public system where low-risk types are required to contribute to the population-wide pool and

---

[7] Akerlof's market for "lemons only" is where the line indicating average risk meets the 45-degree line at the highest level of risk. In Akerlof's model, this holds since he assumes that people are risk-neutral. Our model assumes risk-averse agents.

hence subsidize those at higher risk (whereas in a private system, they would opt out). In other words, it is a matter of majoritarian coercion.

To see this, we can use our example of the individual with the median risk (equal to 0.25) spending 3.9 percent of their income on insurance in the private market and getting a replacement rate of 6.7 percent in the case of income loss.[8] By contrast, in a public system with a proportional tax, the median voter would choose a 12.5 percent tax rate and get a 37.5 percent replacement rate (which would equalize net income across the two states).[9] MASs offered some insurance before the rise of the welfare state, but they were also notorious for under-provision of insurance, which is quite consistent with our logic (see Chapter 3).

An alternative to a public system would be to acquire more information about potential members of insurance pools and to exclude "bad" risks. In our analytical history in the next chapter, we will see that this is what some MASs attempted to do based on social networks and personal recommendations. But it was a very imperfect method that tended to turn MASs into small exclusive clubs, which could only address a narrow range of risks based on shaky information, such as a past history of illness.

The Symmetric Information Case

Akerlof (1970) and Rothschild and Stiglitz (1976) did not discuss the case of symmetric information, since they were interested in exploring the consequences of private information. This is also true of more recent studies, such as that of Barr (2001, 2012). For our story, however, the symmetric information case is important, and it comes in two varieties. In the first, *neither* buyers nor sellers have individual information about risk (low information). In the second, *both* do (high information).

Symmetric but Low Information

In the case of *no* individual information, people will have to rely on the same aggregate information as insurers. Each person will have to form an expectation of their risk based on the observed number of unemployed, disabled, sick, and so on. In our model, this is simply the mean risk in the

---

[8] The median risk is 0.25, and the average risk in the pool is 0.36 when in equilibrium (see Figure 2.1). This gives the optimal spending from Eq. (5). The replacement rate can then be calculated from Eq. (4).

[9] Net income in the good state is $(1 - 0.125) \cdot y_i = 0.875 \cdot y_i$, and net income in the bad state is $(0.5 + 0.325) \cdot y_i = 0.875 \cdot y_i$ ($s = 0.325$ and $\pi_i = 0.325$).

population: $p_i^o = \overline{\overline{p}}$, where p_i^o is i's observed level of risk and $\overline{\overline{p}}$ is the overall population mean (as distinct from the mean among the insured, $\overline{p}$). Since everyone has the same expectation, including the insurer, and $\overline{\overline{p}} \cdot (1 - s)$ is everyone's preferred level of spending (from Eq. (3)), $\overline{p} = \overline{\overline{p}}$ is an equilibrium. In Figure 2.1, this special case is indicated with a circle at the bottom left corner (which is still on the 45-degree line).

In the real world, there may, in fact, be no examples of such a complete lack of information, but the case is instructive, nonetheless. The reason for this is that uncertainty reduces the variance in policy preferences: whereas the range of preferences in the private information case is $p_i = [p_{min}, p_{max}]$, in the case of no information, in other words in the presence of uncertainty, the range is $p_i^o = [p_{min}^o, p_{max}^o]$, where, again, p_i^o is an observed risk. The latter range will be narrower than the former, which can be captured using a simple Bayesian logic:

$$p_i^o = \alpha \cdot p_i^s + (1 - \alpha) \cdot \overline{\overline{p}}, \tag{7}$$

where p_i^s is a noisy signal drawn from a distribution that is centered on the individual's true risk (p_i) and α is a measure of the "precision" of that signal, which in our model equals the private information available to i.[10] With no information $(\alpha = 0)$, i only observes the population mean, $p_i^o = \overline{\overline{p}}$, and the range is therefore zero. At the other extreme, with complete information, $p_i^o = p_i$, the range equals the difference between those with the lowest and those with the highest risk. A very simple way of expressing this general insight is that *class conflict increases with information*. Behind the veil of ignorance, everyone can agree that a robust level of public insurance is a good thing; without the veil of ignorance, there is disagreement about the level of public insurance (and potentially also its public nature). Even if markets are not feasible, information shapes politics.

Symmetric and High Information
The final, and undoubtedly important, case is where information is plentiful and can be shared between buyer and provider. Even when legal privacy protections limit the ability of insurers to acquire individual

---

[10] We can think of the "precision" of the signal as the accumulated information over a specific period of time. In the case of unemployment risks, signals are both an individual's actual experiences of unemployment and observed unemployment in the industry, occupation, or network to which the individual belongs. Formal proof for Eq. (7) can be found in Iversen and Soskice (2015b, appendix B).

information – which we discuss in the empirical chapters – insurers may not need to gain access to private information because people may share it voluntarily. As mentioned in the introduction, some people are willing to use monitoring devices to reduce car insurance premiums, for instance.

This logic also applies to the important area of private health data, where the level and credibility of information have vastly improved. There are three related forces behind this trend. First, the general advance of medicine has made diagnostics much more detailed and reliable (Shojania et al. 2003). Second, the explosion in the number and variety of tests that can be carried out by certified labs has made it possible to share this information credibly. DNA diagnostics in particular promises to offer an order of magnitude more information about health risks than in the past. Lastly, computing power combined with AI has made it possible to classify individuals in risk groups much more accurately than in the past. AI image recognition, for example, can assist radiologists in correctly interpreting data from CT and MRI scans. Machine learning is also increasingly used to combine data from imaging with genomics and proteomics, as well as physician-generated patient data.

The fact that individual information can be acquired by, and credibly shared with, would-be insurers mitigates the asymmetric information problem and opens the possibility of insurance being provided efficiently through the market. For each group with identical risk profiles there would now be a separate insurance plan with its own cost and replacement rate, corresponding to a particular point on the 45-degree line in Figure 2.2. More realistically, we can expect there to be some modest risk heterogeneity within groups, which the insurer is not aware of, or that the insurer pools adjacent risk groups for reasons related to economies of scale. Provided that insurers have enough information to distinguish members of different groups, we will get a series of distinct (pooled) equilibria/insurance plans as illustrated in Figure 2.2. The analysis of each of these equilibria follows the exact logic set out in Figure 2.1.

In this brave new world of near-complete information, there would be an effectively functioning market for the "creampuffs" – people with low risks that insurance companies crave (the opposite of Akerlof's "lemons"). In fact, anyone below the mean ($\bar{p} = .5$ in Figure 2.2) would, in principle, be better off in such a world, assuming (as before) that private provision is no more or less efficient than public provision.[11] This is

---

[11] This is of course, as already noted, an issue of considerable debate. Suffice it to say here that the assumption helps focus on the effect of information on the direction of change in distributive politics. All causal arguments require a ceteris paribus clause.

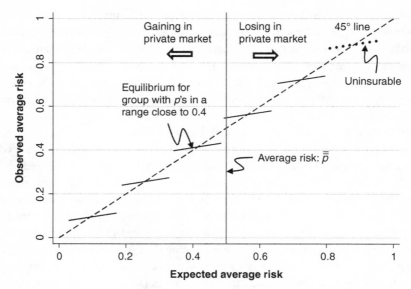

FIGURE 2.2 Equilibria in the private insurance network game with shared information

because, in a public system, all those with below-average risk subsidize those with above-average risk. Another implication is that those with the highest risk, who also tend to have the lowest incomes, may be unable to afford private insurance tailored to high risks. For example, low-income people at serious risk of diabetes may be unable to effectively insure against that risk if there is no pooling with lower-risk groups. They are priced out of the market. In Figure 2.2, such non-insurability is indicated with a dotted line. In contrast to the low-information case, those who are left without insurance are now those at high risk. We will not end up with a market only for creampuffs, but it will be a market with very few lemons!

Note that the possibility of credible information sharing even has implications for those who want to protect their privacy. The reason is that "refusers" will automatically be placed in a high-risk group with high premiums, and everyone in that group with risks below the group average has a financial incentive to divulge their information to reduce the cost of their plan. If they do share their information, the same will be true for those below the average in the remaining group, and this process will continue until all the "lemons" have been called out. As Michael Doughty, president and general manager of John Hancock Insurance, which offers a life insurance policy using data from people's fitness trackers to calculate individualized premiums, explains: "You do not have to send us any data you are not comfortable with," though he points out: "The trade-off is you won't get points for that."[12] It is clear from this analysis that privacy laws are *not* a remedy for the problem.

Would there be majority support for privatization? Based on our assumptions, the answer would be *yes*, provided that the risk distribution is right-skewed. This is unequivocally true in the case of health risks,[13] and it is ordinarily also true in the case of unemployment risks (Rehm 2016). In an "up or down" vote, self-interested voters would therefore support privatization. Again, this conclusion only holds in a world of complete and shared information (and without other types of market failure), and we do not live in such a world. At the same time, we are almost certainly moving in this direction, and as we do, the public system will become increasingly contested and either give way to private alternatives or be reformed in a more market-conforming way.

Nontechnical Summary

The Akerlof model provides a compelling logic for the inefficiency of private insurance markets under conditions of incomplete information. If insurers cannot distinguish between good and bad risks, they need to pool everyone in a single plan, where the price is equal to expected payouts divided by the number of people in the pool. With a single plan, the calculation is very simple: divide the total costs by the number of insured, and you have the insurance premium. This is essentially what a universal public plan does. Yet, if such a plan were to be offered as a private option, it would quickly run into difficulties. This is because people with low risks would opt out of the plan as the price is too high relative to the benefits.[14] They would rely on wealth and savings for insurance. Such opt-outs in turn change the composition of the pool by increasing the share of high-risk

---

[12] The *New York Times*, April 8, 2015, p. B1.

[13] While there is no direct data on risk, health spending is highly concentrated. In 2009, about half of US healthcare spending went to just 5 percent of the population (National Institute for Health Care Management 2012). Of course, much of this spending is on the elderly, and everyone grows old, so people must become increasingly worried about insurance as they age. We consider this issue later.

[14] Similarly, people with low-risk aversion may also opt out of such a plan. However, in our model, for simplicity, risk aversion is constant across individuals.

types, and the price will increase accordingly. This is the adverse selection and will lead to more opt-outs until the marginal utility of having at least some insurance outweighs the cost. The poor may or may not be able to afford such a plan, but one thing we know for sure is that insurance will be costly and under-provided.

For the middle class – loosely those with average income and risk – a better option is to create a universal public system that everyone pays into. This reduces the price because low-risk, high-income members will subsidize everyone else – in other words, public insurance systems are redistributive. Yet, while those who are big net contributors will oppose the system, their opposition will be moderated by uncertainty about where they are in the risk distribution. The more the uncertainty, the broader the support for a public system.

This helps explain the broad cross-class support for the welfare state in the wake of industrialization and the huge shocks of the Great Depression and WWII. Deindustrialization, which started in the 1970s, was an extra boost because many people were worried about losing their jobs and private benefits (Iversen and Cusack 2000). Yet, eventually, the dust settled, and it is becoming increasingly apparent who is at risk of losing their job and who is not, even as health risks continue to be difficult to pin down, especially for insurers. The data revolution promises to accelerate this change as the availability and accuracy of tests improve at an exponential rate. This is causing a growing bifurcation of preferences, with demands for differentiation and choice in public healthcare, complemented by better access to private providers (where costs are proportional to benefits).

SECOND ARGUMENT: THE TIME-INCONSISTENCY PROBLEM

At the time of the transition to democracy, with industrialization and urbanization well underway, countries faced huge unmet social needs, especially among the old, the disabled, and the unemployed. An obvious solution was to transfer resources from younger, healthier, and more employable workers while promising these workers the same benefits in the future. Indeed, this kind of "risk redistribution" is what we often think of as fundamental to social insurance. However, it involves a challenging time-inconsistency problem, which can be understood as a special case of adverse selection but is better treated as a separate problem. This time-inconsistency problem is not part of standard insurance models, including the one presented previously. When the time-inconsistency problem is taken into consideration, we find that even if information is complete, insurance is more likely to be provided publicly. For private insurance companies, the problem is that younger, healthier, and more employable workers will vote with their feet by leaving the insurance plan, although they would stay if there was a credible commitment to future benefits.

Our basic model assumes that people look one period into the future and that the majority decision taken in the first period will be implemented in the second period. This is a standard approach in the literature, but it ignores an important feature of the real world. There is often a significant lag between taxes/contributions and (potential) benefits, and political majorities can shift over time. Under these more realistic conditions – where the stickiness of majority decisions can be a questionable assumption – why would a majority of voters ever agree to a (possibly uncertain) benefit in the future that incurs real costs today? We argue that political parties play an important role in solving this problem.

To account for the possibility that future benefits will not be paid, we can amend the basic utility function with parameter φ, which is the likelihood that benefits will actually be paid:

$$U_i = \ln(y_i - c_i)(1 - p_i) + \varphi \ln(k_i + b_i)\, p_i \qquad (8)$$

In Eq. (1), we assume that $\varphi = 1$, that is, that benefits are certain. More realistically, however, there is a possibility that benefits may not be paid, for example, because the insurer goes bankrupt or because a majority of voters in the future reneges on past majority decisions. Hence, we can think of parameter φ as a measure of how sticky, or certain, past policy promises are.

If $\varphi < 1$, the individual's cost-benefit calculations change to the degree that they may not want to buy (private or public) insurance to begin with. In some domains – such as health and old-age insurance – the certainty of promised benefits being paid out in the future is a particular issue of concern because the time between contributions/taxes and benefits can be very long. For example, young people might be reluctant to support a PAYG pension system if they fear that they might not receive a public pension themselves. Yet, time and again, PAYG pension systems have been introduced and sustained – typically also with the support of young voters. These systems rely on an implicit "intergenerational contract" in which the current contributors are assured that they will receive benefits when it is their turn. Of course, such contracts are merely political metaphors, not legally binding documents, since it is not possible to conclude contracts between generations. The politicians using this meta-phor are trying to solve the time-inconsistency problem by convincing voters that $\varphi = 1$.

How can the current majorities of young voters bind the actions of future majorities? This is a prisoner's dilemma game because if current and future young generations cooperate, they produce valuable insurance that is beneficial to everyone, yet, at any given moment in time, the young generation has an incentive to renege. It is very hard to see how this problem could be overcome through the standard solution of iterated interactions, since present and future "median voters" (really middle-class voters) would not even know each other's identity. In small groups, such self-enforcing equilibria might be conceivable, and we discuss in Chapter 3 how (quasi-democratic) MASs attempted just that using intru-sive monitoring (in fact a common criticism of MASs).

Overlapping generations models are often proposed to solve the problem (e.g., Dickson and Shepsle 2001; Rangel 2003),[15] but such models are not persuasive if the generations are represented by atomistic ("median") voters since these do not interact directly, let alone in a repeated game. That said, a version of the overlapping generations argument that focuses on the mediat-ing role of political parties is, in our view, persuasive. In well-organized political parties, incentives are structured such that ambitious young politi-cians will promote the party program as a way of rising up through the organization, while older leaders will set policies to maximize joint benefits that is, stick to the collectively agreed party program, in order to maintain the support from below (Soskice, Bates, and Epstein. 1992). If voters see political parties as being able to credibly commit to a party platform, a majority will vote for a party that offers optimal insurance. This idea of parties is of course not new but has roots in the responsible party model (Aldrich 1995; Downs 1957; Schattschneider 1942), which in turn reflects party system formation in the early twentieth century (Duverger 1954; Lipset and Rokkan 1967).[16]

The time-inconsistency problem is particularly pronounced in PAYG-financed systems. But even in the case of fully funded systems with little or no intergenerational redistribution, people worry about the likelihood of

---

[15] An alternative solution allows for the possibility of binding intergenerational contracts (Kotlikoff, Persson, and Svensson 1988) or of giving all generations a weighted influence over policies (Grossman and Helpman 1998). Neither seems plausible in the set of advanced democracies being examined here.

[16] This model has been far less successful in new democracies, and it could be argued that failure is one reason why many new democracies have failed to develop effective welfare states.

future payouts, and politicians and companies have enacted a set of policies and regulations to address such worries. Life insurance is a good example. To mitigate the risk of bankruptcy (where $\varphi < 1$), private life insurance markets are subject to a great deal of regulation to ensure solvency, and the insured are typically backed by government guarantees. In the USA, for example, all states have a "life and health insurance guaranty association" to which private insurance companies must contribute. These guaranty associations "provide a safety net for their state's policyholders, ensuring that they continue to receive coverage (up to the limits spelled out by state law) even if their insurer is declared insolvent."[17] Other advanced democracies have similar arrangements.

Well-functioning life insurance markets share some features with private retirement plans: people pay into the scheme in the expectation of a(n) (uncertain) future return on the investment. The insurance aspect is that the families of insurance holders who die at an unexpectedly young age are "compensated" by a lump-sum payout or a continued stream of income. Fully funded individual pension schemes, such as 401(k) plans in the USA, have no insurance component, and it is perhaps not surprising that these plans have gradually replaced most PAYG public pensions as financial markets have matured and governments have sought to shift some of the burden of an aging population to individuals. Other aspects of financial markets serve insurance functions because people use credit markets to bridge increasingly nonlinear careers (moving from job to job, between employment and education, between work and family, etc.). Chapter 5 argues that the combination of financialization and nonlinear life cycles makes access to credit, and the terms of such access, major determinants of welfare and inequality – both closely tied to information about risks.

But why do health insurance markets not use funded solutions more? We noted previously that there *are* some examples of health savings plans in Germany and the USA, and the market also offers some long-term care plans. Yet none of these plans have been particularly popular or successful.[18]

---

[17] www.nolhga.com/home.cfm (last accessed June 3, 2021 [https://perma.cc/WU5H-CLFC]).

[18] A prominent recent example for the failure of long-term care insurance are the Penn Treaty and American Network Insurance Companies, which were liquidated in 2017 (www.media.pa.gov/Pages/Insurance-Details.aspx?newsid=228, last accessed June 3, 2021 [https://perma.cc/EHL6-GSXD]). Of the 76,000 policies, 98 percent were long-term care insurance, with a combined net liability in terms of state guarantees of US$2,583,637,523 (www.nolhga.com/factsandfigures/costs/PennTreaty16.pdf, last accessed June 3, 2021 [https://perma.cc/BD5C-W69D]; https://www.spglobal.com/marketintelligence/en/news-insights/trending/dx7wnoac-xke08m8ygwvpa2, last accessed June 3, 2021 [https://perma.cc/9SSM-FA3H]).

A plausible reason is that for health insurance to be effective, the insurance component needs to be much larger than the savings component, and then plans run into the double issue of adverse selection and time inconsistency. Most health problems tend to be concentrated at the end of life, but compared to life insurance, the risks are much more dispersed, with a long right tail for those who end up with debilitating conditions (such as Alzheimer's). In comparison, the risk of dying is universal, and the distribution of life expectancy around the mean is much narrower and symmetrical. This increases the importance of the savings component relative to the insurance component. For private health insurance to effectively cover an entire lifetime, there needs to be sufficient information to clearly distinguish long-term risks (so those with a high risk of, say, Alzheimer's pay much higher premiums). We return to this topic in more detail in Chapter 4. For now, suffice to say that almost everywhere, the combination of information and time-inconsistency problems has limited private health insurance plans to the non-elderly population.[19]

Table 2.1 gives some examples of different types of insurance, distinguishing private from public provision (rows) and whether or not the domain is characterized by a severe time-inconsistency problem (columns). Insurance domains that do not suffer from a time-inconsistency problem are often

TABLE 2.1 *Time inconsistency and public versus private provision (examples)*

		Time-inconsistency problem?	
		No	Yes
Provision	Private	Car insurance Life insurance Credit markets Short-term disability insurance	Individual health saving plans Long-term care insurance (failed)
	Public	Unemployment insurance	Early PAYG programs Most health insurance for the old

[19] The German exception of private primary healthcare is discussed previously.

covered by private markets. (As mentioned, one exception is long-term care insurance, which is sometimes offered privately. However, the private market for long-term care insurance has largely collapsed.) As expected, the absence of a time-inconsistency problem is a near-necessary condition for private insurance markets to work. The example of unemployment insurance – which does not suffer from a severe time-inconsistency problem – shows, however, that it is not a sufficient condition. Information asymmetries and correlated risks are other problems that make private markets difficult. The biggest social insurance programs at the beginning of the democratic era – PAYG pensions and health insurance – suffered from severe time-inconsistency problems, and it is therefore not surprising that these were historically provided publicly (in the presence of well-organized parties).

The effects of the information revolution should be particularly pronounced in private markets that allow risk discrimination, and we therefore examine the cases of life insurance and credit markets in later chapters. However, the information revolution should also impact the politics of conventional forms of social insurance, through two mechanisms. First, the information revolution may make new areas for private insurance feasible, which changes the calculus of support for public systems. Second, even where private markets are blocked, more and better information can change the patterns of public support for social insurance, leading to polarization and demand for greater differentiation.

THIRD ARGUMENT: PREFERENCE FORMATION

The effect of information on preferences was discussed previously: As people acquire more information about risks, their preferences will diverge. But this of course depends on the extent of variance in risks, and even those who are at low risk will want some social protection. Also, in the model presented previously, when there are no market alternatives, income does not matter for preferences, and this is true even if tax and spending are redistributive. This may seem counterintuitive, so by way of explanation, we return briefly to the formal model. Assume that benefits paid out of taxes are divided equally (lump sum) to all recipients, regardless of income:

$$b_i = \frac{\pi_i \cdot \sum y_i \cdot (1 - p_i)}{N \cdot p_i} = \pi_i \cdot \bar{y} \cdot \frac{1 - p_i}{p_i}. \qquad \text{(from 2)} \qquad (9)$$

Ignoring the role of private saving ($k_i = 0$), the tax rate that maximizes the basic utility function in Eq. (1) is then simply:

$$\pi^* = p_i. \tag{10}$$

As before, income does not matter in this result, only indirectly because income is correlated with risk. The reason for the (perhaps surprising) irrelevance of income is that the risk aversion implied by the log utility function exactly counterbalances the redistribution implied by lump-sum benefits. Most estimates suggest that people are in fact more risk-averse, and this will shore up support for the welfare state among the well-off, even if they are considerably lower risk (and also have more savings, an aspect which we have ignored here). Like uncertainty, this helps explain the broad cross-class support for the welfare state in the first decades after WWII.

But this conclusion changes dramatically if we introduce private alternatives (Busemeyer and Iversen 2020), and one of the consequences of better information is that such alternatives become more feasible. We therefore amend the baseline model to add a private alternative to public provision. This alternative is assumed to be universally available and financed by individuals spending a proportion, γ_i, of their own income on these alternatives:[20]

$$U_i = \ln[(1 - \pi - \gamma_i) \cdot y_i] \cdot (1 - p_i) + \ln(\gamma_i \cdot y_i + \pi_i \cdot \bar{y} \cdot \frac{1 - p_i}{p_i}) \cdot p_i, \tag{11}$$

where $\gamma_i \cdot y_i$ is the amount spent on private alternatives.

Eq. (11) assumes that all individuals receive a share of the public benefit, even though people are allowed to supplement it with private alternatives. One common example would be buying a private health insurance that "tops up" the public plan with additional coverage and care. Another would be supplementing a basic public pension with an individual private account.

The amended utility function (11) has an individual maximum, which is:

$$t_i^* = p_i \cdot [1 - \gamma_i \cdot (1 + r_i)], \tag{12}$$

---

[20] The balanced budget constraint is satisfied, since total per capita revenues are $t \cdot \sum y_i/N = t \cdot \bar{y}$ and total per capita outlays are also $t \cdot \sum y_i/N = t \cdot \bar{y}$.

where $r_i = y_i / \bar{y}$ is relative income. Note that if $\gamma_i > 0$, the preferred level of taxation and public spending is lower than in a public-only system. Moreover – and this is key – with private alternatives, higher income is now associated with lower support for public spending. This is because higher income makes the private alternative relatively more attractive as it is directly proportional to income, whereas the public system is a flat rate. This result holds regardless of the degree of risk aversion (or concavity of the utility function), and it means that the preferences over taxation and public spending are now divided by income class.

The effect of more information is therefore something of a triple whammy for the solidaristic welfare state: (i) information directly increases polarization in policy preferences as people become more aware of their risk profile; (ii) it makes private markets more feasible; and (iii) private options further polarize preferences over public provisions (and reduce overall support). By contrast, in an uncertain world, preferences tend to converge on a public system.

FOURTH ARGUMENT: THE ROLE OF REGULATION AND GOVERNMENT PARTISANSHIP

With regard to partisanship, our conjecture is straightforward and echoes long-standing arguments in the literature (Esping-Andersen 1990; Huber and Stephens 2001). Since left parties tend to represent low-wage, high-risk groups, while the opposite is true for right parties, we expect left-leaning governments to try to inhibit the development of private insurance markets and shore up support for the public system. This may also be true for some types of insurance that are not provided publicly, such as life insurance, if such markets are "fungible" with other areas that *are* public, such as health insurance. Life insurance companies are often also health insurance providers and therefore build up expertise and organizational capabilities in the health insurance market.

Governments affect private insurance outcomes via two main mechanisms. The first mechanism is a simple crowding-out effect. By promoting public spending on social insurance and making it mandatory for people to pay into it, the scope for private markets is diminished. Private insurers can offer attractive plans to individuals, but since people cannot opt out of the public system, they face a double-payment problem that undermines demand for private insurance. Yet whether there are tax "discounts" for people who do not use the public system, or even tax subsidies for those purchasing private insurance, is of course a political decision (as we will see in our Swedish case study in Chapter 6, politics favored privatization, at least initially).

The second mechanism used by governments is regulation. Governments can impose nondiscrimination clauses on the private insurance industry. Insurers may have the necessary information to offer differentiated plans, but they may not be permitted to use it. In this case, the analysis is indistinguishable from the asymmetric information case in Figure 2.1: adverse selection will undermine markets. One example is the US Genetic Information Nondiscrimination Act of 2008 (GINA), which prohibits health insurers from using individuals' genetic information to price discriminate against otherwise healthy individuals. It does not, however, prohibit such discrimination in life insurance, disability insurance, and long-term care insurance markets, at least in most US states (states have considerable discretion in the regulation of insurance). Nor does it apply to nongenetic information. Again, at the end of the day, regulation is always a political choice.

SUMMARY

Our information argument is summarized in Table 2.2. We distinguish two dimensions of information: (i) the level of individual information and (ii) whether information can be credibly shared with insurers. If private information cannot be credibly shared, markets will be inefficient as low-risk types leave and push up the price of insurance for all others. In this case, a majority will typically have an interest in a public system. With low information, support for a public system with a high degree of risk redistribution may increase, as everyone has to assume that they may be beneficiaries of the system. We call this the solidaristic welfare state outcome.

When information can be credibly shared with insurers, however, private markets become feasible. Credible information sharing is usually accompanied by high information, and this opens the possibility of a segmented private insurance market where each risk group is offered its own plan (the size of each pool will depend on the level of detail of the information available as well as economies of scale by insuring more people under the same plan). When tailored private insurance is feasible, those with below-average risks will prefer private provision, and with a right-skewed distribution of risk, this will be a majority. Those with high risks will typically be lower income and thus priced out of the market.

Broadly speaking, our argument implies that the information revolution results in pressures to increase market provision (as indicated by the arrow in Table 2.2). Yet these pressures will be tempered by left governments using measures such as "price nondiscrimination" clauses to rule out private markets and tax rules that make it expensive to opt into private alternatives (the double-payment problem). Highly correlated risks may also prevent some markets from emerging or at least require the state to play a key role as the "payer of last resort." When markets are blocked for any of these reasons, increased information will cause polarization in preferences over the level of public provision and the distribution of the costs. If private options are ruled out, however, conflicts over the public system will be diminished by the demand of those with high incomes for a high level of protection and high-quality services (social insurance as a normal good). With private options, the risk of polarization over government programs rises. This is the contested welfare state outcome in Table 2.2.

Finally, it stands to reason that by allowing greater differentiation in the public sector, markets can be preempted to some extent. In this case, we can think of private markets as having an effect through "shadow prices": to some degree, the public sector mimics the private in terms of choice and prices (LeGrand 2009). Busemeyer (2012), for example, shows

TABLE 2.2 *Information and social insurance*

		Credible information sharing?	
		No (Asymmetric information)	Yes (Symmetric information)
Level of information	Low	Solidaristic welfare state	Pooled private insurance
	High	Contested welfare state	Segmented (private) insurance

that in the case of education, greater stratification in the public system increases support among the rich. In general, this logic applies to all policies that allow more differentiation and choice in the public system, the use of credits for supplementary private insurance, cuts in benefits for high-risk groups (such as disallowing coverage of procedures for conditions such as obesity), and introduction of high co-payments, which makes the system less progressive.[21] We have indicated this possibility by placing "private" in brackets in the high-segmentation cell – the segmentation logic of markets may arise in the public sector.

APPENDICES

Appendix 2.1: Graphical Representation of the Pooled Equilibrium with Private Information and Adverse Selection

In Figure 2A.1, there are three risk groups: L, M, and H. With no insurance, income is y in the good state and k in the bad (which are assumed here to be the same for all groups). The solid downward-sloping "fair-bet" (FB) lines are the feasible sets of allocations of income between the two states that would have the same expected value (in the model, the slopes of these lines are $-(1 - p_i)/p_i$). Each risk group would want to allocate enough income for insurance to equalize income in the two states, which are where the FB lines intersect the 45-degree line and the indifference curves (IC) are tangent to each FB line. If the risk was common knowledge and insurance markets competitive, each group would be offered a contract corresponding to these points, denoted x, y, and z in the figure (assuming no costs of provision and zero profit). The benefit, b, stipulated in each contract is the difference between income in the good and bad state, which is $b_i = \frac{\pi_i \cdot y_i \cdot (1-p_i)}{p_i}$ in our model (illustrated here along the x-axis in the case of L).

However, insurers cannot observe the risks of different groups and instead have to pool these so that the expected combined payouts are equal to total insurance payments. When risks are pooled across all three groups, the lines are drawn so that this expected payout (contract) line is equal to M's FB line.

---

[21] Relatedly, publicly funded social policy can be outsourced to private actors, presumably to increase choice and quality. Such "hidden" (Howard 1997), "submerged" (Mettler 2011), "delegated" (Morgan and Campbell 2011), or "divided" (Hacker 2002) welfare state provision typically undermines social solidarity. Privatization and delegation can also lead to governance challenges (Morgan and Reisenbichler n.d.; Taylor-Gooby 1999).

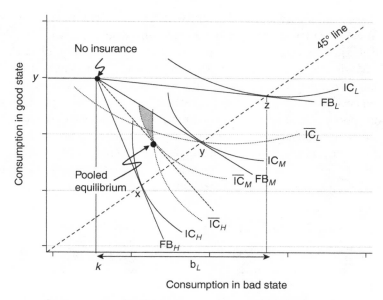

FIGURE 2A.1 Example of a pooled equilibrium with three risk groups

Imagine now that the insurer offered *y* as an insurance plan. If everyone bought the plan, the insurer would break even (the zero-profit condition would hold), and the outcome would be sustainable from the perspective of the insurer. But it is easy to see that *L* would not buy this plan since *L*'s IC is below the "no insurance" point: *L* would be worse off with insurance than without. With *L* opting out, there is a new pooled FB/contract line between *M* and *H*, which is the downward-sloping dashed line. A pooled equilibrium is now feasible, since any point on that line (above the 45-degree line) is superior to the no insurance point for both *M* and *H*.

Note that there is a shaded area above the pooled equilibrium point where *M* would be better off (while *H* would be worse off). In the Rothschild–Stiglitz model, a competitive firm could move into this space and make a profit by selling to *M* (the lower-risk group) only. This would undermine the pooled equilibrium. But this assumes that insurance companies can monitor the quantity of insurance bought by different groups, since otherwise, they might end up selling to a high-risk type at a loss. In this example, *H* would buy the cheaper plan up to the permitted limit and supplement with the high-cost plan to be fully insured. If insurers cannot observe purchases or if they cannot distinguish between low-risk types with high-risk aversion and high-risk types with low-risk aversion, they would not want to move away from the pooled plan and the pooled equilibrium would be feasible (albeit inefficient). This would also be true if insurers could observe purchases and risk aversion but are able to coordinate on not moving away from the pooling outcome. Regulators should, in principle, not object to such agreements, since they preserve the market at a competitive price. In our model, pooling equilibria are allowed for one or all of these reasons.

Lastly, the pooled equilibrium is represented as a single point on the contract line, whereas in the model, we have entered different points on the line in proportion to how much people pay into the system. In this case, the point in Figure 2A.1 represents an average.

Appendix 2.2: Satisfying the Insurer's Balanced Budget Constraint

Assuming zero profit, the total insurance payout is the area under the cost function from the critical threshold given by Eq. (6) to 1 (the insurance pool):

$$\int_{\frac{1}{\bar{p}}-1+s}^{1} (p_i \cdot b_i)\, dp = \int_{\frac{1}{\bar{p}}-1+s}^{1} \left(p_i \cdot \pi_i \cdot y_i \frac{(1-\bar{p})}{\bar{p}} \right) dp.$$

The total insurance revenue is the corresponding area under the revenue function:

$$\int_{\frac{1}{\bar{p}}-1+s}^{1} \left((1-p_i) \cdot y_i \cdot \pi_i \right) dp.$$

The difference between revenues and costs is profits (which we assume to be 0):

$$\text{Profits} = \text{revenues} - \text{costs} = \int_{\frac{1}{\bar{p}}-1+s}^{1} \left([(1-p_i) \cdot y_i \cdot \pi_i] - \left[p_i \cdot \pi_i \cdot y_i \frac{(1-\bar{p})}{\bar{p}} \right] \right) dp.$$

To assess whether the zero-profit condition holds in equilibrium, we need to choose a particular distribution of risks. If this distribution is uniform, as in Figure 2A.1, the amount paid out as insurance in equilibrium is the number of insured, N, times the average payout, which is equal to the mean risk times the mean replacement rate: $N \cdot \overline{p} \cdot \overline{y} \cdot \frac{(1 - \overline{p})}{\overline{p}}$; and the amount paid into the insurance is the number of insured, N, times the average insurance premium: $N \cdot (1 - \overline{p}) \cdot \overline{y}$:

$$\text{Profits} = \text{revenues} - \text{costs} = \left[N \cdot (1 - \overline{p}) \cdot y \right] - \left[N \cdot \overline{p} \cdot \overline{y} \cdot \frac{(1 - \overline{p})}{\overline{p}} \right]$$

$$= \left[N \cdot (1 - \overline{p}) \cdot \overline{y} \right] - \left[N \cdot \overline{y} \cdot (1 - \overline{p}) \right]$$

$$= 0$$

The insurer's budget is thus balanced in equilibrium.

3

A Brief Analytical History of Social Protection

During the period of industrialization in the nineteenth century, many workers across the developed world joined voluntary mutual aid societies (MASs) to cope with new risks (Leeuwen 2016). MASs became quite widespread, and by the end of the nineteenth century, they had millions of members and covered as many as half of all male adults in England/ Wales and Prussia (de Swaan 1988, 144) and at least a third in the USA (Beito 2000, 14). Yet, despite their size, growth, and importance, European MASs protected workers "only against a small fraction of the risks of death, disease, disability, old age and unemployment" (de Swaan 1988, 144). In the USA, MASs were limited to some forms of sickness pay, funeral benefits, and life insurance. In the end, they disappeared and were replaced by alternative arrangements, the most important of which were compulsory public social policy programs (de Swaan 1986, 1988, chapter 5) but also private health insurance in the USA. Why did this happen?

BEFORE THE WELFARE STATE

We begin by considering a successful example of an MAS because it helps us identify features that are conducive to the success of social insurance. The Scottish Presbyterian Widows Fund is commonly credited as the world's first modern life insurance scheme, and it has survived as such to this day (Dow 1971; Dunlop 1992). The story begins with the Scottish Presbyterian Church legalizing clerical marriage in 1560 (as part of the Scottish Reformation). This created the inevitable problem that some ministers would leave widows and occasional orphans without the means to support themselves. Ad hoc collections among the brotherhood did not prevent widespread destitution among survivors, which was a considerable embarrassment to the church. A solution was eventually devised in 1744 by two clergymen, Robert Wallace and Alexander Webster, who teamed up with a mathematician, Colin Maclaurin from the University of Edinburgh, to create a life insurance scheme based on what we now call actuarial tables (they called them "life tables").[1]

These tables relied on detailed data on the life expectancy of ministers and their wives, which made it possible to calculate how much each minister would have to contribute to an insurance fund to ensure every widow and orphan would receive a benefit that was sufficient for them to live comfortably. The scheme is identical to the theoretical model outlined in Chapter 2 with complete risk information, and it proved highly accurate. The projection of the capital in the fund, which was invested in government bonds, was reportedly only one pound off after twenty-one years. This may be a myth, but the calculations were accurate enough that the potential commercial applications became clear, and in 1815, the MAS was transformed into a successful commercial life insurance company named simply Scottish Widows (as it still is today).

Other MASs did not fare as well, and it is important to note the very unique conditions that got Scottish Presbyterian Widows Fund off the ground. First, the membership was small (less than 1,000 ministers), and it was very homogenous. Ministers were chosen from within the religious congregation based on their deep commitment to the teachings of the church. They also attended the same divinity schools to attain their theology degrees. Not only did this guarantee that ministers would have similar life expectancies, but also that outsiders had no feasible way of gaining access to the group's life insurance benefits. In other words, the adverse selection was not a concern. In addition, the fund was built up gradually and resembled fully funded retirement schemes in the sense that most collected benefits only after a life of contributions. The fund was designed for future, not current, widows and orphans. This gradualism, and the fact that life expectancy did not vary very much among ministers, prevented what we referred to in the previous chapter as the time-inconsistency problem. Moral hazard was also not a problem: most ministers led ascetic lives and had no reason or proclivity to put their own lives at risk.

---

[1] The foundations of actuarial science were being established simultaneously in England and were explained for the first time by James Dodson in his "First Lecture on Insurances" in 1756 (Brackenridge and Brown 2006).

Where other MASs were similar to the Scottish Presbyterian Widows Fund – small, homogenous, fully funded, and with strict entry requirements – they generally succeeded. It is no coincidence that many MASs in the USA were organized by immigrant ethnic groups, which brought together people with the same culture, language, and history (Beito 2000, chapter 2). Reciprocity, solidarity, and shared norms of sacrifice – hallmarks of all MASs – were facilitated by a common ethnic identity. But many MASs had wider ambitions. They were cross-ethnic and set up to deal with the huge social needs emerging among the fast-growing urban industrial working class. Unemployment, sickness, and old-age poverty were the issues that increasingly preoccupied the expanding MASs. In the end, however, they were unable to cope, as a brief analysis of their rise and demise will highlight.

No form of insurance eluded MASs like unemployment protection. Such insurance was at the opposite extreme of the widow's fund in terms of feasibility. Risks varied and were hard to observe (except at the tails), and workers at high risk flocked to the funds and drove out good risks. Furthermore, the risks were often highly correlated, since MASs tended to recruit industries and occupations that could be decimated by technological change or foreign competition (Glenn 2001). When this happened, the funds would go bankrupt, which created an incentive not to join and pay dues in the first place. Indeed, if the solution to adverse selection was to seek a more homogenous membership, this only made the problem of correlated risks more severe. Unlike life insurance, all unemployment insurance was organized on a PAYG basis, and it was politically impossible to cut replacement rates as fast and as much as would be necessary for the scheme to remain solvent in private hands. Attempts were made, but no MAS ever managed to create an effective and sustained unemployment insurance scheme.

Episodes of large-scale unemployment before the introduction of major public schemes were also a major constraint on other activities of MASs. During the Great Depression in the USA, Cohen (1999, 220) reports that about three-quarters of unemployed MAS members in Chicago stopped paying their dues. In previous recessions, people relied on savings and short-term credit to remain in good standing, but the persistence of unemployment during the Great Depression meant people simply ran out of money. Dues could be raised by relying on other members to pay for the unfortunate, but redistribution was not a serious option in voluntary associations. Unable to insure against one of the greatest risks in the

Fordist mass production economy, MASs therefore reduced their membership instead.

MASs proved only marginally more successful in providing benefits to older workers. Here, the problem was time inconsistency. MASs instantly attracted workers who sought not only insurance but also more or less immediate income support. Older workers could often anticipate old-age poverty, but accommodating their needs required transfers from younger generations – again organized on a PAYG basis – and for that, MASs had to be able to solve the time-inconsistency problem: current net contributors had to be certain that future contributors would support them when they grew old. But, again, since MASs were voluntary, quasi-democratic organizations, they lacked both the capacity to impose mandatory payments and the institutional mechanisms to enforce commitment to such intergenerational bargains. Some MASs developed "endowment plans," which offered a fixed payout after a certain number of years. This was similar to a funded savings plan, except that it entailed an element of insurance against old age. The "risk" of living past the end of your working age and having no means of sustenance was "insured" against by guaranteeing an income from the common fund (Beito 2000, 207–8).

Interestingly, these plans were opposed by MASs offering life insurance, and they lobbied state governments to outlaw them or at least remove any tax or other protections. While endowment plans were denounced as selfish and flying in the face of fraternalism, it is not hard to fathom the real reason they were opposed (Beito 2000, 208). Endowment plans appealed to the healthy who expected to live long lives, while life insurance did the exact opposite. Any tendency for good risks to exit life insurance was thus magnified by the availability of endowment plans. Simply put, good risks would insure their families by betting on living for a long time, while bad risks did the same by betting on dying early. In the long run, both types of insurance survived in the commercial market where they could be offered more efficiently – like life insurance, individual retirement accounts, annuities, and so on. Old-age poverty, however, could only be addressed by the state, and this was thus the origin of Social Security in the USA.

Across countries, MASs were perhaps most successful in the area of burial insurance. A decent funeral was of considerable importance to most people, so members continued paying their small contributions to the fund even in hard times. It was fairly easy for the MASs to deal with adverse selection – they simply did not admit already sick or old people, and they adopted a funded approach by requiring members to make a minimum number of contributions to qualify for the benefit. Moral hazard in burial insurance is also not of great concern because no one would end their own life just because their funeral is covered. Lastly, while actuarial knowledge was still limited and (burial) insurance systems were often underfunded, increases in life expectancy tended to alleviate the problem and make these systems sustainable in the long run.

MASs were also relatively successful in the area of sickness pay. Every worker faced the risk of falling ill and thus forgoing wages that were essential to their families' welfare, so this was an important matter for all workers (Andersson and Eriksson 2017). As a result, there was widespread willingness to pay into sickness funds, and many were successfully set up. Moral hazard, which is an otherwise serious problem when it comes to illness, could usually be dealt with through community monitoring and peer pressure (checking on colleagues failing to show up at work, requiring doctors' notes, etc.). Gottlieb notes that "intrusive monitoring and social pressure may have been an effective way of mitigating moral hazard" (2007, 278), and such monitoring can be seen as an extension of MASs "fraternizing" function (which sometimes turned abusive). In this respect, MASs had a real advantage over commercial insurance, which was anonymous and arm's length.

Nevertheless, it was hard to avoid adverse selection in the case of sickness pay, and the time-inconsistency problem was never far behind because older workers were more likely to fall sick or have accidents. Unlike the case of burial insurance, rising life expectancy made the adverse selection problem worse (Beito 1990, 725), and the implied direct transfer between younger and older generations was severe enough that it has been likened to a Ponzi scheme (Kaufman 2002, 47). Indeed, much effort went into recruiting younger members to pay for older insiders, which was not easy. That said, the logic is no different than a public PAYG scheme, which would ordinarily be welfare enhancing. The problem was that MASs, unlike strong political parties coupled with the coercive powers of the state, could not credibly commit to future generations.

Over time, nearly all MASs faced an increasingly crippling double bind. These organizations were intended to help workers, irrespective of their means, deal with major risks during the greatest economic transformation in history, but seeking inclusiveness, they only ended up triggering an exodus of younger, healthier, and more employable workers. The problem, as Thane explains, "was ensuring a steady flow of young, healthy entrants to balance the costs of providing sickness and, effectively, old-age benefits to older members, especially as the numbers of older members grew later in the century" (Thane 2012, 414). In practice, MASs could only control who was *excluded* from membership. Organizing around ethnicity, religion, residency, and occupation was one strategy; excluding unskilled laborers and the infirm was another; requiring certain periods of membership/a certain number of contributions before qualifying for benefits was yet another. But all these restrictions reduced the relevance of MASs, especially in an industrializing economy with rising residential and occupational mobility, which implied the need to expand, not narrow, insurance pools.

Even as MASs sought to exclude bad risks, they faced increased competition for good risks from commercial insurance companies. Life insurance provides an early example. While MASs sought to limit adverse selection by religion, ethnicity, or occupation, modern life insurance companies were based on actuarial science and modern underwriting principles, notably the requirement of a medical examination. The Equitable Life Assurance Society in London, Scottish Widows (described previously), New York Life Insurance Company, and the New England Mutual Life Insurance Company of Boston are some of the pioneering companies in the first half of the nineteenth century (Brackenridge and Brown 2006). The business took off due to the use of medical selection criteria, and "insurance medicine" became a certified field, organized by specialized professional associations in both Europe and the USA. The expansion of life insurance has been intimately linked to the growth of medical data, initially based on simple urine, body size, and blood pressure markers but now including the whole range of modern diagnostics, which are linked to mortality tables to predict life expectancy. The next chapter shows how the expansion of such data drove the growth of the life insurance business.

The US healthcare market provides another, related, example of commercial competition for MASs. Initially, writes Robert Gordon, the market "suffered from all the abuses of modern health insurance, including 'cream skimming' to find the healthiest patients, age limitations to avoid insuring the old, medical exams to detect preexisting conditions, and reluctance to insure the lower classes" (Gordon 2016, 235). Trying to exclude bad risks using crude indicators limits the size of the market, but the introduction of group health plans gave private insurance much greater reach.

Group plans succeeded in large part because they could rely on third-party enforcement. When an employer signed up for a group plan for its employees – usually through Blue Cross or Blue Shield (which later merged into an alliance of thirty-six insurance companies) – the cost was shared with employees and health insurance was treated as a fringe benefit. The system was reinforced by the state making contributions tax deductible in exchange for government regulation. The system still left out a significant share of the employed – especially those in smaller firms – as well as everyone outside of employment and not covered by the policy of an employed spouse, but for the insured, it provided state- or region-wide risk pooling.[2] Some MASs tried to offer their own group-based policies, but since membership was voluntary and not tied to employment, they immediately encountered problems of adverse selection. MASs were essentially eliminated from the health insurance market by 1940 (Beito 2000, chapter 11).

The MAS double bind of having to exclude bad risks and lose good risks to commercial insurance is eloquently summarized by de Swaan (1988, 150):

> As modern means of communication and publicity created a nationwide market, commercial insurers began to reach out to a public which had traditionally supplied the members of the workers' funds. The mutual societies found them-selves outpriced, their potential clients usurped by the commercial societies and their actual members increasingly isolated on relatively unfavorable terms. The commercial-insurance market threatened to do to them what the autonomous mutual-aid funds had done before to a lower social stratum: exclude them and join on better terms with more attractive company.

The double bind ultimately led to the homogenization of MASs but at the same time greatly limited their reach.[3] As Thane observes, "[m]utual societies were the preserve mainly of regularly employed, better paid men" (Thane 2012, 413). At the end of the nineteenth century, MASs were widespread, but they could not address the mounting social prob-lems faced by the growing working class. Even for those who were members, only a small range of risks were covered, and three major

---

[2] As we discuss later, however, since the 1974 Employee Retirement Income Security Act, employers have been able to "self-insure" using plans that only cover their own employees, which breaks up state and regional pools into more risk differentiated ones (Hacker 2004). This fragmentation has been magnified by the growing segmentation of labor markets into low- and high-skilled occupations, which has left many of the former uninsured – a trend only recently counteracted by the ACA.

[3] Gottlieb (2007) claims that MASs providing sickness insurance did not face an adverse selection problem. But the evidence is not entirely persuasive. He essentially tests whether members (compared to nonmembers) were more likely to be sick (or suffer an accident). According to his data, this does not appear to be the case, but membership composition already reflects efforts to deal with adverse selection. In our view, the adverse selection was in fact a serious problem for MASs.

insurance areas – unemployment, health, and pensions – were grossly under-provided.

MASs experienced their heyday in the second half of the nineteenth century, a period during which they counted perhaps as much as 50 percent of the working-age population as members. However, by the eve of the democratic revolution in the early twentieth century, when industrialization, urbanization, and longer life expectancy multiplied risks, MASs were in decline. The democratic state soon offered a superior alternative to MASs for a majority of workers by devising state-sponsored and enforced plans. The state had the fiscal capacity to cover a broader range of risks, including unemployment, and it promised to cut costs for the majority by forcing good risks into one national pool. Organized "class-mass parties" on the center-left, with detailed party programs and institutionalized intergenerational commitment mechanisms, stood ready to mobilize the support of the working and middle classes by meeting their mounting electoral demands, and they did so mainly by offering expansive, and compulsory, social programs. The shift, writes de Swaan, can be seen as a transition "from individual providence by private savings [to] collective forms of insurance against income loss to nationwide compulsory social security arrangements" (de Swaan 1988, 165) – what we referred to previously as the solidaristic welfare state.

There is a debate about whether state programs "crowded out" MASs, which would have otherwise survived (Beito 1990, 2000; Gottlieb 2007; Siddeley 1992), but we see this as a largely moot issue because electorates everywhere made their preferences clear through the ballot box. It is certainly true that as publicly provided benefits expanded, MASs lost their raison d'être; at the end of WWII, they had largely disappeared, and virtually all demand for social insurance was directed at the state (with private health insurance in the USA being the main exception). But for the vast majority of workers, this new equilibrium was superior to the old fragmented system. It presupposed democracy or majority rule because the upper classes were generally able to self-insure and had no interest in a large fiscal state. Parties on the right opposed the expansion of state power for that reason, but they could not prevent it.

A different crowding-out argument from the right is that the welfare state undermines family and community, as well as any sense of mutual responsibility toward fellow citizens – the presumed virtues of MASs. Broadly formulated, in this view, the welfare state is antithetical to social capital and vibrant civic society. In the words of Charles Murray (2013, 286):

Communities are strong and vital . . . because the community has the responsibility for doing important things that won't get done unless the community does them. Once that imperative has been met . . . then an elaborate web of expectations, rewards, and punishments evolve over time . . . When the government says it will take some of the trouble of doing the things that families and communities evolved to do, it inevitably takes some of the action away from families and communities. The web frays and eventually disintegrates.

Variations on this theme were often espoused by leaders of fraternal societies in the 1930s USA (Beito 2000, chapter 11), but their focus on organizational survival clouded their judgment. The comparative evidence lends no support to the idea. In fact, Rothstein and Stolle (2003) find a positive relationship between large encompassing welfare states and social capital. The causality is of course hard to establish, but even after seven decades of the postwar welfare state, the positive cross-country relationship persists. This is hardly consistent with the notion of the welfare state substituting for social capital. Rothstein and Stolle argue instead that a large welfare state induces "generalized trust" (a hallmark of social capital) by tying together the fate of people across classes and treating individuals equally; a view much closer to our own.

At any rate, the problem has now shifted. The choice is no longer between the state and MASs but between the state and market-based alternatives. These alternatives appeal to self-interest, and they induce segmentation of risk groups. This is the exact opposite to the early development of the welfare state, which marked a shift toward more encompassing and solidaristic forms of insurance.

A perhaps more plausible argument is that MASs "survived" in the form of "Bismarckian" social insurance. In line with Esping-Andersen's (1990) "conservative" welfare state, payments and benefits in the Bismarckian model, as in the case of MASs, are based on income-related contributions, usually organized by occupation and industry, with employer and employees sharing costs (Palier 2010). The term "Bismarckian" refers to the pre-democratic origins of the system in Bismarck's attempt to foster loyalties to the state instead of to class, famously extended first to civil servants, or "Beamte," and then to the professions. Yet it was only with democracy that social insurance was generalized to the majority through compulsory membership in public schemes.

The contribution-based logic of the Bismarckian welfare state is sometimes referred to as an insurance principle, though payments were never organized according to risks but rather according to occupation (Hinrichs

2010). While there is a correlation between occupation and risk, which has probably increased over time, the Bismarckian welfare state still implied considerable risk redistribution by requiring payments by earnings and awarding benefits by risk incidence. Old-age insurance was organized based on the PAYG principle. The largest occupational class was skilled industrial workers, which represented a very large heterogeneous risk group, implying significant redistribution. Empirically, Bismarckian welfare states are notably more redistributive than "Beveridgean" welfare states, even though the Beveridge model is based on a more deliberately redistributive, needs-based principle. Conde-Ruiz and Profeta (2007) solve this paradox by showing that the Bismarckian welfare state produced greater support for spending among the middle classes and thus pushed overall spending to the point where the redistributive impact exceeded that of Beveridgean systems, an argument harking back to Korpi and Palme (1998).

Still, the differentiation built into the Bismarckian system can be seen as a source of political resilience, even as we simultaneously see the proliferation over time of private pensions, "funded" health opt-outs, and supplementary private insurance. As we discuss later, the link between occupation and insurance has been strengthened in otherwise redistributive Nordic welfare states, and this shift is directly connected to the growing coincidence of risk and occupation. Increasing de facto sorting across risk groups within the state can also be seen as a Bismarckian feature that is graduated by status, but the politics is driven by risk segmentation and middle-class demands, not by any counter-democratic force.

INFORMATION AND THE EMERGENCE OF SOCIAL SOLIDARITY

The rise of the welfare state is a story that has been told many times before (for excellent reviews, see Cousins 2005; Myles and Quadagno 2002; Palier 2010; Quadagno 1987; Van Kersbergen and Becker 2002; Van Kersbergen and Manow 2008, among others), including from a risk perspective (Baldwin 1990; Iversen and Soskice 2015a; Mares 2003; Rehm 2016; Swenson 2002). Our contribution aims to underscore (i) the underlying information conditions that rendered private provision ineffective and (ii) the role that the state played in overcoming not only market failure but also the distributive battles that have received less attention in the literature. These battles were between good and bad risks, which are overlapping with and yet distinct from class and occupation, and between generations. (iii) With the rise of information and private alternatives, however, divisions are increasingly along income and class lines. If people can opt out of the public system, it will face a double bind similar to that of the nineteenth-century MASs but with a twist: high-income, low-risk types will want to opt out (and into private plans), while low-income, high-risk types will try to hang on. The middle class can either seek to shore up the public system by making it costly to exit (and more attractive to stay), or it can join the exodus. The political reality today is fundamentally different from the Golden Age of the welfare state because there are now viable options in both the public and private systems.

The analysis in the previous section highlighted the limitations of private solutions, whether in the form of MASs or commercial businesses, in responding to the rising demand for social insurance. Adverse selection and time inconsistency loom large in this account, and together they set the stage for a revolutionary shift toward a public system that pooled risks across risk groups, income, and policy domains. The state had one trump card that other institutional domains did not: the power to tax. Everyone was in, and no one could opt out. This new public system was massively redistributive because those with higher income and lower risks paid a disproportionate share of the costs and claimed a smaller share of the benefits. It was therefore a boon to the working and middle classes who acquired insurance at an unprecedented level. Others were forced into the system and heavily subsidized it.

Yet the rise of the welfare state was less contentious than it might have been, for three main reasons. First, insurance is a normal good with demand rising with income. When there are no viable private alternatives, this helps shore up support among upper middle classes who may be at sufficient risk to support the system despite paying higher taxes. Second, as long as most people are uncertain about their position in the risk distribution, they must assume that their risks are not vastly different from those of an average person. If everyone assumes their risk is average, those with higher income may in fact be no less supportive of the welfare state, depending on their exact degree of risk aversion and the extent of progressivity in taxation and benefits. Of course, the assumption of average risk is not realistic, but it highlights a key insight in Rawls's theory of justice: behind the veil of ignorance, most will go along with some equalization of income. Finally, because insurance is welfare-enhancing and because many employers depended on workers making risky investments in firm- and industry-specific risks, some government-backed guarantees of benefits, such as healthcare, may have been necessary for skill-intensive product market strategies to emerge (Estevez-Abé, Iversen, and Soskice 2001). Pooling of risk was also attractive to employers in industries with above-average risks (Mares 2003; Swenson 2002).

Figure 3.1 summarizes our historical analytical narrative about the rise of the welfare state in very broad strokes. The main left-right axis captures the key role of information, which can also be loosely read as a timeline starting at the turn of the previous century and moving into the current period as the information revolution unfolded. In this subsection, we focus on the early twentieth century depicted on the left side of the figure; we then turn to the consequences of the information revolution in the late twentieth century and beyond – as summarized on the right side of Figure 3.1 – in the next subsection.

Initially, highly incomplete information – with individuals holding some information about their own risks but most being quite uncertain about their position in the risk distribution – is not conducive to the formation of insurance markets. The commercial health insurance in the USA is highly unusual for the developed world, and its establishment required heavy involvement by both large employers and the state. MASs for artisans and high-skilled occupational groups provided some private insurance to the privileged, but these arrangements only survived in highly modified forms through state compulsion, or they transitioned into charities or occasionally commercial firms (as in the case of Scottish Mutual). The vast majority of MASs appealing to the working and middle

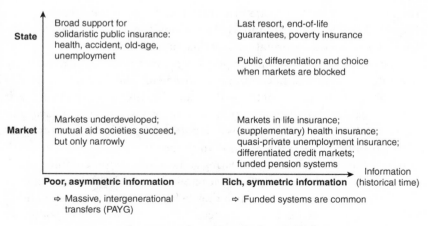

FIGURE 3.1 Summary of our historical-analytical argument

classes were replaced by the welfare state in the 1930s and 1940s, and they were all but gone by 1950.

Across industrializing democracies, the rise of state-guaranteed or state-sponsored social insurance set the stage for decades of relatively equitable social protection. A low-information environment joined with a strong state in the context of majoritarian politics to forge the relatively consensual inter- and post-war welfare state. States trumped markets and MASs in insurance, and the effect was to integrate and redistribute across classes.

As noted, this egalitarian trend was reinforced by the huge demo-cratic demands for solutions to intergenerational transfers, especially in old-age pensions but also in healthcare concentrated among the old. Such intergenerational transfers involve time-inconsistency problems because young people cannot be sure that by paying into a PAYG system, benefits will be available when they themselves need them. Markets could not solve the problem, and it fell on political parties to create overlapping generations organizations that rendered promises about the future credible – what in the party literature is called the responsible party model.

Figure 3.2 illustrates the political-economic logic of the argument. Figure 3.2(A) shows a hypothetical but plausible underlying "objective" risk distribution, which may or may not be directly observed by either individuals or insurers. Since there has always been a small, privileged group of high-income and secure upper-class individuals able to insure privately, sometimes via markets but more often through personal wealth, there is a small "hump" on the left. But for most people in the first half of the twentieth century, private insurance was not an option, in large part because insurance markets and MASs could not solve the pervasive prob-lems of asymmetric information and time inconsistency.

The emergence of compulsory public insurance occurred in a relatively low-information, high-uncertainty environment, and this was undoubt-edly conducive to the rise of the welfare state because, in most instances, it created a solid majority for public solutions (assuming standard risk aversion). We have illustrated this in Figure 3.2(B) with a more homogen-ous distribution of *perceived* risks than the underlying distribution, which can be modeled as a Bayesian updating game where people combine priors based on average (observed) risks with noisy signals about their own risks (or the risks of the group to which they belong). Such "homogenization" of risk perceptions made tax-financed public provision less politically contentious and facilitated expansive social protection coalitions.

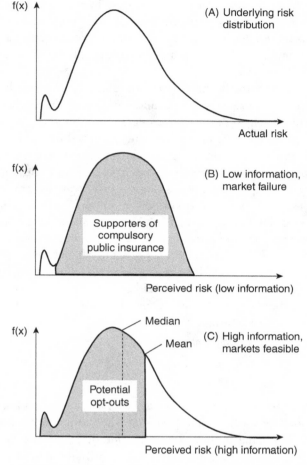

FIGURE 3.2 Information and the actual and perceived distribution of risks
Note: Panel (A) shows the underlying distribution of risk with a small group of very low-risk individuals able to self-insure (this is a hypothetical distribution). Panels (B) and (C) show the distribution of *perceived* risk when information is low and high, respectively. In the low-information case, it is assumed that market failure is widespread and that a large share of the population therefore has a preference for a public system; in the latter case, markets are feasible, and those with below-average risks are potential candidates for opting out of the public system since they are net contributors to that system.

The gradual transfer of social insurance functions to the state was of course not uniform across countries. As MASs were collapsing everywhere and markets were not up to the task of protecting people from large-scale health, employment, and income insecurity, the main questions became "how much state protection?" and "with what design?" In response to these questions, all of today's advanced industrial societies developed mandatory social policy programs but in different forms (Esping-Andersen 1990).

As we have seen, the Bismarckian welfare state used compulsory membership in social insurance schemes, and it preserved the privileged status of those in the strongest professions to a greater extent than elsewhere, but the major role of the state in guaranteeing a compulsory social insurance system still vastly expanded risk pools and generated very significant risk redistribution. In countries with strong churches and Christian democratic parties, compulsory social insurance was complemented by non-state entities, often with the traditional family as an institutional focal point (Hinrichs 2010; Kalyvas and van Kersbergen 2010; Van Kersbergen 1995). In countries with strong and (more or less) unified unions and left political parties, most social functions were left entirely to the state, resulting in more redistribution. Even in liberal welfare states, the extensive social protection programs in health, old age, and employment were shifted to the public sphere, albeit combined with some employer-based coverage in the USA and Japan.

THE INFORMATION REVOLUTION AND THE FRAGMENTATION OF SOCIAL SOLIDARITY

Over time, information about risks has become far more widespread and the technology for credibly sharing risk data has improved exponentially – we are in, or moving toward, the right side of Figure 3.1 and toward Figure 3.2(C). This matters not only for the feasibility of markets but also for the potential for differentiation and segmentation of insurance premiums and interest rates. Where markets are allowed, they generally thrive in a high-information context, as can be seen in life insurance, supplementary private health insurance (in the case of the USA, increasingly differentiated primary insurance), and financialized markets in pensions. The latter has been facilitated by the gradual transition to privately funded systems that have replaced government PAYG schemes.

The information revolution has helped bring the observed risk distribution into line with the actual distribution (Figure 3.2(C)), and it has at the same time enabled private insurance markets to emerge. These markets are inevitably more differentiated and less redistributive than the public solutions that preceded them. It is true that their spread is limited by the fact that all else being equal, everyone with above-average risk would be better off in a public system, but since most risk distributions can be assumed to be right-skewed, the assumption of overwhelming support for public solutions is no longer tenable. It is this shift in the politics of social insurance as a result of increased availability and quality of information that we want to draw attention to in this book, using examples from a variety of (social) insurance markets.

Partisanship and institutions that shape partisanship continue to matter because different income-risk groups have different preferences over the form and level of social insurance. We therefore follow Gingrich (2011) in hypothesizing that the political left and right respond differently to the pressures of privatization. For the left, the objective is to shore up support for the public system, even if this means the introduction of internal markets, and sometimes even private opt-out options that put pressure on public providers to better cater to the preferences of middle-class constituencies. Where demand for services rises with income, the strategy pursued by the left is to spend more on high-quality public provision, often coupled with an expanded set of choices within the public system. The right, by contrast, seeks a more wholesale substitution of private markets for public provision, constrained by situations (such as Medicare) where there is broad popular support for a public option. But while we allow for partisan effects, our key claim is that the information revolution has expanded the scope for private markets in social insurance and that the result has been rising segmentation of social insurance across income-risk groups.[4] This has made appeals of the traditional left for solidaristic public solutions less politically viable, despite the fact that provision is not likely to move out of the public domain entirely. In short, the costs and benefits of social insurance have changed with the growing availability and quality of information in a manner that is generally inequality increasing.

Hicks (2016) has argued that in proportional representation systems, the left can sometimes facilitate privatization because in these systems governments are better able to internalize dispersed benefits of privatization while ignoring concentrated costs, whereas the opposite is true for the left in single-member district systems. Hicks considers

---

[4] We abstract from geographic variation in risk pools, which have their own interesting political implications and can lead to more or less territorial fragmentation of social solidarity (Beramendi 2007, 2012). We find it plausible that the information revolution heightens geographical cleavages.

privatization of state-owned businesses, where the logic is compelling, but insurance markets work differently because the costs and benefits are both concentrated. In this case, privatization is always problematic for the left.

In the remainder of this chapter, we illustrate these conjectures across three "classic" social insurance domains: health, pensions, and unemployment. In the next three chapters, we will examine these domains in greater detail, using a variety of evidence. What follows is thus essentially a short preview of the rest of the book.

Health Insurance

The availability of more and better information promises to be of particular importance for health insurance. Health risks are not as closely related to "class" (education and income) as unemployment risks are, but the financing of public health insurance is almost perfectly correlated with income because public health systems are financed either by contributions or general tax revenue, both of which are disproportionately paid by the rich. For this reason alone, health insurance is redistributive. When markets, or at least quasi-private insurance organizations, form because information about risks rises, risk pools will fragment, and inequality will increase.

The case of US health insurance offers a fascinating study in the tug-of-war between a centralizing, risk-distributive state and a fragmenting market-driven process – what Jacob Hacker (Hacker 2002, 2004) called "risk privatization." Until the ACA in 2010, healthcare in the USA consisted of two public segments – Medicare and Medicaid – and one private segment, namely, the employer-provided healthcare described earlier. The private segment was heavily regulated by US states until 1974, and almost all plans were organized collectively across firms and industries, usually on a state- or region-wide basis (Swenson 2018). Covered by the huge nonprofit Blue Shield Blue Cross insurance alliance, all employers were charged the same per-employee "community rate." Most employees therefore enjoyed equal access to benefits, making this a rare example of private risk redistribution – although the unemployed, many outside the labor market (unless covered by an employed spouse) and many workers in small firms were still left uninsured.

The 1974 Employee Retirement Income Security Act opened the possibility of the provision of insurance by individual employers, called "self-insurance," which was not subject to state regulation. Many large firms with relatively educated and well-paid, as well as low-risk, workers took advantage of this option, which undermined the cross-subsidization of more risky workers, especially those in smaller and medium-sized firms (Hacker 2004, 253). This is a classic example of segmentation of risks, and it greatly increased the inequality in insurance coverage and in rates. For some, health insurance became much more expensive, and the uninsured rate soared (Catlin and Cowan 2015).

With many middle-class voters worried about costs and coverage, the ACA of 2010 created a new layer of regulation that sought to improve access and lower prices by shifting more people onto publicly subsidized plans. This introduced much broader risk pooling than in the employer-provided private system. But, at the same time, private insurance outside of the ACA has been allowed to further fragment. It is thus a complex picture with much uncertainty about the future. But the American health-care system is a good illustration of the powerful centrifugal force of increasingly fragmented private insurance taking advantage of new opportunities to subdivide risks, even as the centralizing force of government provision garners significant popular support with so many worrying about whether they will be able to insure themselves and their families through the market.

In the short run, it is conceivable that the COVID-19 pandemic will boost support for public insurance as more people have been exposed to the fear that their employer-provided insurance plans will not survive the lockdowns. Even more than the financial crisis, the pandemic has created a sense that no one is safe. But any solidarity "bump" from the pandemic is likely to be dwarfed by the most important long-term driver of the politics of health insurance: more and better information. Public insurance cannot be assumed to be safe as long as private alternatives are ubiquitous and likely to metastasize and divide into new forms.

There certainly seems to be no limit when it comes to the technological possibilities for identifying and parsing health risks. In 1965, Gordon E. Moore, the cofounder of Intel, made his famous prediction that the number of transistors on a microchip would double every two years. Moore's Law has held up remarkably well, and the number of transistors per integrated circuit chip has increased from less than a thousand to over 50 billion. This increase in processing power has been complemented by no less spectacular growth in storage – by a factor of several thousand between 1950 and 1990, a thousand between 1990 and 1996, and about tenfold since then. This expansion of data storage and increase in processing speed were essential to one of the greatest accomplishments of science: the sequencing of the human genome. The prototype version developed in 2001 cost about US$300 million, but since then the price of sequencing has dropped to about US$1,000 in 2014, to less than US$200 in 2018, and it continues to fall. In fact, according to the National Human Genome Research Institute, the cost of sequencing the human genome has been falling much faster than implied by Moore's Law.[5] If a complete sequencing of the gene is not required, a company such as 23andMe can provide a pretty comprehensive genotyping of individuals for less than US$200,[6] though the accuracy of consumer genomics products still leaves much to be desired.

Gene-based diagnostics and treatment are in their infancy but progressing fast. The number of available personalized gene-based diagnostics and treatments approved by the Food and Drug Administration (FDA) in the USA rose from 13 in 2006 to 113 in 2014 (Personalized Medicine Coalition 2016), and it continued to climb sharply, reaching 184 in 2019. The number of standard tests on a simple penetration blood sample increased from 130 in 1992 to 319 in 2014 (Pagana and Pagana 1992; Pagana, Pagana, and Pagana 2014). Perhaps more tellingly, all the leading technology companies – Alphabet, Amazon, Apple, IBM, Microsoft, and so on – have committed huge resources to developing a new data-based health industry that draws on large databases stored in the cloud. In one project called Verily, the self-proclaimed aim is to "accelerate precision health and medicine by integrating state of the art testing, longitudinal monitoring and participant engagement."[7] One longitudinal monitoring device is "Study Watch," which shares real-time health data with a cloud-based database (Apple Watch works similarly). Combined with data from the NHS, AI can be used to diagnose and predict a broad range of illnesses including eye disease, diabetes, kidney disease, Parkinson's, heart failure, and multiple sclerosis. Verily is part of Google Health, which comprises two related initiatives: DeepMind and Calico. Microsoft has created a parallel health initiative called HealthVault, and Amazon Care offers both virtual and in-person AI-assisted healthcare.

The potential application of such data by insurance companies is obvious. In the extreme, it could render broad swaths of the population

---

[5] See www.genome.gov/about-genomics/fact-sheets/DNA-Sequencing-Costs-Data, last accessed June 3, 2021) [https://perma.cc/5KW5-AAJV]).

[6] Unlike complete gene sequencing, genotyping requires that variants of genes are identified in advance.

[7] https://verily.com/blog/better-data-better-care/ (last accessed June 3, 2021) [https://perma.cc/FAB7-KZHX].

uninsurable in a private market (Rosanvallon 2000). The real question is not whether Big Data can be used to create more differentiated risk pools but whether and to what extent insurance companies will be allowed to use the data in this manner. The constraint is not primarily privacy, despite the huge attention privacy policies have received, amplified by the public sharing of data that were not properly anonymized. Instead, people who are deemed to be at low risk may be perfectly willing to share their data with insurers, and those who refuse would be placed in higher-risk pools by default. Insofar as health data can be acquired by, and credibly shared with, would-be insurers, it mitigates the asymmetric information problem and opens the possibility that insurance can be provided efficiently through the market. This dynamic is already well underway in life insurance, as we show in the next chapter.

An effective constraint on insurers is for governments to prohibit private firms from making use of actual or potential data. A good example here is the nondiscrimination clause in the ACA. This clause does not extend to non-preexisting conditions, which may nevertheless be highly predictive of future illness. A more thorough attempt to shut down such discrimination is GINA in the US, which prohibits insurers from using individuals' genetic information to engage in price discrimination against otherwise healthy individuals. As mentioned, it does not however prohibit such discrimination in life insurance, disability insurance, and long-term care insurance markets, at least in most US states.[8] Nor does it apply to nongenetic information. This highlights an important point: nondiscrimination regulations are political choices, and we cannot assume that democracy will necessarily adopt and sustain such regulations if a majority perceives them as an implicit tax on their good health.

Outside of the USA, voluntary private health insurance (VPHI) – which gives preferential access to procedures, doctors, and hospitals outside the public system – is now available to individuals in most countries, subject to health tests designed to weed out bad risks. Private providers emphasize that their services should be seen as a complement, not a substitute, to the public system, but it is unambiguously increasing segmentation and may undermine support for the public system in the long run as decisions are

---

[8] For a brief overview of the topic of genetic information and how it is (not) regulated by the Health Insurance Portability and Accountability Act of 1996 (HIPAA), the GINA, and the Federal Trade Commission in the USA and the General Data Protection Regulation (GDPR) in the EU, see Harbord (2019). Privacy regulations with respect to genomic data raise thorny questions, many of which remain unanswered (Mitchell et al. 2020).

made about what is and is not covered under the two tiers (Fabbri and Monfardini 2016). Again, regulation is always a political choice, and if a majority sees the advantage of pro-market regulation, it could obviously carry the day. In the high-information scenario in Figure 3.2(C), the median voter has risks below the mean and knows this, which gives them an obvious reason to be critical of a redistributive public system. Given an underlying right-skewed distribution of risk, the politics can change with more information. The main case against the fragmentation of risk pools is a normative one; politically, there can be no presumption that it will win out.

Pensions and Credit-Based Insurance

"Privatization of risks" (Hacker 2004) has also occurred through the spread of "funded" retirement plans (individual or collective), which are much less redistributive than public PAYG schemes. Younger workers, either individually (as in the case of American 401(k)s or individual retirement accounts [IRAs]) or collectively (as in the case of collectively bargained occupational plans in Europe), have gradually moved into funded systems, which are usually defined-contribution (but not necessarily: annuities would be defined-benefit). Privately funded systems now make up an average of 72 percent of GDP (2017), up from 37 percent in 2002 (OECD 2018c).

This shift has important implications for inequality. First, there is little or no redistribution going on in funded systems because benefits are directly tied to contributions (with some qualifications for collectively bargained plans). Where pension schemes are individualized, a second source of inequality is information about optimal investment strategies, which typically increases with income and education. Finally, private equity, unlike public pensions, can be transferred to the next generation via inheritance (Rehm 2020).

Private pension plans have helped fuel a huge expansion of credit markets, which also increasingly serve to smooth personal income and hence act as insurance. "Nonlinear" career patterns where workers move between family and work and between work and education are much more common in today's knowledge economy than in yesterday's industrial economy, and credit markets have accommodated this shift. In just over twenty years, from 1995 to 2016, private debt in advanced democracies increased from an average of 90 percent to about 157 percent of GDP (OECD 2018b). Insofar as credit is used to smooth income, interest rates are essentially equivalent to insurance premiums – they are the cost of insurance against income volatility. Access to credit, and the terms of such access, has become an important determinant of stratification, just like other private insurance schemes.

The same is true of mortgages for house purchases – which are increasingly seen as a key to a middle-class life – with home equity acting as a buffer against bad luck (Ahlquist and Ansell 2017; Ansell 2014). Chapter 5 explores the consequences of financialization for economic inequality, with a focus on the role of information and how it is conditioned by the regulation of financial markets and social transfers. We show that in the wake of the financial crises, Fannie Mae and Freddie Mac (FM/FM) – two major quasi-public financial institutions created by the US government – were required to shift a greater share of mortgage risk to the originators (mostly banks), which created a scramble to acquire more information in order to separate good from bad risks. In European countries, where mortgage markets are often less regulated, protection against income losses has helped equalize interest rates and access to loans. Removing these protections, as occurred under the Hartz IV reform of unemployment benefits in Germany, should create greater rate differentiation by risk and induce efforts by lenders to cut out bad risks.

Unemployment Insurance

Unemployment insurance is one of the "classic" forms of social insurance that has historically been in the public domain. As we have discussed, one reason for this is that individual risks of unemployment are correlated over time, sometimes highly, thereby violating the actuarial principle of equating the current values of revenues and outlays. A major shock to an industry, or sometimes the entire economy, could wipe out an insurance fund, and it often did just that in the case of unemployment MASs (until such insurance was abandoned altogether). Second, even in stable environments, adverse selection would often either deter membership among good risks and/or leave a large number of workers uninsured. The state solved these problems by compelling workers and firms to pay into a common unemployment pool and by using deficit spending to bridge the business cycle.

But while there is no example of a truly private system of unemployment insurance, information – coupled with regulation of insurance pool entry – is nevertheless having a major transformative effect on the politics of unemployment insurance. Over the past four decades, the risk of unemployment has been increasingly tied to occupation and education because of what economists call skill-biased technological change. This shift is not lost on unions and professional associations, and we will argue in Chapter 6 that it is increasingly acknowledged in the social network in which economic information is shared informally. Stable differences in unemployment risks eventually become known, at least approximately, when workers share them through their networks or organizations, and this is when preferences over the level of protection begin to diverge or polarize. As we discuss in Chapter 6, this is happening in the USA, and it undermines the solidarity that was once forged by uncertainty or incomplete information.

The bifurcation of risks, and information about such risks, has parallels in a number of historical cases. Japan is a case in point because of starkly divergent unemployment risks between high- and low-skilled workers – a bifurcation that has been reinforced by a system of employment protection and company-provided benefits that substitute for labor mobility (Aoki 1988). In Latin America, formal sector workers have historically enjoyed a much higher level of protection than those in the informal sector, with an order of magnitude difference in labor market risks (Wibbels and Ahlquist 2011). To a lesser but still significant degree, this has also been true in certain European countries where strict hiring and firing rules adopted in the post-1970 period have divided labor into "insiders" and "outsiders" (Rueda 2005, 2007).

Segmentation of unemployment risks may not only polarize spending preferences but also lead to a differentiated system of benefits. A paradigmatic case of universalism, Sweden, has experienced episodes of significant segmentation along these lines. The Swedish unemployment system is organized around unemployment insurance funds (UIFs) run by unions but backed by commercial insurance companies. Because Swedish unions are strongly segregated by occupation and socioeconomic status, and because unions serve as gatekeepers for entry into the UIFs based on detailed information about workers' education and current and past employment, differences in occupational unemployment rates translate directly into differences in fees, *unless* there are deliberate policies to pool across funds. Much like the case of American healthcare, with more of the funding burden shifting from a common pool to individual UIFs starting under a conservative government in the early 1990s, there was a notable rise in insurance rates for some, while others paid less (when accounting for savings on taxes). The increasing linkage between contributions and benefits can also be seen as a new Bismarckian aspect of the system, although the participation of private insurers is a genuinely novel feature. During the reforms many Swedish workers gave up on unemployment insurance altogether and now depend on minimal social benefits if they lose their jobs. With the partial rollback of the reforms in 2014, fees converged again but the general lesson is that when risks become closely associated with observables, such as occupation, solidaristic forms of insurance are likely to come under political attack. In Chapter 6, we show how this interaction of information about risks and labor market segmentation is translated into polarized policy preferences through social networks.

CONCLUSION

Faced with the uncertainties of life, people have always pursued risk-coping strategies and set up "systems of social security" (Platteau 1991). In the early phases of the Industrial Revolution, MASs became a key institution for coping with social policy risks. But they proved inadequate and ineffective to deal with market failure and widespread destitution, especially among the old. MASs could not solve information problems and faced the double bind of losing good risks to commercial insurers or self-insurance and attracting bad risks from among the broad target constituency of workers. They were also unable to solve the commitment problem at the heart of intergenerational redistribution (PAYG systems), which was much needed in the face of poverty and disease among the old and infirm.

Only the emerging modern democratic states had the capacity to address these challenges. Governments could overcome adverse selection by mandating the take-up of insurance. Such mandatory risk pooling did not come about for efficiency reasons – as economists tend to imply – but instead for reasons of distributive politics. Under the proverbial "veil of ignorance" (Rawls 1971) – in times of uncertainty or in low-information environments – a majority of risk-averse citizens have an economic interest in publicly provided social insurance. This is especially true because public insurance compels even the best risks to contribute to the system, thereby subsidizing those with higher risks. In terms of the commitment problem, political parties in democracies developed into organizations that could credibly promise the young and healthy that the system would still be around to assist them when they became old and needy, which is a precondition for majority support of a PAYG system. From this perspective, a dearth of information and the immediate need for transfers played critical roles in bringing about the welfare state under conditions of democracy.

How does the information revolution – the lifting of the veil – change these dynamics? Does lack of information *cause* the welfare state, while ample information causes it to wither away? The story is not that simple: we see some unraveling of welfare states but also remarkable resilience. In reality, the information revolution changes the political economy of insurance by (i) making markets more feasible through the separation of good and bad risks and (ii) dividing preferences over public provision between those groups.

For insurance markets to work efficiently, it has to be possible to divide people into a large number of small and homogenous risk pools. This enables "actuarially fair" insurance, but coverage, contributions, and replacement rates will vary widely. Welfare states do not depend on detailed information – instead they are forcing everyone into a common pool. This insurance will not be actuarially fair but rather highly redistributive – what we might call "socially fair." When information is incomplete and markets are infeasible, the majority tends to prefer socially fair insurance to no insurance, but when information makes it possible to offer actuarially fair private insurance, this becomes an attractive option for many who would otherwise support public insurance.

This is not an argument for the inevitability of private insurance. The welfare state is still very much with us. Markets do not offer insurance against poverty, and insurance for the poor in a liberal welfare state like the USA enjoys broad popular support, as is the case for Medicaid. Social investment policies focused on the development of human capital and skills also enjoy broad support in the middle and upper-middle classes (Garritzmann, Busemeyer, and Neimanns 2018; Hemerijck 2018), and such investments, in turn, promote labor market mobility, which tends to spill over into support for generous public insurance (Alt and Iversen 2017). In addition, fiscal and regulatory constraints sometimes crowd out private markets by creating a "double-payment" problem for those who might otherwise opt into private plans. When this occurs, and assuming that insurance is a normal good, those with high income sometimes exhibit surprisingly high support for public spending (Busemeyer and Iversen 2014).

More often than not, however, high-end demand has been allowed to trickle through to supplementary private insurance schemes. Alternatively, demand for high-quality provision has been accommodated by choice and internal markets in the public sector, which puts those with the education and cognitive resources to use these opportunities at a significant advantage.[9] In this sense, the market casts a long shadow over the state. More generally, as the information revolution facilitates both more private market formation and differentiation between risk groups, it becomes harder to sustain a highly solidaristic welfare state and the broad middle-class support that gave rise to it.

---

[9] Choice and competition mechanisms are more beneficial for people that have better information and can navigate a system's complexities – typically those with higher education and income. LeGrand, a proponent of such mechanisms, suggests the employment of "choice advisors" (LeGrand 2009) to offset this effect.

4

Private Markets for Life and Health Insurance

After pensions, health is generally the second largest form of social insurance in wealthy democracies. In 2018, healthcare spending amounted to nearly 17 percent of GDP in the USA and more than 10 percent in Western Europe (OECD 2019, figure 7.3).[1] Arguably, no single form of insurance matters more to the welfare of people than health insurance, and any differentiation in access and cost is therefore highly consequential for inequality. For these reasons, the potential for the information revolution to create increasingly segmented health insurance markets is a topic of great importance to both political economy and public policy.

It is hard to accurately gauge the potential for segmentation, however, because most health insurance is (still) public (in the case of Europe) or heavily regulated (in the case of the hybrid US system). The continued importance of public provision is itself an interesting aspect, which we will discuss later, but to explore the consequences of information in terms of risk segmentation, we first turn our attention to two smaller, but increasingly relevant, insurance markets that have much in common with the health insurance domain: life insurance and supplementary (private) health insurance.

Life insurance relies heavily on the same kind of health data that is critical to health insurance, and since it is entirely in the private domain, and less regulated, it can serve as a window into the potential future of health insurance as discussed in the "Life Insurance Markets" section. We

[1] These numbers refer to government, compulsory and voluntary, or out-of-pocket health expenditures (https://doi.org/10.1787/888934016816, last accessed June 3, 2021 [https://perma.cc/8K4A-UARY]).

offer both qualitative evidence on the way information is used in the underwriting practices of the industry and quantitative evidence on the relationship between information and market penetration.

In the "Supplementary Private Health Insurance Markets" section, we extend this analysis to voluntary health insurance markets, which have increased as a supplement to, and sometimes substitute for, the public system. Even when these markets do not directly replace the public system, access follows the same logic of "cream skimming" that characterizes all private markets and turns them into a source of inequality. It is too early to say whether supplementary insurance markets will act as a bridge to a more privatized healthcare system – this depends critically on how the middle class views the costs and benefits of a system with more opt-out options – but one thing that is fairly clear is that it leads to more differentiation in the access to and quality of healthcare, even when healthcare remains in the public sector.

Finally, we consider the collective choice of public versus private insurance and how this choice interacts with individual decisions to opt out or stay in the public system (see "The Choice between Public and Private Health Insurance" section). Although we expect major partisan clashes over this choice, it is possible to imagine relatively stable equilibria with predominantly public or private provision. Even in the latter case, however, we are likely to observe pronounced public elements that compensate for the lack of private insurance against poverty and the difficulty of overcoming time-inconsistency problems through private markets. Whatever the balance between private and public insurance, we make the case that the information revolution will introduce greater differentiation in the healthcare system, to the detriment of equality and solidarity.

LIFE INSURANCE MARKETS

Life insurance companies go to considerable lengths – described later – to decide who can get insurance, under what conditions, and at what rate. Why? In its most basic form, life insurance guarantees the payment of a stated benefit if the covered person dies during a specified time period in exchange for premium payments.[2] From an insurer's perspective, therefore, the ideal customer is someone who never dies. Because such customers are hard to come by, life insurance companies try to sign up people less

---

[2] In permanent life insurance policies, the agreed time period is the customer's lifetime. Many customers choose twenty-year time periods.

likely to die during the covered period (term life insurance) or have high life expectancy (permanent life insurance). Insurance companies use information to pick those "cream puffs" and to adjust premiums based on assessed mortality risk. They might even nudge you to keep the grim reaper at bay. As one provider puts it, insurance companies want you to "live a longer, healthier life"[3] – though, in truth, they mostly care about whether you outlive your life insurance (which is good for them) or not.

Life insurance companies walk a fine line between insuring as many customers as possible at competitive rates and remaining financially viable. Accurate risk classification is crucial for their financial survival and success. They collect all sorts of information – as described later – to screen out undesirable applicants and to charge appropriate premiums, based on an applicant's assessed mortality risk. In the language of our theoretical framework, information mitigates the adverse selection problem and helps companies set actuarially fair premiums. As shown in Figure 2.2, customers are placed into risk groups and charged different premiums, while some people are denied insurance altogether.

In the previous chapter, we briefly discussed the origins of life insurance in the early nineteenth century. In the next subsection, we describe current underwriting practices in the (American) life insurance industry. Even though the industry still largely functions as it has since its inception, many readers will be surprised by just how much information life insurance companies collect, where they are getting it from, and how it is used for underwriting purposes.

More and better information helps companies improve their risk classification, and we agree with one insider that "[t]he life insurance industry is in the early stages of a digital transformation that has only accelerated since the onset of the pandemic."[4] In the "Innovations in Underwriting Practices" section, we describe some elements of this digital transformation, how completely new types of data sources are being exploited for more granular risk assessments, and how the pandemic has fast-tracked these developments. More and better information can improve risk classification, which enables private insurers to offer insurance policies for well-defined and relatively homogeneous risk pools and improve their

---

[3] www.johnhancockinsurance.com/home.html (last accessed June 3, 2021 [https://perma.cc/N4H3-Z72M]).

[4] According to Brian Winikoff, President and CEO of MIB (www.mibgroup.com/news/2020_11_psg.html, last accessed June 3, 2021 [https://perma.cc/VGW8-YDU7]). As we will see later, the MIB plays an important yet largely hidden role in life insurance underwriting.

bottom line and expands markets. This is the *first argument* we developed in detail in Chapter 2. For the purposes of this chapter, we divide the argument into two hypotheses:

H1: As the quantity, quality, and credible sharing of information improve, private insurance markets will rely on such information when it becomes available, for purposes of risk classification and premium calculation.

H2: Where private insurance markets are politically tolerated, they expand as information and credible sharing of information improve.

The life insurance market is just beginning to be transformed by the information revolution. Micro-targeted insurance products are still a thing of the future. For the most part, the industry continues to function as it always has: Applicants fill in a form with medical information; the company verifies that information, potentially requires they undergo a medical exam, pulls some records, and places the applicant in a particular risk group that determines the insurance conditions. Medical information and medical records are still the primary source of information for risk classification. Yet these too have expanded, and in the "Life Insurance Market Penetration" section, based on a sample of rich democracies, we explore the effects of medical information and the viability of life insurance markets in the past few decades.

We will also engage with another argument from Chapter 2, namely, that left and right governments have different approaches to the regulation of insurance markets depending on the constituencies they represent. In the case of life insurance, the political left is not primarily concerned with the spread of insurance itself – it has always been provided privately, and while it discriminates against bad risks, the distributive consequences are modest – but instead with how medical information is treated, since this has implications for private health insurance markets, which have huge distributive consequences. Placing regulatory roadblocks in the way of private insurers' access to medical information will slow the expansion of both private health and life insurance markets:

H3: Private insurance markets will expand more rapidly under right than left governments.

Current Underwriting Practices

Underwriting is a secretive business. But a Google search for "life insurance underwriting guidelines not for public use" (without quotation marks) turns up interesting results that shed light on how life insurance companies try to solve the asymmetric information problem. The first few hits include detailed underwriting guidelines from more than half a dozen American life insurance companies that are "not for public dissemination"[5] but easily accessible to anybody with an internet connection. If you walk into a broker's office to get a quote for life insurance, he/she will need to collect the information set out in these guidelines.

Generally, the documents state what information must be collected and how. They typically cover at least three topics. The first topic included in underwriting guidelines is insurability. All guidelines list the conditions under which life insurance coverage is declined. These range from (a long list of) medical preconditions to unfavorable family histories, certain occupations or hobbies, risk factors such as bankruptcy or addiction, and even driving violations. The list of disqualifying preexisting conditions is lengthy and can be quickly updated. In response to the COVID-19 pandemic, for example, many life insurance companies immediately tightened their underwriting rules. Common adjustments included the postponement of applications from consumers who had recently traveled internationally, a temporary freeze on applications from older people, and refusal to offer policies to customers with COVID-19, at least for the time being. Changes of this kind were clearly designed to screen out applicants with a high probability of contracting COVID-19 or a high probability of dying because of it.

The second topic covered in underwriting guidelines pertains to necessary medical information for the purposes of risk classification.

---

[5] Examples of these qualifiers read as follows:

- "For Agent Use Only – Not For Use With The Public" (National Life Group)
- "For Producer or Broker/Dealer Use Only. Not for Public Distribution" (Legal & General)
- "For Financial Professional Use Only. Not For Use With the General Public" (Metlife)
- "FOR BROKER/DEALER OR AGENT USE ONLY. Not for public dissemination. May not be distributed, reprinted or shown to the public in oral, written or electronic form as sales material" (Allstate)
- "For Financial Professional Use Only. Not For Public Distribution" (Brighthouse Financial)
- "For producer use only. Not for use with the general public" (Mutual of Omaha)

The guidelines establish detailed rules about what medical tests and other check-ups are required. A third topic in the guidelines concerns how those deemed insurable are grouped into risk classes – based on age, BMI, health history, heart rate, cholesterol, and so on. Insurance companies consider their customers to be "Preferred Plus," "Preferred," "Standard Plus," "Standard," or "Substandard (Table-Rated)," and insurance premiums vary accordingly. Substandard customers pay the highest premiums (if they can even get insurance at all).

Additionally, even for basic coverage, insurance companies typically acquire information from at least three sources. The first source is the Medical Information Bureau (MIB; tagline: "Risk Revealed"). This little-known not-for-profit is owned by 600 or so life and health insurance companies. It has existed since 1902 and stores the information from life, health, disability income, critical illness, and long-term care insurance applications and allows insurance companies to compare the information from current applications to previous applications dating back up to seven years. Customers shopping for insurance, therefore, cannot hide information they have shared in the past.

The second source life insurance companies routinely consult is one of several available prescription databases. For a small per case fee, they "run a quick search that provides the names of medications taken, when and how often they were filled and the prescribing doctor. Even better, there's no additional client contact required – it's quick and invisible."[6] Prescription histories are now pulled on more than 90 percent of life insurance policies (Balasubramanian, Chester, and Milinkovich 2020, 6). Therefore, applicants cannot conceal their prescription drug history from life insurance companies, either.

The third source life insurance companies customarily use is the Department of Motor Vehicles. They request Motor Vehicle Reports, which provide data on an applicant's driving history, including violations and accidents. This information is predictive of mortality and used to help determine eligibility and premiums.

---

[6] www.scorgloballifeamericas.com/en-us/knowledgecenter/Pages/Emerging-Value-of-Rx-Datab ases.aspx (https://web.archive.org/web/20180219144455/www.scorgloballifeamericas.com/e n-us/knowledgecenter/Pages/Emerging-Value-of-Rx-Databases.aspx, last accessed June 3, 2021).

On top of that, life insurance companies typically also query existing databases to acquire information on an applicant's financial situation, such as credit reports. Interestingly, they use financial information not only to determine the financial viability of high-value policies but also to assess mortality risk. For example, the "Lexis Nexis Risk Classifier" is a tool that "accurately stratifies mortality risk using public records, consumer credit history and motor vehicle history" since "customers with superior public records and credit history information have better relative mortality."[7]

Innovations in Underwriting Practices

More, better, and more shareable information is already affecting underwriting practices in the life insurance industry and is likely to bring transformative change to the entire insurance industry. We identify three broad trends triggered by technological progress: the digitalization of existing data, the collection of new types of data, and the mining of these old and new data. We discuss these three developments – digitalization, tracking, and artificial intelligence – in turn.

Digitalization

In 2009, former President Obama signed the Health Information Technology for Economic and Clinical Health Act, as part of the Recovery Act. Its goal was to accelerate the adoption of electronic health records (EHRs) in order to improve the safety, quality, and coordination of healthcare. But entrepreneurs quickly realized that this digitalized information would be of use for other, commercial, purposes as well, including underwriting, provided it could be standardized. It did not take long for this general idea to be converted into money-making businesses. Even for insiders, the pace of this development came as a surprise. In July 2019, one such insider concluded that "the use of electronic health data is in its infancy for underwriting."[8] Less than a year

---

[7] www.munichre.com/content/dam/munichre/marc/pdf/stratifying-mortality-risk/lexis-nexis/L exisNexis-Risk-Classifier-stratifying-mortality-risk-using-alternative-data-sources.pdf/_jcr_c ontent/renditions/original./LexisNexis-Risk-Classifier-stratifying-mortality-risk-using-alterna tive-data-sources.pdf (last accessed June 3, 2021 [https://perma.cc/RX9E-ZA7K]). TransUnion offers TrueRisk scores, a similar product that "has been validated by Reinsurance Group of America" (Balasubramanian, Chester, and Milinkovich 2020, 6).
[8] Katie Devlin: "Leveraging Electronic Health Data for Insurance Operations" (http://clar eto.com/wp-content/uploads/2019/09/8.8.19-Clareto-White-Paper-DRAFT-KFD.docx, last accessed June 10, 2021 [https://perma.cc/RV5P-SH4J]).

later, the use of digital health data in underwriting has become standard, at least in some companies.

The reliance on digital health data was greatly accelerated due to COVID-19. The pandemic made many traditional underwriting practices impossible, most importantly in-person medical examinations. Life insurance companies immediately sought to replace in-person medical exams – long the centerpiece of risk classification – with alternative ways of credibly assessing an applicant's health status and history. Advances in data sciences came to the rescue. The approach taken by John Hancock life insurance is instructive here. In early April 2020, John Hancock rolled out access to the "Human API portal," which allows applicants to give the company direct access to their health records.[9] Human API has built up a large infrastructure that allows John Hancock to guzzle up, standardize, and interpret health information from users that authorize access to their data. This includes clinical data (diagnosis and conditions, doctors' visits and encounters, vital signs and behaviors, doctors' notes and narratives, procedures and lab tests, medications, and prescriptions) and data from wearables (steps and activity, heart rate, weight and BMI, sleep quality, meals and calories, and blood pressure). Human API makes money by selling these data to other interested businesses, such as life insurance companies. As explained in the company's mission video:[10]

Consumers today generate health data in all kinds of ways, from doctors' visits to fitness devices to trips to the pharmacy. Unfortunately, this data lives in disconnected systems with no easy way to access all of it when we need it most. ... New and exciting technologies meant to improve our daily lives need data access. But our health data is unstructured and fragmented which makes accessing it complicated, time-consuming, and expensive. ... We built the first national consumer-controlled health data platform that covers 90% of US hospitals along with over 300 wearable devices and fitness apps. We give consumers a free, easy, and transparent way to connect and share their health data with the businesses they trust no matter where or how it was stored. ... Human API gives businesses a simple way to allow consumers to share their health data ....

At about the same time, John Hancock also entered into a strategic collaboration with Clareto, to "further enhance [their] electronic health

---

[9] https://advisor.johnhancockinsurance.com/financial-professionals/NLI/life-insurance/collateral/covid-19/Producer_msg_underwriting_4_8.html (last accessed June 3, 2021 [https://perma.cc/XG5U-66W7]).

[10] www.humanapi.co/videos (last accessed June 3, 2021 [https://perma.cc/RX3V-LEPV]). Also available at https://vimeo.com/416429521 (last accessed June 3, 2021 [https://perma.cc/37AJ-5UNL]).

record (EHR) access capabilities."[11] Clareto collects and standardizes much of the same clinical data as Human API, but accessing it does not require the involvement of the applicant, other than their signature on a HIPAA waiver. HIPAA refers to the Health Insurance Portability and Accountability Act, and it contains strict privacy rules for medical records. But it cannot prevent the voluntary sharing of data on which underwriting relies.

Once health information is digitally available, standardized, and portable across systems, there is no going back to the old status quo – companies will inevitably continue to seek more and better information about their potential customers. For example, the abovementioned secretive nonprofit MIB – run by life insurance companies – has recently taken the exchange of medical information for underwriting to another level by developing an infrastructure of EHR, known as "MIB EHR" (tagline: "The Future Is Here Today"). Since the start of this effort in 2018, MIB has gained access to tens of millions (likely hundreds of millions) of patient records and patient' real-time clinical data.[12] To date, more than fifty US life insurance carriers have signed up to use the MIB EHR platform,[13] greatly facilitating their access to an applicant's medical information.

Some of these practices operate in gray zones of privacy laws, but we think it is highly unlikely that stricter consent rules would reverse or even slow the digitalization tsunami. As we have emphasized throughout, there are strong incentives for "good risks" to share their information, and

---

[11] https://advisor.johnhancockinsurance.com/financial-professionals/NLI/life-insurance/c ollateral/covid-19/Producer_msg_underwriting_5_7.html (last accessed June 3, 2021 [https://perma.cc/NU3L-2YNC]).

[12] Since the inception of MIB EHR in 2018, the company has rapidly gained access to tens of millions of medical records. According to press releases, it has partnered with the following EHR providers (all links last accessed June 3, 2021): (1) Uhin, June 2020, 6 million records (www.mibgroup.com/news/2020_06_uhin.html [https://perma.cc/R9 E7-BJKJ]); (2) Midwest Health Connection, June 2020, 24 million records (www.mibgroup.com/news/2020_06_MHC.html [https://perma.cc/RQM2-9ZVM]); (3) Healthix, April 2020, 20 million records (www.mibgroup.com/news/2020_04_heal thix.html [https://perma.cc/5RWC-3PXR]); (4) Allscripts/Veradigm, February 2019 (www.mibgroup.com/news/2019_02_allscripts.html [https://perma.cc/63Z7-M5XK]), estimated 50–150 million records (www.healthcareitnews.com/news/ehr-vendor-veradigm-and-partners-creating-new-shared-data-tools-researchers [https://perma.cc/6 5BM-ZR5P]); and (5) Epic, November 2018 (www.mibgroup.com/news/2018_10_epic .html [https://perma.cc/F73T-Q7E4]), estimated 250 million records (www.epic.com/a bout [https://perma.cc/2EZF-M6C9]).

[13] www.mibgroup.com/news/2020_08_ehr.html (last accessed June 3, 2021 [https://perma .cc/X5E6-ASX4]).

those who do not will face an insurance "penalty." MIB is not likely to run out of data any time soon.

Tracking

Besides this increased standardization, portability, and connectedness of existing medical data, life insurance companies increasingly collect and rely on new types of data. Just as in the car insurance market, companies are increasingly making use of trackers to identify attractive risks and setting premiums based on verifiable information, such as fitness protocols. Information obtained through these channels allows companies to offer individually tailored insurance plans, based on detailed risk classification.

In this business model, insurance companies worldwide team up with firms like Discovery Limited, which develops wellness programs branded as "Vitality – A wellness solution that changes the way insurance works." Vitality uses data on consumer behavior, which are collected by fitness trackers (such as Fitbit, Jawbone, Misfit, and Apple Watch) and transmitted directly to the company or insurer. Additional information, such as purchasing data, is sometimes collected as well. This detailed, constant, and instant tracking of consumers is useful for health and life insurance companies alike, as explained on the company's (now defunct) website:

Insurers traditionally use risk rating factors to access and underwrite risk. These include age, gender, socio-economic status as well as smoker status and medical history. These risk factors are mostly static and offer a limited view of a person's risk. A person's health behavior, however, provides a more accurate risk indication. Vitality, with its 17 years of wellness experience, data and understanding of wellness behavior, adds an additional dynamic underwriting rating factor. It takes into account the impact of chronic diseases and lifestyle factors, such as smoking, level of exercise, diet, alcohol consumption, blood pressure and cholesterol on a person's risk profile. By integrating Vitality with insurance products, we have developed a scientific and dynamic underwriting model that uses high-quality data about a person's health, wellness, credit card spending and driving behavior to assess their risk more accurately over time. This results in: better benefits, lower and more accurate risk pricing, better selection, lower lapse rates, [and] better mortality and morbidity experience.[14]

Tracking devices ("wearables") are increasingly common in the life insurance market. And health insurance coverage plans tied to these tracking devices – frequently in combination with workplace wellness programs,

---

[14] https://web.archive.org/web/20160322151205/www.vitalitygameon.com/vitalityga meon/ (last accessed March 11, 2021).

which often perform their own health risk assessments and biometric screenings – are gradually being rolled out as well. At one point, policy-holders with Oscar Health Insurance in the USA, for example, received a free step tracker and could earn up to US$1/day for taking a particular number of steps. In a similar vein, health insurance company UnitedHealth and chipmaker Qualcomm have teamed up to develop a wearable device tied to a coverage plan that incentivizes health behavior by paying up to US$4/day to a covered employee and their spouse if they reach certain targets.[15] John Hancock Life Insurance marketed a life insurance policy that calculates annual premiums based partially on data collected by an "activity tracker," which policyholders received for free when they signed up as "a whole new approach to life insurance – one that can protect your loved ones while allowing you to save money and earn valuable rewards by simply living a healthy life. In fact, the healthier you are, the more you can save."[16]

The new tracking systems have become widespread in the life insurance market and are used by John Hancock Life Insurance (USA), Prudential's Vitality Health (UK), AIA Australia life insurance and MLC On Track (Australia), and Generali (Austria, France, and Germany). But they are equally useful for health insurers, and currently, more than 100,000 employees at an undisclosed number of companies in a dozen US states are using wearables through UnitedHealth plans. But this is undoubtedly just the beginning. Implanted sensor technology takes health monitoring to the next level and is already being used widely by the medical profession (Dey et al. 2019).

Regulators are trying to play catch-up. For example, in response to reports of a number of insurance companies "creeping" on potential customer's social media profiles, New York State Department of Financial Services – the state's primary insurance regulator – issued one of their "circular letters" "to advise insurers authorized to write life insurance in New York of their statutory obligations regarding the use

---

[15] Technological progress makes tracking devices ever more sophisticated. One example is the Kolibree toothbrush whose three-axis accelerometer, three-axis gyrometer, and three-axis magnetometer can decipher detailed subtle movements in order to provide real-time feedback, which gets transferred to the brusher's smartphone via Bluetooth and from there can be shared with a dentist. Of course, it could also be shared with a dental insurance company.

[16] www.myadvisorschoice.com/sites/default/files/pdf-files/ProspectingLetterforLifeInsuranc e.pdf (last accessed June 3, 2021 [https://perma.cc/4V4M-LBCU]). See also the FAQs on the John Hancock Vitality Program (www.johnhancockinsurance.com/vitality-program /vitality-faq.html, last accessed June 3, 2021 [https://perma.cc/6U2W-NQ5W]).

of external consumer data and information sources in underwriting for life insurance." Such data include "consumer's retail purchase history; social media, Internet or mobile activity; geographic location tracking; the condition or type of an applicant's electronic devices (and any systems or applications operating thereon); or [a consumer's appearance] in a photograph." The agency allows the use of such information but mandates that "the insurer must establish that the external data sources, algorithms or predictive models are based on sound actuarial principles with a valid explanation or rationale for any claimed correlation or causal connection" (New York State Department of Financial Services 2019). So, for the time being, it is legal for insurance companies in New York to snoop on social media to collect information used for risk discrimination, at least if they can explain to regulators why they are doing it.

Artificial Intelligence

All the data that are being collected must be stored and analyzed, and Big Tech is committing huge resources to the advancement of a new data-based health industry, using a variety of related strategies. Alphabet has recently created a new research unit, called Verily Life Sciences, to develop AI-based approaches to data analysis, and Microsoft's Healthcare NExT is focused on collecting massive amounts of individual data from a variety of sources and transferring it to cloud-based systems, including a virtual assistant that takes notes at patient-doctor meetings using speech recognition technologies (Singer 2017). AI-enabled machine learning is used to make sense of the data for diagnostic purposes, which are of course also highly relevant for underwriting.

One of the sources of data is independent laboratories, which have greatly proliferated over time, and these data can be combined with other health data to produce detailed profiles of individual health parameters with enormous predictive power. The promise of "personalized medicine" is based on such individual information, and former US President Obama's Precision Medicine Initiative reads like an impassioned call for more data on people's underlying health risks – "including their genome sequence, microbiome composition, health history, lifestyle, and diet."

As AI crunches the numbers, unexpected predictors of health and mortality may turn up as well. For example, it turns out that mortality outlook can be informed by charitable giving and pet ownership (Balasubramanian, Chester, and Milinkovich 2020, 6) or floor of the residence (Panczak et al. 2013). Whether these associations are causal or correlational matters little, since AI can use them to facilitate greater risk differentiation in insurance policies, which in turn expands the reach of markets and simultaneously results in greater inequality in coverage and cost. The expectation is that advances in technology and medical knowledge will enable companies to predict someone's medical future with remarkable accuracy, rendering bad risks uninsurable in private markets, while offering good risks a whole range of attractive options.

Life Insurance Market Penetration

Insurance companies have always relied on a variety of ways to mitigate the information problems they face. It is also clear from the previous discussion that their methods of risk classification are becoming increasingly sophisticated and targeted at individual consumers. Our anecdotes and vignettes are therefore consistent with the idea that private insurance markets are plagued by information problems, that companies employ a variety of strategies to mitigate them, and that the information revolution offers new opportunities that insurance companies will exploit to improve risk classification and underwriting. Ultimately, more, better, and more shareable information should deepen private markets.[17]

To further explore the effect of information on private market penetration more systematically, we now turn to information about health and the development of life insurance markets. Apart from modest programs for survivors' ("widows'") pensions, the public system offers no life insurance. This is therefore an obvious area of potential private expansion as more medical information becomes available that can be credibly shared.

The principle of life insurance is very simple, as mentioned previously: people pay a predetermined monthly premium as long as they live, and the insurance company pays a predetermined amount to survivors if the policyholder dies before the end of the insurance contract. If the policyholder dies before the cost of the payout (adjusting for interest) is covered, the insurer loses, while the family of the insured gains. For the insurer to

---

[17] This conjecture follows our *first argument* in Chapter 2. It unambiguously applies to all cases where additional information replaces asymmetric information, which can be reasonably assumed in the vast majority of instances. But it also extends to the case of moving from low, symmetric information to high, symmetric information when it is not common knowledge that information is low. In this scenario, insurers will worry about adverse selection and raise premiums accordingly, limiting the scope of markets. Without common knowledge, insurers are essentially operating in a risky environment and therefore demanding a risk premium. In a high-information environment, common knowledge does not matter because insurers know what they need to know.

calculate the insurance premium, it is therefore essential that they are able to accurately calculate the life expectancy of potential policyholders. The adverse selection problem is obvious in this context because people will buy plans that assume they will live longer than they themselves expect to live. The first life insurance plans were restricted to pools where members shared so many traits that their life expectancy could be calculated with great accuracy. In the previous chapter, we described how The Scottish Presbyterian Widows Fund, commonly credited as the world's first modern life insurance scheme, was restricted to Scottish Presbyterian clergymen – a very homogeneous group with high entry barriers and an average life expectancy that was easy to calculate from carefully kept church records.

In the following regression analysis, our *dependent variable* is life insurance market penetration measured as a ratio of direct gross life insurance premiums to GDP. This measure was developed by the OECD and "represents the relative importance of the [life] insurance industry in the domestic economy" (OECD 2015b). We have data covering twenty-two advanced economies for the period around 1983–2018. (The Appendix provides more details on the data, as well as methods, variables, and results.)

Modern life insurance schemes rely on information about individual health, complemented by demographic and related data. The expectation is that better information regarding health risks leads to larger life insurance markets. Thus, our key *independent variable* is private information that can be credibly shared with insurers. But how can information be measured? This is a difficult challenge – not only for this chapter but also for the entire book: we do not, of course, have direct access to private information. Unfortunately, there is no simple or general – and perhaps not even a satisfactory – answer to the question of how to measure information.

But actuarially relevant information is reflected to some extent in the availability of diagnostic tests. Accurate tests by independent laboratories are one element of what insurance companies need to distinguish risk groups, and such tests – based on blood, saliva, urine, tissue, and increasingly also genetic samples, as well as CT and MRI scanning – have become much more common, accurate, and affordable. A striking example is the cost of sequencing the human genome, which was about US$300 million in 2001, dropping to US$1,000 in 2014 and less than US$200 in 2018, as mentioned previously.[18] Correspondingly, and as also mentioned previously, the number

---

[18] According to *The Economist* (March 14–20, 2020, p. 5), "the first genome cost, by some estimates, $3bn." Moreover, the costs for sequencing a human genome have been falling faster than Moore's law (*The Economist*, March 14–20, 2020, p. 8).

of personalized gene-based diagnostic tests and treatments available in the USA has risen from 13 in 2006 to 184 in 2019. The number of standard tests that can be carried out on a simple penetration blood sample increased from 130 in 1992 to 319 in 2014 (Pagana and Pagana 1992; Pagana, Pagana, and Pagana 2014). This development is shown in the left panel of Figure 4.1. Tests can be used to predict life expectancy by disease, and the more the number of tests, the greater the accuracy of these predictions.

We can also trace the development of diagnostic capabilities via an authoritative and widely used indexing system for diagnostic tests operated by the National Library of Medicine. It maintains a list of 27,000 or so "Medical Subject Headings (MeSH)" (Coletti and Bleich 2001) that are designed to map the entire biomedical field based on English-language academic journals. The MeSH classification includes a hierarchical tree structure where one sub-branch indexes terms related to "Diagnosis" (E01). In 1971, there were 277 index entries; there were 450 in 1981, 600 in 1991, 701 in 2001, 914 in 2011, and 1,067 in 2014. This development is shown in the middle panel of Figure 4.1.

Or we can chronicle the increase in medical information – and hence perhaps even the ability to correctly predict mortality – by the number of yearly entries in Medical Literature Analysis and Retrieval System Online, a bibliographic database of life sciences and biomedical information.[19] These numbers are shown in the right panel of Figure 4.1.

All these plausible indicators of medical information show sharp increases over time. However, while interesting and suggestive, such numbers do not lend themselves to a quantitative cross-national empirical test. Consequently, we choose instead to focus on a quantity of key interest for life insurance companies: a policyholder's probability of dying before the expected age. Measures of life expectancies (or life tables) are one of the oldest and most accurate health measures around. The distribution around these expectancies, accounting for observables like age, gender, and education, represents the risks that life insurance companies can insure against. Some people die earlier than expected, while others live longer. This mortality risk is what individuals seek to insure against in the life insurance market, and it is the source of the information problem for insurance companies.

Life expectancy is the average age at which people die, but some people die younger while others live longer. The more insurance companies know

---

[19] www.ncbi.nlm.nih.gov/pubmed/?term=all[sb] (last accessed June 3, 2021 [https://perma.cc/53B5-E9LZ]).

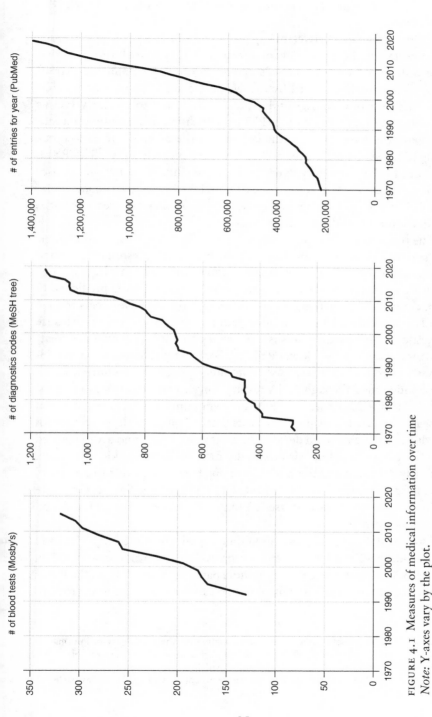

FIGURE 4.1 Measures of medical information over time

Note: Y-axes vary by the plot.

Sources: Left plot: (Pagana and Pagana 1992; Pagana, Pagana, and Pagana 2014). Middle plot: www.nlm.nih.gov/databases/download/mesh.html (last accessed June 10, 2021 [https://perma.cc/26R3-U6KR]). Right plot: www.ncbi.nlm.nih.gov/pubmed/?term=all[s b] (last accessed June 3, 2021 [https://perma.cc/53B5-E9LZ]).

about the difference between people's actual mortality risk and average life expectancy, the more relevant information they have. It turns out that "the difference between people's actual mortality risk and life expectancy" is a statistic collected by the World Health Organization (WHO) for a wide set of countries and years. It is referred to by the WHO as "Potential Years of Life Lost" (PYLL), which is the absolute difference between how long people actually live and the average life expectancy (weighting deaths occurring at younger ages more heavily). The PYLL data are broken down by cause of death, including details on diseases (cancer, cardiovascular diseases, AIDS, etc.). PYLL has become more detailed and accurate over time; it varies by country and year; and it is available for a broad set of countries.

The business of life insurance is to predict life expectancy, and PYLL is the sort of information insurance companies need to estimate expected payouts for people with particular conditions. For healthy buyers, insurers will have to rely on diagnostic information that is predictive of such conditions, something we as researchers do not have access to. Yet PYLL carries useful indirect information about risks. This is because accurate and timely diagnosis is a necessary condition for effective treatment and therefore for a lower PYLL.[20] For example, hereditary amyloidosis is a condition that is caused by an inherited genetic mutation, which can be identified through DNA testing – even with an affordable home testing kit like 23andme – long before symptoms arise. Once symptoms appear, there are blood and tissue tests that can pinpoint the exact form of the disease, which in turn decides the treatment. Most who are diagnosed with hereditary amyloidosis eventually die from heart or kidney failure, but early detection and treatment – ranging from a strict diet to drugs and even liver transplants – create a wide PYLL range. Needless to say, a late or inaccurate diagnosis increases PYLL, so a lower PYLL is an indication of better information.

In general, better diagnosis should be negatively related to PYLL, and this is indeed what we find when we regress the diagnostics data (based on the MeSH tree structure, i.e., the middle panel of Figure 4.1) on the PYLL series, along with a set of control variables.[21] Better diagnostics leads to

---

[20] A low PYLL is, however, not a necessary condition for the availability of information because some diseases, especially soon after they are discovered, are not treatable even if they can be accurately diagnosed (AIDS and Covid-19 being examples).

[21] Controls are health insurance coverage (percent of the population), total health expenditures (percent of GDP), and GDP/per capita levels.

better treatment, which reduces premature death. Hence, PYLL is also a good indicator of underlying risks that are not directly observed as a disorder.[22] Specifically, countries using fewer and less precise diagnostic tests will see people die earlier from any given disease than countries with more and better tests. Life insurance companies thrive when they have access to accurate information about life expectancy and can exclude tail risks, which in turn depends on an established infrastructure of laboratories, testing technology, and expertise.

Our assembled data set contains close to 600 country-year observations, covering 22 countries over the period from the early 1980s to the late 2010s. Year coverage varies by country, giving us an unbalanced cross-section time-series data set`. To emphasize the dynamic nature of our argument and data, we estimate an error correction model (ECM) with panel-corrected standard errors and with an AR1 autocorrelation structure. We include controls for three variables that may influence life insurance penetration: (i) the percentage of the population covered by public or primary private health insurance, (ii) total health expenditure (all financing agents) as a percentage of GDP, and (iii) GDP per capita. The estimation results are illustrated in Figure 4.2 (detailed results can be found in the Appendix). We find that going from the lowest to the highest level of information (0 to 1) – as measured by negative PYLL – raises life insurance market penetration by an average of about five percentage points. This substantive effect is indicated by the solid upward sloping line in Figure 4.2.

Figure 4.2 also includes separate estimates for countries with frequent left and frequent right governments (H3). The effect of information on life insurance penetration is much stronger in countries with frequent right governments (p10 in terms of left government, top line), whereas it is muted in countries with frequent left governments (p90 in terms of left government, bottom line). The difference between frequent right and frequent left governments is just about statistically significant at $p < 0.1$, throughout the range of values on information (based on Model (2) in Table 4A.1). Left governments tend to favor more restrictive regulations on what information insurers are allowed to use for underwriting because

---

[22] The assumption is that if good diagnostics is a necessary condition for treatment; ipso facto effective treatment (fewer years of life lost) is a sufficient condition for accurate diagnostics. We realize that this will be a noisy indicator, since some diagnoses may not be followed by treatment, and some treatments may make more effective use of information. But as long as the variance is not systematically related to our dependent variable (market development), it will only bias our results toward zero.

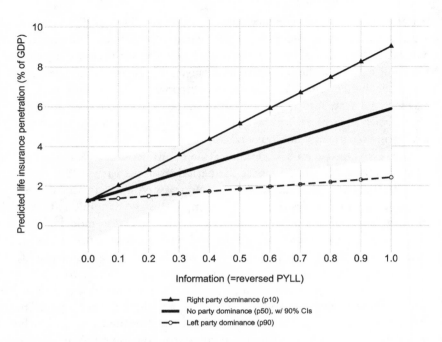

FIGURE 4.2 Predicted life insurance penetration
Note: Based on model (2) in Table 4A.1.
Sources: See Appendix.

they (rightly) worry about how such data could also be used to determine access to health insurance. While there are no readily available data on the regulation of the life insurance industry, a typical restriction is that insurance companies cannot use genetic information to set premiums. This in turn creates an adverse selection problem for insurers.

The quantitative results are clearly only suggestive – we do not claim to have identified causal effects – but they lend credence to the proposition that the increased availability of diagnostic testing has facilitated life insurance markets, barring regulations designed to prohibit discrimination on the basis of health information.

SUPPLEMENTARY PRIVATE HEALTH INSURANCE MARKETS

Are the developments in the private life insurance market – fueled by the information revolution – a harbinger of what is to come in the (public) health insurance market? Life and health insurance share many similarities. Anything that improves risk classification in life insurance can also be used for risk classification in health insurance. Thus, more and better information has the potential to decisively alter health insurance markets as well. In particular, our argument implies that as more information can be credibly shared with insurers, private health insurance markets become more feasible, undermining an important rationale for public provision.

However, as discussed in Chapter 3, pressure for marketization is not the same as actual privatization. Even under conditions of much more and much better information, private markets may not emerge, due to, inter alia, the time-inconsistency problem or the double-payment problem discussed in previous chapters. Furthermore, demand for private markets can be diminished by allowing greater differentiation (segmentation) in the public sector, and private markets can be regulated to undermine actuarially fair pricing. Political parties represent different constituencies – characterized in terms of income and risk – and parties continue to "matter." In particular, left governments are more likely to oppose privatization because they represent constituencies that are on average lower income and higher risk – groups that lose out in private markets; the opposite holds for right governments.

We can get a sense of the importance of private health insurance by looking at the OECD Health Statistics. This health database provides a measure of "voluntary schemes and out-of-pocket" spending, which captures private spending over and above tax-financed public outlays. It includes VPHI, which either tops up public insurance in instances of high user charges ("complementary insurance") or offers parallel services where public provision is seen as inadequate because of perceived low quality and long wait times ("supplementary insurance").[23] As Foubister et al. put it, supplementary VPHI promises "faster access to treatment, a more comfortable care environment, and a wider choice of specialists, treatment facilities and timing of treatment" (2006, xi).

The OECD data are shown in Table 4.1 – both as a percentage of GDP and as a percentage of total health spending – for eighteen advanced democracies for which there are comparable data since 1980.

---

[23] This distinction is made by Mossialos and Thomson (2004). They also identify a type of private spending "substitutive" VPHI, which allows people to opt out of public provision and into private. This is common in the USA but rare in Europe (although we discuss an important exception in the next chapter for the case of Germany where those above a certain income threshold can substitute private for public insurance).

TABLE 4.1 Private spending on health as a percentage of GDP and total health spending

	Private health expenditure (% of GDP)						Private health expenditure (% of overall health expenditure)					
	1980	1990	2000	2010	2019	1980 => 2019	1980	1990	2000	2010	2019	1980 => 2019
Australia	2.2	2.2	2.4	2.6	3.0	0.9	37	34	32	31	33	-4.5
Austria	2.3	2.0	2.3	2.6	2.6	0.3	33	26	24	25	25	-8.0
Canada	1.6	2.2	2.5	3.2	3.2	1.6	24	26	30	30	30	5.7
Denmark	1.1	1.4	1.4	1.7	1.6	0.6	13	18	17	16	16	3.5
Finland	1.3	1.5	1.8	2.1	2.1	0.8	22	20	26	23	23	0.7
France	1.4	1.9	2.0	2.7	1.8	0.4	20	24	21	24	16	-4.2
Germany	1.8	2.0	2.2	1.9	1.7	0.0	22	25	22	17	15	-7.2
Ireland	1.4	1.5	1.3	2.5	1.8	0.3	19	27	22	24	26	6.5
Italy	1.0	1.3	2.1	1.9	2.2	1.3	na	19	27	22	26	*7.2
Japan	1.8	1.3	1.4	1.7	1.7	-0.1	29	22	20	18	16	-13.0
Netherlands	1.7	2.0	2.4	1.7	1.7	0.0	27	29	31	17	17	-9.5
New Zealand	0.7	1.2	1.6	1.8	1.9	1.2	12	18	22	19	20	8.5
Norway	0.1	1.2	1.4	1.4	1.5	1.4	2	17	18	15	15	12.8
Portugal	1.8	1.9	2.5	3.0	3.7	1.9	38	35	30	30	39	1.2
Spain	1.0	1.3	1.9	2.3	2.6	1.6	20	22	29	26	29	9.2
Sweden	0.6	1.5	1.1	1.5	1.6	1.0	8	20	14	18	15	6.8
UK	0.5	0.8	1.7	1.8	2.3	1.7	10	16	24	18	22	11.7
USA	4.8	6.8	7.0	8.4	^8.3	^3.6	58	60	56	52	51	-6.5
Average	1.5	1.9	2.2	2.5	2.5	0.8	23	25	26	24	24	1.0

Note: 1980 => 2019 refers to absolute change from 1980 to 2019.

* Change from 1990 to 2019.

^ The last US observation is from 2013 (pre-Obamacare). The change is therefore from 1980 to 2013.

Source: OECD Health Statistics 2020 (www.oecd.org/els/health-systems/health-data.htm, last accessed June 3, 2021 [https://perma.cc73SW-SYH7]).

Private spending as a share of GDP has increased in every country, except in Germany, Japan, and the Netherlands where it remained stable (or dropped slightly in the case of Japan). In eleven of the eighteen countries, the private sector also expanded as a share of total health spending. The latter numbers must be treated with caution, however, because some countries have seen a significant expansion of public schemes, notably long-term care (Gingrich 2011, chapter 4), where markets are absent or lacking for the reasons discussed previously. In the case of the Netherlands, the drop in the share of private spending is due to public healthcare being extended to the entire population for the first time in 2006. In the USA, the private share dropped considerably after the passing of the ACA simply because of the individual mandate requiring everyone to have health insurance. While this reform did not change the fact that most American citizens were covered by private insurance, we end the American time series in 2013 for better comparability over time. All told, private spending increased by an average of about 1 percent between 1980 and 2019, measured both as a share of GDP and as a share of total health spending.

Another indicator of privatization focuses on providers. Rothgang et al. (2008) find that public provision has declined in nearly all of the fifteen OECD countries for which they have comparable data. Our focus is on the finance side, but the two are closely related because most private insurance uses private providers, and where the public insurance system turns to private providers it often gives those patients with the greatest resources an opportunity to secure better care inside the public system. As noted previously, choice and private competition are ways for governments to introduce differentiation within the public system without any outright rollback.

Overall, the numbers suggest a significant increase in the use of private insurance, but the rate of growth is still small compared to life insurance markets. Unlike the latter, the starting point for health insurance is the public provision, which permits growth in private markets only as a result of deliberate political decisions to open up regulatory and fiscal space for such markets. That said, private markets are a reality in today's healthcare systems in a way they never were before.

The Nordic countries are instructive cases in point because they share a history of universal and virtually exclusive public health insurance systems, yet have seen a significant expansion of VPHI in recent decades. This is evident in the finance data in Table 4.1 and also from the sharp increase in the number of people covered by VPHI (Alexandersen et al.

2016). The trigger for purchasing VPHI is typically a buildup of dissatisfaction with the public system – long waiting times in particular – among those with higher income and education (Besley, Hall, and Preston 1999; Gingrich 2011, chapter 4). Supplementary private insurance typically offers immediate access to high-quality private providers, often for procedures that otherwise have long public waiting lists.

But VPHI is not simply about satisfying rising expectations among the middle and upper-middle classes. These expectations could be met in the public sector by committing greater resources and by introducing more competition and choice, which are of course among the solutions offered by the political center-left, in particular. What makes private insurance especially attractive to those best able to afford it is that it is only offered to "good risks" on attractive terms. In all VPHI systems, private insurers can and do reject people based on preexisting conditions, and the combination of preferential access and rising demand among high-income, highly educated individuals turns VPHI into a significant source of health inequality (Kullberg, Blomqvist, and Winbald 2019; van Doorslaer 1999; van Doorslaer and Masseria 2004; Wagstaff and van Doorslaer 2000). In the public system, improvements must ordinarily be offered to everyone, and those with high income will usually pay disproportionately. The inequalities build into VPHI apply not only to individual insurance but also corporate insurance, with the latter being bought by employers on behalf of their employees. In the corporate segment, this is because employers with younger, better-educated, and usually white-collar employees can secure better rates and therefore more valuable benefits for their workers.

These inequities are conditioned by tax (dis)incentives for the purchase of private insurance, which has emerged as a polarizing partisan issue. Denmark (2002) and Norway (2003) introduced tax deductions under center-right governments to offset the cost of private insurance – essentially reducing or eliminating the double-payment problem – but center-left governments subsequently repealed them (in the case of employer-based plans, by making health insurance benefits taxable) (Alexandersen et al. 2016, 77–78). A reform introduced in Sweden in 2009–2010 under the center-right Reinfeldt government that greatly expanded the choice of private healthcare centers likewise brought deep partisan divisions in its wake (Bendz 2017).

Insurers' reliance on health information to determine eligibility and pricing is not well-documented, in large part because insurers treat underwriting as proprietary information, which makes research into their practices hard. However, there is no reason for it to be systematically different from underwriting practices in the life insurance industry, which we described previously based on leaked sources. The European Observatory on Health Systems and Policies (EOHSP), an intergovernmental organization hosted by WHO, has systematically analyzed the British VPHI system (Foubister et al. 2006). Their findings confirm that similar to the Nordic cases, the VPHI system in the UK also excludes preexisting conditions, specifically referring to "conditions suffered in the five years prior to insurance purchase," but some insurers also exclude a range of conditions that are correlated with past conditions. Age is a separate risk factor, with premiums rising with age, and some insurers even refusing customers over a certain age (65 or 75). The same study illustrates that additional data on gender, occupational status, smoking, and related demographic and lifestyle information are also routinely used to develop algorithms for estimating individual risks and prices.

In the corporate market, for groups of more than fifty employees, premiums are based on companies' history of claims ("experience rating"), which in turn is a function of the average health of employees and therefore also well-known socioeconomic correlates, such as occupation and education. This practice resembles "self-insurance" in the USA (discussed in Chapter 3). Small group insurance (<50) in the corporate market is priced much like individual insurance using detailed risk information. Reflecting both screening policies and composition of demand, Besley, Hall, and Preston (1999) find that VPHI is much more widespread among those with higher incomes, higher education, and homeownership. One survey of British companies found an overrepresentation of firms and employees in pharmaceuticals, financial services, advertising, media, and communications – all with a mostly highly educated white-collar workforce (Foubister et al. 2006, 53).

The EOHSP report (written in 2006) does not mention genetic information, and such information is in principle excluded from underwriting by the UK's Code on Genetic Testing and Insurance (formerly the Concordat and Moratorium on Genetics and Insurance). Like the GINA in the USA (discussed in Chapter 3), Code on Genetic Testing and Insurance prohibits the use of genetic information in deciding who to insure and at what terms. Many OECD countries have similar genetic nondiscrimination regulations (Bélisle-Pipon et al. 2019), and while genetic information often enters through the back door (e.g., via primary care physician records), there is little doubt that genetic nondiscrimination rules limit insurers in their underwriting practices.

However, it would be reasonable to ask why genetic information is banned, while preexisting or past conditions, as well as lifestyle and demographic information, are not. The almost unlimited potential of using genetic testing seems to be a major concern for consumers and politicians alike, but more conventional types of diagnostics have also markedly improved (as discussed in the previous section), and we suspect that the use of genetic data will emerge as an increasingly contentious partisan battleground in the near future. Nondiscrimination regulation protects those at high risk, but it simultaneously constrains those at low risk, and risks are correlated with politically salient socioeconomic divisions. The Republican Party in the USA, for example, is committed to repealing not only the ACA but also GINA. In general, most current genetic tests identify tail-end risks that the majority need not worry about, at least among the working-age population (and again, many insurers turn away people above a certain age anyway). Freedom to share information is logically compatible with strict laws to protect privacy, and combining the two may prove to be a winning policy mix. If so, segmentation of insurance markets will proceed unabated.

THE CHOICE BETWEEN PUBLIC AND PRIVATE HEALTH INSURANCE

In the "Innovations in Underwriting Practices" section, we described how the information revolution influences underwriting practices in life insurance. We conjecture that many of the same developments can, in principle, influence health insurance as well, with one major difference: the availability of public insurance. Since public health insurance was born of market failure, while public life insurance never existed in the first place (with minor exceptions for widows' benefits), the analysis is quite different. As the historical institutionalist literature reminds us, institutional evolution is path-dependent (Hacker, Pierson, and Thelen 2015; Hicks 2013; Mahoney and Thelen 2010; Pierson 2000). Once public insurance is in place, those with high income may be able to opt out into private insurance, but they may have to continue to subsidize the public system if there is a political majority in favor of maintaining it.

Having to pay for one's own private insurance, while still paying into the public system, is an obvious deterrent against opting out. This double-payment problem (discussed in Chapter 2) makes leaving the insurance fund a less viable option. The choice is also shaped by regulatory policies and above all depends on the expected behavior of others. As more opt out, the private option will become more attractive because the double-payment problem is reduced with fewer people in the public system. Using this logic, for each (nonpoor) potential policyholder, there is a critical threshold of participation in the private scheme that will make private insurance sufficiently attractive to the individual that they will decide to opt out. With a normal distribution of critical thresholds, the opt-out response function is S-shaped, and equilibria are where this function intersects the 45-degree line. With a normal distribution of critical thresholds, there are two stable equilibria: one with low opt-out and one with high opt-out. In the high opt-out equilibrium, there will be convergence in preferences to the private option among those for whom this option is optimal ("first-best"); the low opt-out is one where there will be convergence in preferences around the public option. In the latter, some might like to move into a private system but are prevented from doing so by the double-payment problem; it can therefore be problematic to infer back from "revealed preferences" to "first-best preferences." The latter requires a level of coordination that is typically not feasible.

Specifically, some people with high income may prefer a private system because it better reflects their preferences, but if they cannot unilaterally choose such a system, they may well support an expansion of the public system to better mirror their desire for high-quality healthcare. We observe the same with regard to education, where the rich are often the strongest supporters of more spending, even though they are the first to opt out when private options become available (Busemeyer and Iversen 2020). The differences in preferences will thus manifest themselves mostly in the form of conflicts over the structure of spending or, if it is possible to buy supplementary insurance for high-end procedures, in the form of "partial opt-out": everyone relies on the public system for basic healthcare, but some pay a premium for access to high-end providers and procedures. When differentiation is introduced in a purely public system, the costs may be indirect, for instance, in the form of a premium on house prices when the quality of local public provision is high, or the time and cognitive resources required to exercise choice in the public system when identifying and selecting the best doctors, hospitals, procedures, and so on.

Building on the theoretical analysis presented in Chapter 2, the causal story is as follows: (i) Improved medical information enables private health insurance markets; (ii) if, because of the double-payment problem, those attracted to private insurance face major hurdles to leave the public system, they might seek differentiation within the public system and, as a consequence, may continue to support the public system; and (iii) if it is cheap to exit the public system, those with the means and incentive to take advantage of private insurance will opt out. Once they do, public opinion on healthcare is likely to polarize because people leaving drives up the price of the public option.[24] The exception is "catastrophic" health insurance, where the government serves as the equivalent of a "lender of last resort." Health insurance in the cases of poverty or old age is an example that we will now explore in a little more detail.

The American health insurance system is a unique case where major public and private health insurance programs coexist.[25] For the working-age population, health insurance is mostly private, and it displays many of the elements of individualization of risks and premiums that our argument implies (discussed in Chapter 3). Yet there are two elements of the American system that remain entirely public: Medicare and Medicaid, and they are instructive for understanding the limits of privatization. Medicare provides healthcare for the elderly and Medicaid for the poor. We contend that both exist largely because of what we have called the intergenerational time-inconsistency problem in social insurance.

Many health risks are concentrated at the end of life, and in public systems, these risks are covered through PAYG transfers from younger to older generations. As discussed in Chapter 2, all PAYG systems face a time-inconsistency problem, and private insurance cannot easily solve this problem because there is usually no way for private insurers to credibly offer lifetime coverage to justify younger people paying for expensive PAYG plans. Individually "funded" old-age healthcare plans are conceivable, but health "savings plans" are usually restricted to young people who use them to "bridge" short bouts of illness, rather than serving as a path to private insurance at the end of life. The widespread bankruptcies, frequent premium hikes, and limited take-up in America's private long-term care insurance market attest to the difficulties. Similarly, the German primary private health insurance market, which, in theory, strives to achieve stable premiums by balancing pay across younger and older members, in practice sees frequent premium hikes as people age. If offered purely as savings plans, funded retirement schemes provide better

---

[24] The main difficulty of testing this logic for healthcare preferences is that access to private alternatives is likely to be associated with many other individual circumstances, such as good health or income and education, which may also explain lower support for public insurance.

[25] Germany is the only other advanced industrialized country with a significant private primary healthcare market, but it is very different from the American case.

alternatives; if offered as genuine insurance, it is difficult to get young people to sign up for plans that are mostly used in old age.

The implication is that public systems designed to overcome time-inconsistency problems will enjoy broad support because they have no effective private substitutes. This is true everywhere, but the USA is the only case where it is possible to observe this clearly because it is the only system where healthcare for the non-elderly is mostly private; in other cases, we cannot distinguish support for healthcare in general from support for healthcare for the elderly in particular. The hypothesis of widespread support most obviously applies to Medicare (health insurance for the elderly), but it may also help us understand middle-class support for Medicaid. As noted previously, a large portion of the Medicaid budget goes to long-term care, and many middle-class people needing such care end up spending down their savings and becoming eligible for Medicaid. There are complex rules regulating this to prevent gaming the system, but Medicaid is truly a last-resort insurance for many.

No long-term time series of attitudes toward Medicare and/or Medicaid exists (see Corman and Levin 2016 for available data), but the American National Election Survey (ANES) Time Series contains a survey item that tracks support for government versus private health insurance plans. Specifically, the item reads:

There is much concern about the rapid rise in medical and hospital costs. Some people feel there should be a government insurance plan which would cover all medical and hospital expenses for everyone. Suppose these people are at one end of a scale, at point 1. Others feel that all medical expenses should be paid by individuals through private insurance plans like Blue Cross or other company-paid plans. Suppose these people are at the other end, at point 7. And, of course, some other people have opinions somewhere in between, at points 2, 3, 4, 5, or 6. Where would you place YOURSELF on this scale, or haven't you thought much about this? (item VCF0806 and V201252)

Over the years on which data is available (1972–2020), the average response mildly fluctuates around the mean point of the survey item. About 40 percent of non-elderly Americans support private health insurance (answers 1 to 3 on the item), while around 40 percent support government health insurance (answers 5 to 7). Support for private versus public provision of healthcare varies by partisanship as we would predict, and partisan polarization on the topic has intensified, probably in the wake of the strongly partisan debates about the ACA. As expected, wealthier respondents are less supportive of government-provided healthcare, but the income gradient is relatively gentle and often not statistically significant (see Figure 4.3).

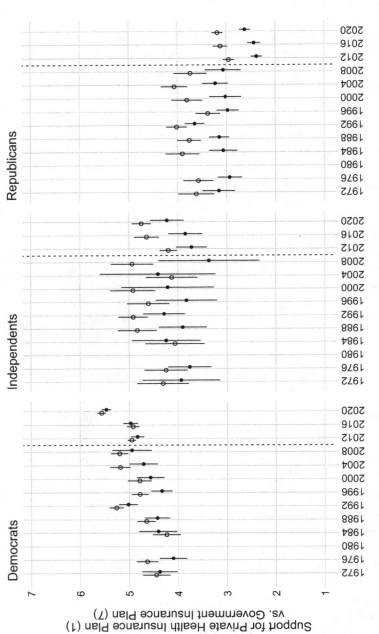

FIGURE 4.3 Support for private health insurance plan versus government insurance plan (USA)
Note: Average support per group (items VCF0806 and V201252), with 95 percent confidence intervals. The sample is restricted to respondents aged 18–65.
Source: The American National Election Studies (https://electionstudies.org, last accessed June 9, 2021 [https://perma.cc/TR2 N-SG-MM]): ANES TS 1948–2016 and ANES 2020.[26]

[26] This material is based on work supported by the National Science Foundation under grant number SES 1444721, 2014–2017, the University of Michigan and Stanford University.

Despite the fairly broad support for private health insurance provision in the USA, the public programs – Medicare and Medicaid – are wildly popular. As mentioned, there are no long-term time series of attitudes toward Medicare and/or Medicaid, but some useful survey items are available. For example, the ANES 1992 asked respondents whether they favor or oppose expanding Medicare "to pay for nursing home care and long hospital stays for the elderly." Only about 15 percent of respondents indicated opposition or indifference ([1] oppose strongly, [2] oppose not so strongly, or [3] neither), while around 21 percent of respondents favored and about 64 percent strongly favored expanding the program. In a similar vein, Grogan and Park (2017) report very broad support for Medicaid, based on a Kaiser Family Foundation Poll from 2015. Their article's title summarizes the findings of their study: "The Politics of Medicaid: Most Americans Are Connected to the Program, Support Its Expansion, and Do Not View It as Stigmatizing" (Grogan and Park 2017).

The very large majorities in support of Medicare and Medicaid are remarkable because – as shown in Chapter 2 – a significant portion of the electorate may well favor a system with a large private component, as is true in the USA. This mix of preferences – support for private insurance and a targeted public program such as Medicaid – was evident in the Democratic primaries for the last presidential election where majorities showed support for plans that promised an expansion of Medicaid, Medicare, or some other "public option" yet balked at giving up their private (employer-provided) insurance. From our perspective, Medicare is a solution to the time-inconsistency problem, and Medicaid is essentially an insurance against poverty.

CONCLUSION

More, better, and more shareable data mitigate the information problems faced by most insurance markets. Insurers can use better information for more accurate risk classification, which broadens their reach and improves their bottom line. Rather than charging rates based on some rough grouping of customers, insurance companies can more accurately calibrate premiums to expected claims of individual customers. As a result, customers pay premiums that are more actuarially fair, which increases the efficiency of the market. This development leads to more accurate pricing – and more unequal pricing. Customers with better risk profiles end up paying less for insurance. Customers with worse risk

profiles end up paying more. Many would consider this outcome fair –
especially if customers can influence their risk exposure, for example, by
driving more carefully or not smoking.

But often, individuals have little or no influence over their risk –
accidents happen; many diseases are either due to what we usually call
sheer bad luck, including disease-prone genes; or other causes people
cannot influence, such as environmental factors. Moreover, risk often
correlates with income and wealth: Those who need the coverage most
are often the least able to afford it. As we explain in Chapter 5, more
accurate risk pricing increases inequality in discretionary income – the
income left after taxes, contributions, and insurance premiums have
been paid. And while more and better information expands the scope
of private markets, it also excludes some customers from that market.
People with bad risk profiles – based on, say, their genes – may be unable
to acquire insurance at all, either because companies refuse coverage or
because premiums are too high. These bad risks must fall back on public
insurance, which may increasingly depend on the goodwill of taxpayers
who are themselves not heavily dependent on such insurance (although
they may support it as a last resort).

In this chapter, we analyzed private life insurance markets because they
are almost entirely outside the state and found that the insurance industry
very deliberately exploits more, better, and more shareable information
for underwriting purposes. Insurance companies eagerly make use of
better diagnostics, micro-level tracking, and liquid health data to assess
the risk profiles of potential customers. The increased use of data is a long-
term development, but the incorporation of more and better information
for underwriting purposes has dramatically picked up speed in the last few
years and, as we have shown, has also further accelerated during the
COVID-19 pandemic.

Supplementary private health insurance, which is widespread across
advanced democracies, uses information in a manner that is very similar
to life insurance, making sure that high-end services are reserved for
people who will not need them very often. That said, we do not expect
public health insurance systems to disappear or to adopt actuarially fair
pricing in the near future. The double-payment problem, regulatory roadblocks such as nondiscrimination rules, and a lack of private alternatives
for the old and the poor militate against it. But we have little doubt that
the information revolution will influence the politics of healthcare provision and will decisively change public systems over time. Barriers to
privatization are themselves political choices, and they are likely to

come under increased partisan attack. The secret underwriting guidelines of private life insurance companies (available by googling "life insurance underwriting guidelines not for public use") give a flavor of what could happen in the health insurance domain, though countervailing forces, notably continued uncertainty among many voters regarding their interests, make a rapid and radical change in public health insurance provision less likely.

APPENDIX: INFORMATION AND LIFE INSURANCE PENETRATION

• Life Insurance Penetration Data
The data are available at: https://stats.oecd.org/Index.aspx?DataSetCode= INSIND (OECD insurance indicators, last accessed June 3, 2021 [https:// perma.cc/D4LH-3E3 T]). See also OECD (2015b).

• Mortality by Cause Data
Our measure of information is based on data about premature mortality, as provided by the OECD (https://stats.oecd.org/index.aspx?DataSetCo de=HEALTH_STAT, last accessed June 3, 2021 [https://perma.cc/D3P4-UGPV]).We make use of the "Potential Years of Life Lost" (PYLL) variable, defined as follows: "This indicator is a summary measure of premature mortality, providing an explicit way of weighting deaths occurring at younger ages, which may be preventable. The calculation of Potential Years of Life Lost (PYLL) involves summing up deaths occurring at each age and multiplying this with the number of remaining years to live up to a selected age limit (age 70 is used in OECD Health Statistics). In order to assure cross-country and trend comparison, the PYLL are standardised, for each country and each year. The total OECD population in 2010 is taken as the reference population for age standardisation. This indicator is presented as a total and per gender. It is measured in years lost per 100 000 inhabitants (total), per 100 000 men and per 100 000 women, aged 0–69" (https://doi.org/10.1787/bd12d298-en, last accessed June 3, 2021 [https://perma.cc/3CK9-A76S]).

We calculate PYLL due to the following diseases:

- Certain infectious and parasitic diseases
- Neoplasms
- Diseases of the blood and blood-forming organs
- Endocrine, nutritional, and metabolic diseases
- Mental and behavioral disorders

- Diseases of the nervous system
- Diseases of the circulatory system
- Diseases of the respiratory system
- Diseases of the digestive system
- Diseases of the skin and subcutaneous tissue
- Diseases of the musculoskeletal system and connective tissue
- Diseases of the genitourinary system
- Certain conditions originating in the perinatal period
- Congenital malformations and chromosomal abnormalities

These diseases account for about 75 percent of PYLL – the remaining PYLL are largely due to "external causes of mortality" (traffic accidents, accidental poisoning, suicides, etc.).

These data are coded using the International Statistical Classification of Diseases and Related Health Problems (ICD). Over time, the ICD has been updated. In the empirical analyses, we include an indicator variable for changes to the ICD classification. The potential breaks occur in the following country-years: Australia (AUS): 1968, 1979, and 1998; Austria (AUT): 1969, 1980, and 2002; Belgium (BEL): 1968, 1979, and 1998; Canada (CAN): 1969, 1979, and 2000; Denmark (DNK): 1969 and 1994; Finland (FIN): 1969, 1987, and 1996; France (FRA): 1968, 1979, and 2000; Germany (DEU): 1998; Greece (GRC): 1968 and 1979; Iceland (ISL): 1971, 1981, and 1996; Ireland (IRL): 1968, 1979, and 2007; Italy (ITA): 1968, 1979, and 2003; Japan (JPN): 1968, 1979, and 1995; Luxembourg (LUX): 1971, 1979, and 1998; Netherlands (NLD): 1969, 1979, and 1996; New Zealand (NZL): 1968, 1979, and 2000; Norway (NOR): 1969, 1986, and 1996; Portugal (PRT): 1971, 1980, and 2002; Spain (ESP): 1968, 1980, and 1999; Sweden (SWE): 1969, 1987, and 1997; Switzerland (CHE): 1969 and 1995; United Kingdom (GBR): 1968, 1979, and 2001; and United States (USA): 1968, 1979, and 1999.

• Partisanship Variable and Controls

Since partisanship only has an effect through slowly changing regulatory measures, we measure it as the average left cabinet participation since 1980, for each country, based on the "Comparative Political Data Set 1960–2018" (Armingeon et al. 2020). Using a cumulative measure (Huber and Stephens 2001) of left seats in government (divided by the number of years), starting in 1980, yields similar results.

• Sample

The following country-years are in our sample, which is determined by data availability: AUS (1985–2017), AUT (1988–2017), BEL (1984–2016), CAN (1985–2017), CHE (1984–2016), DEU (1992–2017), DNK (1984–2015), ESP (1987–2017), FIN (1984–2017), FRA (1985–2016), GBR (1997–2016), GRC (1993–2016), IRL (1984–2015), ISL (1984–2018), ITA (1988–2016), JPN (1984–2017), NLD (1996–2017), NOR (1984–2016), NZL (1990–2001), PRT (1984–2017), SWE (1984–2017), and USA (1984–2017).

• Results

The estimation results are shown in Table 4A.1. The lagged dependent variable is statistically significant, with an estimated coefficient of around −0.2, and the lagged information variable is positive and statistically significant (indicating that more information is associated with higher life insurance penetration). The coefficients on the regressors have specific interpretations: the coefficients on the lagged level variables capture permanent effects of a one-off change in those variables, while the coefficients on change variables capture transitory effects (Beck and Katz 1995). We find that there are short-term transitory effects (most not statistically significant), but that the main effects are long term and permanent.

TABLE 4A.1 *Life insurance penetration, information, and partisanship (ECM)*

	(1)	(2)
	Dependent variable: life insurance penetration (first difference)	
Life insurance penetration	−0.205**	−0.226**
(Lag)	(0.050)	(0.051)
Information	0.821+	2.242*
(Lag)	(0.479)	(0.982)
Information	3.186*	5.342
(First difference)	(1.556)	(6.125)
Left partisanship X information		−0.036+
(Lag)		(0.020)
Left partisanship X information		−0.057
(First difference)		(0.155)
Health insurance coverage	−0.004	−0.006
(% of population)	(0.011)	(0.011)
Total health expenditures	−0.035	−0.039
(% of GDP)	(0.065)	(0.064)
GDP per capita	0.010+	0.011*
(Lag)	(0.005)	(0.005)
GDP per capita	−0.018	−0.019
(First difference)	(0.016)	(0.016)
Constant	−0.030	0.263
	(1.246)	(1.224)
Dummy for breaks in PYLL series	Yes	Yes
Country dummies	Yes	Yes
N of observations	592	592
N of countries	22	22
Adj. R^2	0.134	0.141

Note: Coefficients above standard errors. $+ p < 0.10$, $* p < 0.05$, and $** p < 0.01$

5

Credit Markets

At the turn of the last century, banking was personal.[1] Banks made lending decisions based on personal knowledge of borrowers, which often meant lending was haphazard and not infrequently biased toward friends and family (and against minorities!). The small-town banker and horse trader David Harum, the main character in Edward Noyes Westcott's 1898 novel of the same name, described his approach to lending in the 1932 movie adaptation (with Will Rogers as Harum): "I go a long way on a man's character. And then I go a longer way on his collateral. And if he's got character and collateral both, I let him have half of what he asked for ... anybody can get along on half of what they think they can."

The use of information has come a long way since then, but the objective is the same: separate good risks from bad and lend to the former on the best possible terms (for the bank). The massive improvement in data, a large expansion of risk-sharing financial instruments, and a huge increase in demand have resulted in loans and credit to the household sector increasing exponentially. Household debt has correspondingly risen to new heights (see Figure 5.1). In less than twenty-five years, from 1995 to 2019, private debt in advanced democracies increased from an average of 90 percent to about 150 percent of disposable income. A growing portion of personal income now goes to servicing debt, and this has a sizable effect on discretionary income. With an average interest rate of 10 percent, it would amount to 16 percent of disposable income but obviously with huge variation across countries, time, and individuals. Moreover, access to credit has become an important determinant of individual welfare in a

---

[1] This chapter is based on Iversen and Rehm (2022).

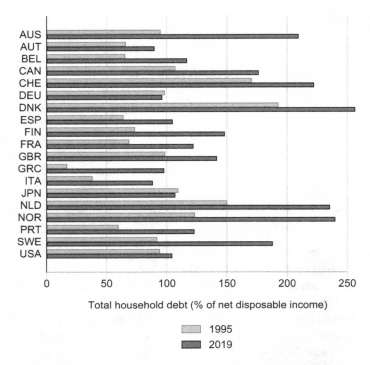

Total household debt (% of net disposable income)

1995
2019

FIGURE 5.1 Household debt as a percentage of disposable income
Note: Second data point refers to 2018 in JPN, NOR, and USA and 2020 in CAN.
Source: OECD National Accounts Statistics: National Accounts at a Glance
(https://doi.org/10.1787/f03b6469-en, last accessed June 3, 2021 [https://per
ma.cc/HE5 R-NR7X]) (OECD 2018b).

new economy where credit is used to smooth income across increasingly
nonlinear life cycles. As owning a home has become commonplace in some
countries, access to mortgage finance is also increasingly seen as a pre-
requisite for a middle-class life style. Therefore, both access to credit and
the cost of such access are becoming important determinants of prosperity
and hence also of inequality. This chapter explores the consequences of
financialization for economic inequality.

As illustrated in Figure 5.2, the financialization of economies took off
in the early 1980s (whether using the International Monetary Fund's
measure of financial development or the closely related expansion of
finance and insurance as a share of total output). These shifts are linked
in complex ways to the transition from a Fordist economy to a new, more

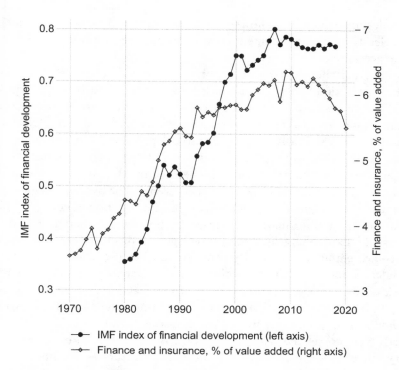

FIGURE 5.2 Financialization of advanced economies, 1970–2020
Note: The line with circles shows the IMF's index of financial development (Svirydzenka 2016). The line with hollow diamonds shows the share of value added accounted for by finance and insurance (OECD 2017). Both lines are averages across nineteen advanced economies: Australia, Austria, Belgium, Canada, Denmark, Finland, France, Germany, Ireland, Italy, Japan, Korea, Netherlands, New Zealand, Norway, Sweden, Switzerland, the United Kingdom, and the USA.
Sources: https://doi.org/10.1787/a8b2bd2b-en (last accessed June 3, 2021 [https:// perma.cc/B6TX-66KW]) and Sahay et al. (2015).

decentralized and globalized, knowledge economy with rising demand for sophisticated financial instruments among firms. Also rising was demand for credit from individuals that pursue nonlinear careers with more frequent changes in jobs, time off for retraining and additional schooling, and moves back and forth between work and family (highly educated women, in particular, are increasingly delaying starting a family) (Iversen and Soskice 2019, chapter 4; Wiedemann 2021). As we argue later, the financialization of economies has also been facilitated by the information revolution, which has allowed credit markets to operate much more efficiently but with unintended consequences for income distribution and access to credit.

As credit becomes more important to individual welfare, it also becomes a significant – albeit largely overlooked – driver of inequality. This is because access to household credit is tied to socioeconomic status, and because the terms of access vary with individual risks of default. Such risk assessments, in turn, depend on individual data on the likelihood of experiencing catastrophic life events – significant loss of income due to unemployment, illness, or involuntary job switches – and ability to financially weather such events. The availability of such data has been greatly facilitated by the information revolution. Big Data combine information disclosed by borrowers themselves with a trove of data on residency, demographic indicators, credit history, income, employment history, and so on. As the data available to lenders improve, they are able to make increasingly differentiated risk-of-default assessments, which means that interest rates increasingly reflect the underlying risk distribution. As interest payments come out of disposable income, and insofar as disposable income is negatively correlated with default risk, the distribution of *discretionary income* – which excludes interest payments – becomes more unequal. And those deemed too high risk will not qualify for loans in the first place.

While nearly all research on inequality focuses on market or disposable income and increasingly wealth inequality, what matters most to individuals' sense of welfare is discretionary income, *after* accounting for the positive direct effects of access to credit. Simply put, financialization and the data revolution combined have increased discretionary income inequality, even if disposable income inequality is held constant. And those excluded from credit markets will not enjoy the benefits of income smoothing or homeownership in the first place.

There is now a large literature showing that the brunt of unemployment and other labor market risks are borne by those with lower incomes (Häusermann, Kurer, and Schwander 2015; Rehm, Hacker, and Schlesinger 2012; Rueda 2007). This generates more inequality in expected income, as captured in insurance models, but in addition to this, a more unequal distribution of (observed) risk also leads to a more unequal distribution of discretionary income, which is not captured in insurance models. As debt-to-income rates rise, this source of inequality will become increasingly important.

Yet the distribution of default risk is not merely a function of individual circumstances but also a function of national-level financial and social institutions. Income losses are cushioned by the social protection system, and financial regulations can absorb some of the default risk by subsidizing debt repayments or providing lender-of-last-resort guarantees. For example, when governments step in to purchase debt, notably by buying and securitizing mortgage debt, they assume risks that would otherwise be borne by lenders, thus enabling the latter to offer loans to more people and on more equal terms. This is a key effect of major quasi-public financial institutions such as Fannie Mae and Freddie Mac in the USA.

The welfare state also matters. When people become unemployed, some of their lost income is replaced by unemployment benefits, and the higher the replacement rate, the more likely an unemployed person will be able to keep servicing debt. Lenders know this and push down rates to reflect the lower risk of default. By directly reducing the effect of adverse life events on disposable income, the welfare state thus has a similar effect on discretionary income to state loan guarantees or interest subsidies by improving the terms of borrowing at the lower part of the distribution.

Yet the underlying political coalitions that sustain these different institutions have distinct historical origins, creating sometimes unexpected cross-national patterns that do not conform to standard cross-national typologies of welfare states or varieties of capitalism. For example, institutions and policies in Denmark and the USA produce surprisingly similar results, and while the difference between social protection institutions is well-established, it is Denmark and not the USA that has a highly market-based mortgage system.

This chapter contributes to a burgeoning literature on the politics of financialization. Ahlquist and Ansell (2017) argue that borrowing is used to compensate for high inequality and that credit has therefore been expanded more in inegalitarian countries. Our objective, however, is to explain the distributive consequences of increased access. Since inequalities tend to be magnified by differences in access and terms of access, financialization is not generally a remedy for rising inequality.

Access to credit, however, can sometimes substitute for social protection. Ansell (2014) shows that house ownership can serve as a form of long-term insurance that reduces demand for redistribution, while Hariri et al. (2017), Wiedemann (2021), and Hariri et al. (2020) find that short-term liquidity constraints and lack of access to credit increase demand for social transfers, such as unemployment benefits. Our argument and evidence are consistent with these findings, but we also ask the prior question of who has access to credit and at what terms – with a focus on discretionary income inequality.

Specifically, we make four contributions to the literature: (i) We show the direct effects of financialization on inequality; (ii) we show that these effects are magnified by lenders having access to increased information about borrowers; (iii) we show how social protection and financial regulation mitigate the unequalizing effects of financialization; and (iv) we present quasi-experimental evidence for strong effects of information, financial regulation, and social protection on both access to credit and the terms of such access. To our knowledge, none of these effects have been identified in the existing comparative political economy literature.

THE LOGIC

We base our presentation on a simple formal model that is developed in detail in Appendix 5A. A lot of lending is for purposes of "income smoothing," where current consumption (say, for a car or daycare services) or investment (say, in further education) is in anticipation of higher income in the future (Hall 1988). This is known as the permanent income hypothesis and presents no problems in terms of repayment. People who stay on their anticipated income path would never default (which would exclude them from future borrowing). Unanticipated drops in income as a result of long-term layoffs or illness, on the other hand, can lead to default, and this is what lenders worry about. The same is true for borrowing to buy a home, which for most people is a long-term investment that greatly enhances their welfare, while also potentially generating wealth – the proverbial nest egg (Ansell 2014). As in the case of other loans, discretionary income is reduced by the interest on the mortgage.

Discretionary Income and Welfare

Utility to the individual is equal to discretionary income (D_i), which is disposable income minus "mandatory" charges and spending on necessities, plus the utility of the consumption that borrowing, L_i, in credit markets $u(L_i)$ enables:

$$U_i = D_i + u(L_i). \tag{1}$$

We focus on discretionary income. Yet access to loans is determined by the same factors that shape the terms of borrowing, so we can extend this logic to access.[2] In our model, mandatory charges are equal to the cost of borrowing (such as mortgage interest payments). To identify the effect of borrowing, we will assume that spending on necessities is constant. Discretionary income for individual i, D_i, over the term of a loan is then equal to:

$$D_i = Y_i - L_i \cdot r_i, \tag{2}$$

where Y_i is disposable income and r_i is the interest rate.

As long as the elasticity of demand for credit is more than -1, higher interest rates will lead to lower discretionary income and also lower utility (assuming that people borrow at an optimal rate). The standard assumption is that the elasticity of demand for credit is close to 0.[3] Since utility increases with both credit and discretionary income and since a rise in interest rates reduces discretionary income as well as borrowing, such a rise also reduces utility.

Given the demand function, the loan amount and the total cost of borrowing are determined by the interest rate, and discretionary income will be a function of the default risk, p_i. We show in Appendix 5A that:

$$D_i = Y_i \cdot \left(1 - \alpha \cdot \frac{\bar{r} + 2p_i}{1 + \bar{r} + p_i} \right), \tag{3}$$

where $\bar{r}$ is the competitive rate in a market with no default risk, and α is a weight that determines the demand for credit. We observe that $dD_i/dp_i < 0$, so that discretionary spending decreases with the default risk. If the probability of default declines with income – which is strongly supported by the data (more on this below) – then *the greater the dispersion of the distribution of risk, the greater the dispersion of the distribution of discretionary income*. Indeed, discretionary income is always more dispersed than disposable income. This is our first result, and it shows a heretofore unrecognized effect, via interest rates, of increasing inequality of risk.

Lenders are not always able to offer credit at the optimal rate because they are constrained by regulation mandating them not to charge rates

---

[2] Since access to borrowing is an important source of wealth accumulation – especially real estate – access is related to wealth inequality. For the purposes of this book, however, we do not attempt to explicitly model the complex relationship between credit and wealth.

[3] DeFusco and Paciorek (2017) estimate the elasticity of demand for mortgages to be around -0.02, but it may be notably higher for credit card debt, which Gross and Souleles (2002) estimate to be around -0.85.

above a certain threshold or because it is too difficult to determine actual default risks above a certain level. In the latter case, the lender may use a simple cutoff rule to limit exposure to bad loans. In the presence of cutoffs, an increase in the dispersion of observed risk will also lead to more people being denied credit. At the same time, the dispersion of the distribution among those who can obtain loans will increase (under standard assumptions about the shape of the risk distribution).[4]

It directly follows from our first result that countries with more unequal risk of default distributions have more unequal discretionary income distributions, *after* controlling for disposable income inequality. This is not captured by the effect of risk on (expected) future income (as in standard insurance models); it is a direct effect on current consumption. This is the *first implication* of the model.

The Effect of Information

We have assumed that borrowers and lenders are all fully informed about the risk of default. This may be a feasible assumption for the borrower, but default risk is hard to observe for the lender, which creates a classic adverse selection problem. If the lending firm has no information about risk type, it will have to set an average interest rate that is proportional in equilibrium to the amount of defaulted loans among all borrowers (which *can* be observed). This average rate is called $\bar{\bar{r}}$ (distinct from $\bar{r}$, which is the competitive rate charged *if* all loans were repaid with interest).[5]

This common interest rate means that high-risk types will pay lower interest rates than low-risk types, compared to a situation with full information. The consequence is a shift in lending toward high-risk types so that the total amount of defaulted debt increases and the average interest rate rises. This is an efficiency cost, but at the same time, it reduces inequality in discretionary spending because those with higher income now pay more for credit, while those with lower income pay less, compared to the full information scenario.

The unequalizing effect of information can be established more generally if we assume that lenders learn about individual risks by observing

---

[4] Imagine a normal distribution with a fixed lower cutoff point. A means-preserving increase in dispersion implies that a greater proportion of the distribution is below the cutoff, while the dispersion of the distribution above the threshold increases.

[5] Note that since the individual loan amount depends on income, if p_i is (negatively) related to income, the average loan amount among those who end up in the bad state is not the same as the amount among those who remain in the good state. Hence, $\sum p_i \cdot L_i = \bar{p} \cdot L$.

credit history. Such history is constructed by collecting information about the speed of debt accumulation, timeliness of repayments, past instances of default, and so on, and such information can be understood as signals in a Bayesian updating game where "observed" risk is a weighted function of a prior and the signal. If $p_i^o = [p_{min}^o, p_{max}^o]$ is the observed risk of individual i by lender l, we can write:

$$p_l^o = \iota \cdot p_i^s + (1 - \iota) \cdot \bar{p} \qquad (4)$$

where p_i^s is a noisy signal drawn from a distribution that is centered on the individual's true risk and p_i, and $\bar{p}$ is the mean among all borrowers, which is the prior. The parameter ι is a measure of the "precision" of the signal, which equals the information about i that is available to the lender. With no information ($\iota = 0$), the lender only observes the population mean, $p_i^o = \bar{p}$, and the range is therefore 0. At the other extreme, with complete information, $p_i^o = p_i$, the range equals the difference between the individual with the lowest and the individual with the highest underlying risk (see also Chapter 2).

If we use the range as a measure of dispersion, we therefore have:

$$[p_{min}^o, p_{max}^o] < [p_{min}^i, p_{max}^i]. \qquad (5)$$

Moreover, the difference in the range falls with increasing information:

$$(p_{max}^i - p_{min}^i) - (p_{max}^o - p_{min}^o) = f(\bar{\iota}). \qquad (6)$$

Alternatively, we could treat the difference in the variance of underlying and observed risks as a function of information. Keeping in mind that discretionary income is a function of default risk, the implication is that *more information increases the inequality in discretionary income* (i.e., increases the range or the variance in income). This is the *second implication* of the model.

The Role of the Welfare State

So far, we have assumed that any "catastrophic" loss of income leads to default. However, people have an incentive to try hard to avoid default, which will exclude them from future borrowing (or significantly raise the cost of such borrowing). If people default on a mortgage, they will lose their home. We do not explicitly model the individual decision to default but instead assume that if the private funds that are available in the bad state, k_i, are at or below a given threshold, T_i, the borrower will default; otherwise, they will not:

$$\text{If} \left\{ \begin{array}{l} k_i \le T_i \text{ then default} \\ k_i > T_i \text{ then do not default} \end{array} \right\}. \tag{7}$$

We can think of k_i as income from selling assets, bringing forward long-term pension savings, or the like. It is natural to think that k_i must be high enough to cover basic needs as well as essential fixed expenses (such as medicine) before debt servicing is possible. But there are clearly also subjective aspects to what individuals consider acceptable sacrifices, and the lender cannot observe these directly. Some people will make great sacrifices to repay their loans; others will be more willing to accept the consequences of default.

In Appendix 5A, we derive the interest rate for the cases where (i) the lender cannot observe either risk of income loss, p_i, or individual thresholds, T_i, and (ii) the lender knows p_i but not individual thresholds. In the former case, there will be a common interest rate for all (see Eq. A11 in Appendix 5A), but in the latter case it will vary according to:

$$r_i = \frac{\bar{r} + 2 \cdot p_i \cdot p_{(k_i < T)}}{1 - p_i \cdot p_{(k_i < T)}}. \tag{8}$$

Intuitively, the interest rate is rising in individual risks and the probability of default. Since the latter depends on personal assets, k_i, such assets are a source of discretionary income inequality, even in the good state, as long as they are rising in income.

Yet social protection mediates this relationship by adding a transfer, b_i, to personal funds in the bad state, which has the exact same effect for the individual as increasing k_i. Even if b_i is a lump-sum benefit paid to everyone from a flat-rate tax (as in a Meltzer–Richard model), we show in Appendix 5B that the distribution of interest rates, and hence the distribution of discretionary income, becomes less dispersed as b_i rises. The intuition is that a flat-rate benefit shifts the distribution of income in the bad state to the right, while the distribution of default thresholds stays constant. If the default threshold distribution is normal, this means that the bottom portion of the income distribution, say, the bottom decile, moves into the "thicker" portion of the default threshold distribution with more people now willing and able to service their debt.[6] This holds for a

---

[6] There are, of course, more people at the top end of the income distribution who move above the default thresholds at the high end of the default threshold distribution, but because the

flat-rate benefit; ipso facto, it also holds for benefits that target those with low income ("means-tested").

The conclusion is that the welfare state diminishes the unequalizing effects of financialization and information and that this dampening effect is *in addition* to the direct effect of the welfare state on disposable income inequality. This is the *third implication* of the model. The existing literature only considers the direct effect of the welfare state on disposable income through redistribution, not the indirect effect through interest rates.

The Role of Financial Regulation

Social protection systems were not created to reduce default rates or to equalize discretionary spending through a lower dispersion of interest rates. They were created to alleviate poverty or to mitigate the risk of income loss, and it is only with financialization that the indirect effect of the welfare state on discretionary income has become important. For this reason, we treat social spending as an exogenous variable that is not caused by the credit regime, although this may, of course, change in the future as the distributive consequences become apparent.

Financial regulation, on the other hand, is specifically designed to shape the terms of lending, as well as the risks that lenders and borrowers take on. Regulations are complex, but what concerns us here is the extent to which they facilitate the transfer of default risk to the state. A very common mechanism of government intervention is credit guarantee schemes (CGSs), where a state agency steps in to provide collateral and some repayment guarantees (which can be less than 100 percent). State-guaranteed educational loans or government-backed loans to small businesses are examples. If these guarantees are credible, it reduces the risk of lending, and since risks are concentrated at the bottom of the income distribution, it has the same pro-poor/pro-high-risk effect as government transfers. Tax deductions for interest payments, another common policy, make loans, usually for housing, more affordable, thus expanding the market.

To illustrate our logic, we use the regulation of the American mortgage market (Thurston 2018), perhaps the most important case of transferring default risks to the state, as an example. At the center of the system are two

---

upper tail of that distribution is "thin," the effect on the default rates of high-income borrowers is small.

government-sponsored enterprises (GSEs) – Fannie Mae and Freddie Mac (FM/FM) – which are required by law to purchase all mortgages meeting certain minimum requirements, issued by commercial banks, savings and loan associations (S&Ls), and other originators, and to securitize them by issuing bonds in the secondary bond market. Before recent reforms, the quasi-public role of FM/FM had two effects on private lenders. First, they became less concerned about default risks because these were largely absorbed by FM/FM. Lenders were given considerable discretion, and minimum requirements were often finessed by the banks since they knew that the GSEs rarely returned loans. Second, less concerned about risk, they stopped acquiring detailed and costly information about individual borrowers and effectively treated all would-be homeowners equally (over and above the minimum requirements set by FM/FM). Once approved, "conforming loans" were offered at essentially the same terms to almost everyone.[7]

This equalizing effect masks significant subsidization of high-risk (usually lower-income) borrowers. The 1990 amendment of the Fannie Mae and Freddie Mac charter made it an explicit goal to "facilitate the financing of affordable housing for low- and moderate-income families," a provision used aggressively under the Clinton administration to extend loans to low-income families (Acharya et al. 2011). It was thought, or at least hoped, that FM/FM's strong market position and the large margins they had been able to sustain between borrowing costs in the securities market and mortgage interest rates were enough to cushion them from the

---

[7] We recognize that lending has a long history of discrimination on the basis of sex, marital status, income, and especially race (Thurston 2018). A comprehensive review of race-based discrimination ("redlining") provided by an edited volume by Goering and Wienk (2018) does not reach an unambiguous conclusion about the extent of the problem today, but no one disputes that it exists. Prejudice is usually bad for business and should be minimized in a competitive market, but the authors make the convincing argument that lenders may well have a strong incentive to use statistical discrimination in pursuit of pure (color-blind) profit maximization (which is against both the Fair Housing Act and the Equal Credit Opportunity Act). This is a matter of considerable concern for data-driven algorithms, which may include many correlates of race (such as detailed geographic information). It seems clear, however, that GSEs on balance had the effect of broadening equal access after the Fair Housing Act of 1968. As Ladd explains, before the financial crisis, the practices of Fannie Mae, Freddie Mac, and Ginnie Mae meant that "the risks of default [were] shifted to investors in the secondary market, and so it is not clear why loan originators such as banks should need to pay attention to any race-specific probability of default" (1998, 47). This is an important area of research, but discrimination of any kind, including discrimination based on actual risk of default (which is legal), was probably less likely at the time when GSEs played a major role in buying mortgages with little threat of "put-backs" (again, after the Fair Housing Act of 1968).

risks of bad debt. Although FM/FM had been private corporations since 1968, it was also widely believed that all their loans were implicitly guaranteed by the government, which enabled the GSEs to borrow very cheaply. Apparently confirming this logic, China and other countries with saving surpluses poured large sums of money into the bonds issued by FM/FM, pushing average interest rates down (Eichengreen 2008).

Faith in the financial health of the GSEs was shattered with the crash of the subprime mortgage market, after which the stock prices of FM/FM collapsed. They were placed into conservatorship in September 2008. Before and after the government takeover, a series of reforms were implemented to reduce the risk exposure of FM/FM and shift more of it to banks and other mortgage originators, as well as to a third government entity, Ginnie Mae, which securitizes mortgages directly guaranteed by the Federal Housing Administration (FHA). Below, we use these measures as a natural experiment whereby lenders are strongly incentivized to acquire more information and use it to screen out risky borrowers or raise their interest rates. The takeover thus serves as a window into both the effect of government regulation and information.

It is remarkable that the USA, which is a laggard in social policy, has pursued such "progressive" policies in the mortgage market. But this can be explained, at least in part, by the unusual overlap in the interests of progressive politicians and housing affordability advocacy groups, commercial banks and S&Ls, home builders, and even some conservatives keen to cultivate an "ownership society." Over time, Fannie and Freddie themselves became powerful lobbyists (Thompson 2009). This "unholy alliance" has created broad support for lax lending rules across the aisle in Congress and, in fact, goes back a long time to the depths of the Great Depression and the establishment of the FHA in 1934 and the Federal National Mortgage Association in 1938 (later nicknamed Fannie Mae).

The contrast to Denmark drives home the point that regulatory variation does not map onto standard political economy typologies. Denmark, a coordinated market economy, has an entirely market-based, securitized mortgage system, whereas the USA, a liberal market economy, is heavily regulated. These are not outliers. The organization of mortgage lending markets varies greatly across advanced democracies, and it does not correlate with the most widely used political economy typologies (Blackwell and Kohl 2018, 2019; Fernandez and Aalbers 2016; Schwartz and Seabrooke 2008; Wood 2019).

EMPIRICAL TESTS

Our theoretical model makes three empirical predictions:

- H1: More information increases the interest rate spread (and hence the inequality in discretionary income).

- H2: The government acting as a backstop in loan markets reduces the interest rate spread (and hence the inequality in discretionary income).

- H3: More generous public income support facilitates access to loans and reduces the interest rate spread.

The reader will recognize H1 as a special case of our *first argument* in Chapter 2 and H2 and H3 as special cases of our *third argument* about partisanship (broadly construed).

For the model and all three hypotheses, the underlying assumption is that risks are correlated with income. We think this is an uncontroversial assumption but nevertheless show in Appendix 5C that it is strongly supported by the data.

A Note on the Relationship between Information and Regulatory Incentives

It is difficult to test H1 and H2 separately because, while information is increasing over time because of the data revolution, discontinuous exogenous shifts in information typically only occur as a result of regulatory changes that incentivize lenders to seek more information (or not). Conversely, changes in public subsidies for lending changes the risks that lenders face but at the same time also their incentives to acquire information. In this section, we briefly show that under certain assumptions, changes in incentives can be treated as equivalent to changes in information. We use this equivalence to infer the effect of information from sudden regulatory changes.

Lenders crave information because it allows them to separate good risks from bad and thus to (i) exclude potential borrowers who are likely to default and (ii) differentiate interest rates among borrowers to reflect individual risks. Yet the benefits of information have to be weighed against the cost of acquiring information. Furthermore, when the state assumes some of the default risk, the incentive to acquire information falls. We can capture this using a very simple lender utility function:

$$U_L = \iota(\delta) - c(\iota, A),$$

where the benefit of information (as before, ι signifies information) is a negative function of δ, which we can think of as the probability that the regulator will assume responsibility for defaulted loans. The cost of information is a rising function of the level of information, depending on the "information technology," A (Big Data and faster processors, plus better algorithms, make the rise in cost "flatter"). A simple concave representation of this utility function is as follows:

$$U_L = \iota \cdot (1 - \delta) - c(A) \cdot (\iota^2),$$

which implies a maximum investment in information of:

$$\iota^* = \frac{1 - \delta}{2 \cdot c(A)}$$

This shows that changes in the regulatory framework that affect the cost to the lender of defaults, δ, have the same effect on information as changes in the cost of information, c, due to new technology. The latter is mostly driven by secular changes in ICT that reduce the costs of compiling and analyzing data. The former is driven by regulatory changes, which can be abrupt. We know that the cost of information is declining, but the gradual nature of this decline makes it hard to identify its effect on interest rates. Sudden changes in the regulatory framework, by contrast, can be used to gauge the causal effect of information, even if this only results in changes in the incentives to use information. In the following section, we test H1 and H2 simultaneously using this logic. We are also able to confirm that the gradual drop in the cost of information is correlated with a gradual increase in the dispersion of interest rates, although it is of course not possible to establish causality using this evidence.

Regulation, Information, and Inequality in Mortgage Interest Rates

To test H1 and H2, we use a data set that contains all single-family loans that Freddie Mac purchased or guaranteed from the first quarter of 1999 to the last quarter of 2019 – more than thirty-six million mortgages. As described above, Freddie Mac is one of the two main GSEs – along with

Ginnie Mae, a government agency – that purchase "conforming mort-gages" from lenders and sell them in the secondary bond market.

The main reason GSEs return mortgages is delinquency or default – even several years after closing – but it is at the discretion of the GSE. Mortgages closed in 2007 and 2008 saw a dramatic rise in put-back rates, which far exceeded the rise in defaults (Goodman et al. 2014, 60); the aggregate amount of repurchase requests increased tenfold. In terms of the notation used in the previous section, an increase in put-backs is equiva-lent to a decrease in δ: the probability that the regulator will assume the default risk. Moreover, the GSEs tightened the underwriting guidelines for conforming mortgages that lenders had to adhere to[8] and increased their quality controls in various ways.

These changes were rolled out starting in early 2008, and the beginning of that year therefore serves as a break after which lenders had strong incentives to use more information to accurately assess mortgage applica-tions. From the perspective of our theoretical framework, the subprime mortgage crisis is a discontinuity, at which the effort lenders expend and the amount of information they use to assess mortgage quality sharply increased. Again, the trigger for lenders to acquire more information was regulatory reforms, put-backs in particular, that raised the costs of not accurately identifying default risks. For this reason, we expect the spread of interest rates to increase at the discontinuity.[9]

This increased scrutiny and intensified information collection clearly shows up in the data as a sharp rise in the number of days to close a loan. In an interesting account of the role of technological innovation in mortgage underwriting, Foote, Loewenstein, and Willen (2019) show that mortgage processing times dramatically dropped between 1995 and 1998 – from close to fifty (1994) to under thirty (1998) days – and continued to trend down-ward until 2005 – to about seventeen days.[10] They attribute this decline in processing times to technology-augmented innovation, very consistent with

---

[8] For example: "In light of [deteriorating] market conditions, we are reinforcing our appraisal standards and underwriting expectations related to maximum financing in declining markets" (Freddie Mac Bulletin November 15, 07, p. 3).

[9] The effect is reduced, however, by the extent to which Ginnie Mae (a pure government entity) increased its share of mortgage-backed securities, since this reduced the exposure of Fannie and Freddie to high-risk, low-income lending.

[10] They rely on the Home Mortgage Disclosure Act (HMDA) micro-data (using confidential variables) and focus on processing times for refinance loans. They report "average processing time [in days] by year after stripping out any variation explained by the size of the lender, the borrower's race and gender, whether the borrower has a coapplicant, and the concurrent monthly application volume. The processing times are calculated as of

the cost of information gradually dropping. More interestingly for our purposes is the sharp increase in processing times in 2008 and 2009, from about eighteen (2007) to about twenty-six (2008) to almost forty days (2009). It is worth citing their explanation in some detail:

After the US housing boom ended, refinance timelines increase sharply as various lender and governmental policies changed. One of the most significant policy changes involved the repurchase policies of the GSEs. Fannie Mae and Freddie Mac occasionally require mortgage originators to repurchase loans that do not meet the agencies' underwriting guidelines. After housing prices fell, both Fannie and Freddie increased their repurchase requests to originators that had incorrectly underwritten loans. This prompted originators to follow GSE policies more carefully, which likely lengthened origination timelines. (Foote, Loewenstein, and Willen 2019, 14)

We consider these findings and conclusions by Foote, Loewenstein, and Willen (2019) as evidence in favor of our assertion that the beginning of 2008 marks a discontinuity at which lenders were very strongly incentivized to seek more and better information on mortgage applications. As argued, we expect an increase in the spread of interest rates at this discontinuity.

To assess the propositions that the interest rate spread increases over time in general and at the discontinuity in particular, we start by calculating the Gini coefficient of interest rates for each year-month between 1999 and 2019, using Freddie Mac's "Single Family Loan-Level Dataset." On average, each cell (year-month) contains about 60,000 mortgages (the median cell size is 55,714, and the minimum and maximum are 11,910 and 207,049, respectively). Figure 5.3 plots these Gini coefficients over time. While the figure shows an upward trend, there only seems to be a short-lived increase in the spread of interest rates at the discontinuity (January 2008).

However, balance tests reveal that the samples to the left and right of the discontinuity are very different. Most importantly, the composition changes in terms of the distribution of FICO scores (and FICO scores are highly correlated with interest rates), right at the discontinuity. This can be seen in Figure 5.4.

This rise in FICO scores is itself very consistent with the claim that early 2008 was a discontinuity at which lenders engaged in more careful screening since it implies that an increased number of potential borrowers with

the year of application and include both closed loans and denials" (Foote, Loewenstein, and Willen 2019, 37 (note of figure 7)).

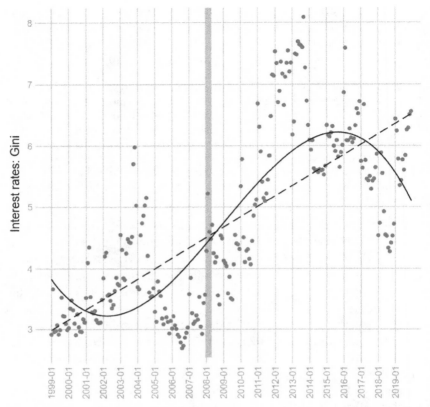

FIGURE 5.3 Interest rate spread over time (year-month level)
Note: Shown are the Gini coefficients of interest rates for each year-month between 1999 and 2019. The dashed line is a linear fit line, while the solid line is a cubic fit line. The shaded area indicates the first quarter of 2008.
Source: Freddie Mac's "Single Family Loan-Level Dataset" (www.freddiemac.co m/research/datasets/sf_loanlevel_dataset.page, last accessed June 3, 2021 [https:// perma.cc/KU32-9TXH]), Q1-1999 to Q4-2019.

low FICO scores were denied loans.[11] But in addition to such censoring, lenders began to differentiate more between borrowers with good FICO scores in the terms they were offered. The obvious interpretation is that lenders acquired additional information among borrowers with similar FICO scores. We focus our analysis on the change in the spread *within*

[11] Our data set does not include denied mortgage applications, but the patterns in Figure 5.4 clearly suggest that lenders screened out applicants with low FICO scores.

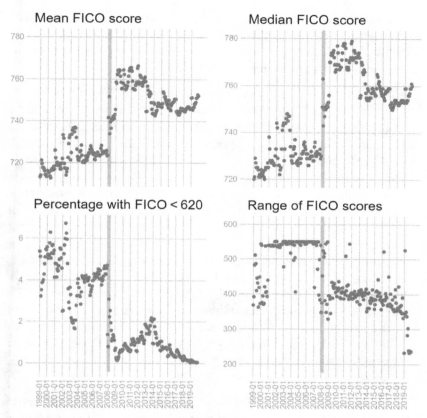

FIGURE 5.4 FICO scores in sample, over time
Note: Shown are mean and median FICO scores, as well as the percentage of FICO scores below 620 and the range of FICO scores within the full sample of the data set. The shaded area indicates the first quarter of 2008.
Source: Freddie Mac's "Single Family Loan-Level Dataset" (www.freddiemac.com/research/datasets/sf_loanlevel_dataset.page, last accessed June 3, 2021 [https://perma.cc/KU32-9TXH]), Q1-1999 to Q4-2019.

FICO tranches to circumvent the potential problem of a changing composition of borrowers. Note that this gives us a conservative estimate of the effect of the discontinuity because (i) we do not capture the rise in rejected mortgage applications (which would otherwise increase dispersion) and (ii) we do not capture the rise in the interest-rate spread *across* FICO groups.

Specifically, to balance the samples before and after the discontinuity – to compare apples with apples – we restrict the sample to mortgages that fulfill the following criteria, and we also shift the analysis from the year-month-level to the year-month-FICO-2d level:

- Credit (FICO) scores in the range of 620 to 819. We drop cases with scores below 620 because this is the minimum score required by Freddie Mac to qualify for a conforming mortgage, at least under normal conditions in most years (this drops 2.19% of the sample). We drop cases with FICO scores in the 820–850 range (the very top-end of the FICO-score distribution) because only a few mortgages are in this category, and they are unevenly distributed over time – leading to unreliable and infrequent estimates of the spread of interest rates for FICO scores above 819 (this drops 0.03% of the original sample).
- Thirty-year mortgages (applies to 67.1% of the original sample).
- Fixed-rate mortgages (applies to 100% of the original sample).
- No mortgage insurance (applies to 82.9% of the original sample).
- Loan-to-value ratio of a maximum of 80 percent (i.e., minimum of 20 percent down payment) (applies to 80% of the original sample).
- Single-family units that are owner occupied (applies to 90.6% of the original sample).
- US states only (applies to 99.8% of the original sample).

This leaves us with a sample of about 15.3 million mortgages. Balance tests show that the composition of mortgages before and after January 2008 is very similar even across bins and assuredly so within bins. We use this data set to calculate measures of interest rate dispersion – such as the Gini coefficient, the coefficient of variation, and others – at the year-month-FICO-2d level.[12] Figure 5.5 plots the Gini coefficient of interest rates within FICO-2d bins over time. Therefore, a dot in the figure represents the Gini coefficient of a year-month-FICO-2d bin.

At least three aspects are noteworthy about the patterns in Figure 5.5. First, the spread of interest rates – as measured by the Gini coefficient within ten-point FICO bands – clearly increases over time, as hypothesized. The spread of interest rates roughly doubled within the twenty-year period under consideration.

---

[12] By FICO-2d level, we refer to the first two digits of FICO scores, which range from 620 to 819 in our sample. For example, FICO-2d score 62 refers to FICO scores 620–629.

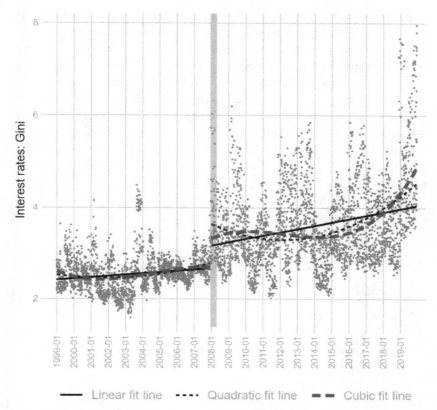

FIGURE 5.5 Interest rate spread over time (year-month-FICO-2d level)
Note: Shown are the Gini coefficients of interest rates for each year-month between 1999 and 2019, within FICO-2d levels (mildly jittered), along with local polynomial fit lines of orders 1 to 3. The shaded area indicates the first quarter of 2008.
Source: Freddie Mac's "Single Family Loan-Level Dataset" (www.freddiemac.com/research/datasets/sf_loanlevel_dataset.page, last accessed June 3, 2021 [https://per ma.cc/KU32-9TXH]), Q1-1999 to Q4-2019.

Second, there is a clear increase of the spread of interest rates beginning in January 2008 (the discontinuity). The figure shows local polynomial fit lines of orders 1 through 3 (fitted over the entire support of the pre- and post-treatment time periods, respectively). All indicate a visual break in the series. To test whether there is, indeed, a break in the spread of interest rates, we rely on regression discontinuity (RD) in time analysis. The outcome variable is the interest rate spread (measured by Gini coefficients within FICO-2d bins at the month-year level). The score/running variable is month-years, with January 2008 as the discontinuity. We employ a (data-driven) mean square error (MSE) optimal bandwidth selection procedure – imposing the same bandwidth on each side of the cutoff – for local polynomial estimation of and inference on treatment effects and report robust bias-corrected confidence intervals, with standard errors clustered at the FICO-2d level. Observations are weighted via a triangular kernel function (i.e., observations closer to the cut-off are weighted more heavily). Our data set has repeated observations in the running variable (20 FICO scores per year-month), for which the estimator controls. Table 5.1 reports the RD estimates based on local polynomials of orders 1 through 4.

Table 5.1 shows that the RD estimate ranges from about 1 to about 1.3, depending on the order of the local polynomial. These estimates are statistically significant at $p < 0.001$. The literature usually recommends (Gelman and Imbens 2019) and chooses (Pei et al. 2021) lower-order over higher-order polynomials. Therefore, we prefer the first model (which uses local linear regressions). The RD estimate of about 1 implies roughly a 40% increase at the threshold in the interest rate spread (from about 2.5 before the threshold on average).

In Appendix 5D, we perform a wide variety of additional tests and show that the finding of a statistically significant (and substantively meaningful) increase in the interest rate spread at the discontinuity is very robust. In particular, we perform the following additional/robustness checks:

- Different bandwidth selection procedures
- Different kernel functions
- Covariate adjusted estimates (controlling for month dummies, lagged dependent variable, and average interest rate) (Hausman and Rapson 2018)
- Different specification of the running variable (months, quarters, trimesters, half years, and years), using the year-month-FICO-2d-level data
- Different specification of the running variable (months, quarters, trimesters, half years, and years), with the outcome variable recalculated at the respective unit level (months, quarters, trimesters, half years, and years)
- Sensitivity to observations near the cutoff (donut hole approach)
- Placebo outcomes

TABLE 5.1 *Regression discontinuity estimates*

	(1)	(2)	(3)	(4)
Order of local polynomial	1	2	3	4
RD estimate	1.003*** (0.0976)	1.300*** (0.113)	1.032*** (0.105)	1.063*** (0.112)
Robust 95% CI	[0.901; 1.283]	[1.14; 1.609]	[0.75; 1.176]	[0.782; 1.259]
BW type	mserd	mserd	mserd	mserd
Kernel	Triangular	Triangular	Triangular	Triangular
Order Loc. Poly. (p)	1	2	3	4
Order bias (q)	2	3	4	5
N	5,025	5,025	5,025	5,025
N (l)	2,147	2,147	2,147	2,147
N (r)	2,878	2,878	2,878	2,878
Eff. N (l)	340	300	320	500
Eff. N (r)	360	320	340	520
BW est. (l)	17.15	15.78	16.52	25.35
BW est. (r)	17.15	15.78	16.52	25.35
BW bias (l)	28.13	25.24	26.03	38.35
BW bias (r)	28.13	25.24	26.03	38.35

Note: Standard errors in parentheses (clustered at the FICO-2d level)
*p < 0.05$, **$p < 0.01$, and ***$p < 0.001$
Estimates adjusted for mass points in the running variable.
The outcome variable is the Gini coefficient of interest rates at the FICO-2d level.
The running variable is time (month-year) with the cutoff in January 2008.
These estimates are based on the user-written Stata commands "rdrobust" (Calonico et al. 2017).
Source: Freddie Mac's "Single Family Loan-Level Dataset" (www.freddiemac.com/research/datasets/sf_loanlevel_dataset.page, last accessed June 3, 2021 [https://perma.cc/KU32-9TXH]), Q1-1999 to Q4-2019.

- Placebo cutoffs
- Mass points adjustments

The third noteworthy aspect in Figure 5.5 is the increasing range of the interest rate spread, with a clear jump at the discontinuity. For example, in 2007, the Gini coefficient of interest rates ranged from 2.3 to 3.5, while it ranged from 2.4 to 6 in 2008. This might suggest that the increase in the interest rate spread at the discontinuity was higher for some of the twenty FICO-2d groups. The obvious hypothesis is that lenders focused their increased screening efforts on applicants with lower FICO scores because it is well-documented that the spread of risks, measured by default rates, is greater for lower FICO tranches (VantageScore 2020).[13] If so, lower FICO scores essentially received a higher dosage of the treatment (scrutiny from lenders). To explore this supposition, Figure 5.6 reproduces Figure 5.5, but with separate panels for each of the 10-point FICO bands. Therefore, Figure 5.5 is a pooled version of Figure 5.6 and a dot within the panels of Figure 5.5 indicates a year-month. Within each panel, the mortgages are very similar. Most importantly, their FICO scores are within 10 points of each other (by construction), and the samples before and after January 2008 are balanced well – the figure therefore offers something close to an apples-to-apples comparison.

Visual inspection of Figure 5.6 suggests that the increase in the spread of interest rates at the threshold was particularly pronounced at lower FICO scores – roughly in the 620–679 range. In contrast, at higher FICO levels, the increases seem to be more minor.

Statistical discontinuity tests confirm this pattern. In particular, Figure 5.7 summarizes the RD estimates for each of the twenty FICO bands as coefficient plots. The three columns display estimates based on linear, quadratic, and cubic local fit lines (the estimates are equivalent to the models 1, 2, and 3 in Table 5.1 – they employ the same bandwidth selection procedure, kernel function, and so on – but they are derived from each FICO-2d bin separately). The figure shows that while all estimates are positive and almost all estimates are statistically significant, they tend to be larger at the lower end of the FICO score distribution. This test therefore adds further evidence that is consistent with the hypotheses. It also ameliorates one of the weaknesses of RD in time designs by adding cross-sectional evidence (Hausman and Rapson 2018).

We interpret the general upward trend in interest rate inequality in general (Figures 5.5 and 5.6), the increase in early 2008 (Figure 5.5), and the sharp increase in early 2008 among lower FICO scores (Figures 5.6 and 5.7) as evidence consistent with our framework and hypotheses H1 and H2. Increasing information, whether gradually rising over time or induced by abrupt regulatory change, does indeed seem to increase interest rate dispersion, as predicted.

---

[13] Taking FICO scores as a proxy for default risk, the risk distribution is right-skewed.

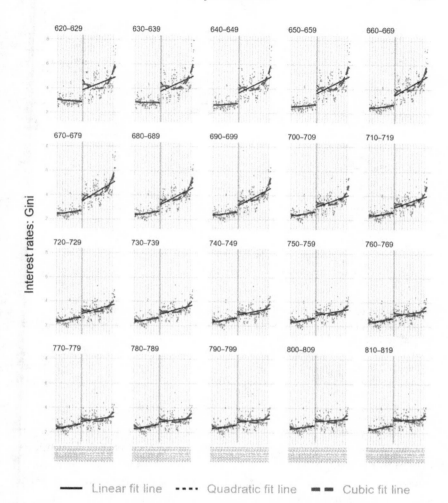

FIGURE 5.6 Interest rate spread over time (year-month-FICO-2d level), at FICO-2d

Note: Shown are the Gini coefficients of interest rates for each year-month between 1999 and 2019, by FICO-2d level, along with local polynomial fit lines of orders 1 to 3. The shaded area indicates the first quarter of 2008. The figure contains the same data points as Figure 5.5 but arranges it by FICO bands.

Source: Freddie Mac's "Single Family Loan-Level Dataset" (www.freddiemac.com/research/datasets/sf_loanlevel_dataset.page, last accessed June 3, 2021 [https://perma.cc/KU32-9TXH]), Q1-1999 to Q4-2019.

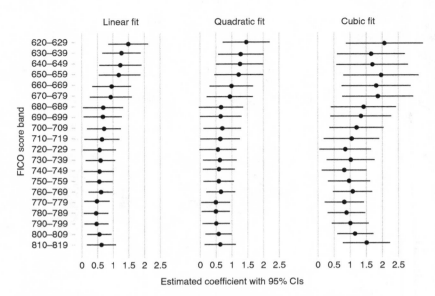

FIGURE 5.7 RD estimate at FICO-2d levels, different polynomials
Note: The figure plots the RD estimates for FICO-2d levels, based on the data displayed in Figure 5.6.
Source: Freddie Mac's "Single Family Loan-Level Dataset" (www.freddiemac.com/research/datasets/sf_loanlevel_dataset.page, last accessed June 3, 2021 [https://perma.cc/KU32-9TXH]), Q1-1999 to Q4-2019.

Regression discontinuity-in-time designs face challenges (Hausman and Rapson 2018). For example, January 2008 was during a tumultuous time, and there might be other candidate explanations for the increase in interest rate inequality. But starting in early January, the evidence clearly suggests the importance of information: The time to close sharply increased; the average FICO scores of loans supported by Freddie Mac increased and lower FICO score loans became much less common in Freddie Mac's portfolio; and lenders began to make more fine-grained distinctions between borrowers. We can infer that they relied on information that went well beyond FICO scores since the spread in rates increased notably even within narrow (two-digit) FICO tranches. Lenders did this, we argue, because regulators provided them with powerful new incentives to separate good from bad risks.

But there are good reasons to believe that the financial industry has been continuously improving its information both before and after 2008.

It is a frontrunner in adopting new ICTs for that purpose (Foote, Loewenstein, and Willen 2019), and even with the increased role of Ginnie Mae (which reduces industry exposure to bad risks), there is a clear upward trend in the spread. This is consistent with the price of information falling over time, which is theoretically predicted to have the same effect on lender behavior as a rise in the cost of defaults (see the "A Note on the Relationship between Information and Regulatory Incentives" section).

The Welfare State and Homeownership

Our model's third prediction is that more (less) generous public income support expands (contracts) access to lending and decreases (increases) the spread of interest rates. The unemployed and those at high risk of unemployment are a greater risk to lenders unless a generous unemployment benefit system enables people to keep servicing their debt. Because unemployment risks are higher for lower-skilled, lower-paid workers, low replacement rates will disproportionately raise borrowing costs and rejection rates at the bottom of the income distribution. Those at the higher end will instead benefit from lenders screening potential borrowers more carefully.

For an initial exploration of this hypothesis, we exploit the profound changes in the German unemployment benefit system resulting from the Hartz IV reforms in 2005 (Arent and Nagl 2013). Because the reform affected the ability to service debt in the event of unemployment, we can compare changes in homeownership rates across groups (un)affected by the reform, from before to after the reform – a difference-in-difference approach.

Unlike in the US system, government entities play no major role in the lending market in Germany,[14] and banks offer mortgages, which are typically fixed rate, on a competitive basis. The system has strong built-in prudential safeguards, including low loan-to-value ratios and limited equity release options, so any changes in the assessed creditworthiness of borrowers show up immediately in lending decisions, and because of civil

---

[14] An exception is the state-owned promotional bank "Kreditanstalt für Wiederaufbau" (KfW) that has various programs to support home ownership, but it is not allowed to compete with commercial banks. There are also subsidies incentivizing homeownership through the state-run aid for pension schemes (Wohn-Riester).

usury law, lenders tend to cut off risky prospects rather than charge high interest rates.[15]

The most consequential changes of the Hartz IV reform occur after a year of unemployment benefit recipiency. Before the reform, the unemployed could qualify for "unemployment assistance," a benefit proportional to previous wages – 67 percent in the first year and approximately 57 percent in the second – that could be collected indefinitely, subject to annual renewal. To qualify, assets had to be below a certain threshold (~520€ times age), though certain assets were protected ("Schonvermögen"), including owner-occupied housing of reasonable size. For banks, default was not a major concern if the income-to-loan ratio was high enough because unemployment assistance was proportional to previous wages at a fairly generous rate and paid indefinitely.

After the reform, the reasonably generous, proportional, perpetual unemployment assistance in the second year was replaced with a meager, flat rate, conditional benefit (Arbeitslosengeld II). Owner-occupied housing of reasonable size is treated as a protected asset as before, but the overall limit for *other* protected assets is significantly lower (~150€ times age). This somewhat odd (Kaiser 2018) differential treatment of assets means that a mortgage provides an opportunity to protect assets from the government by shifting them into owner-occupied housing. Consequently, for those at risk of unemployment, incentives for seeking a mortgage increased with the Hartz IV reforms. For banks, however, there is now much more reason to worry about default among those with risk of long-term unemployment.

Overall, the reforms had two potential effects on financial markets: (i) They made it more difficult for some people to qualify for a loan, and (ii) they increased the risk of default among some borrowers who did qualify. The logic is illustrated in Figure 5.8, where the solid line is the pre-reform distribution of default risk, and the dashed line is the post-reform distribution. The share with observed risk above the threshold for approval increases, and the distribution of those below the threshold "flattens" (becomes more dispersed), reflecting a more right-skewed default-risk distribution. The implications are a reduction in the number of loans granted among higher risks and an increase in the interest rate spread of loans that are granted. We have data that can illuminate the former effect.

---

[15] Interest rate may not be more than twice the comparable market rate in relative terms and not more than 12 percentage points in absolute terms (BGH, Urt. vom 13. März 1990 – XI ZR 252/8).

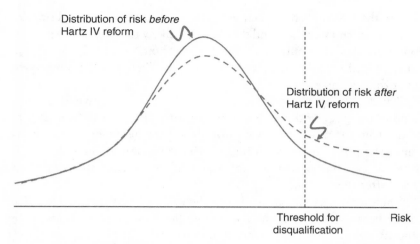

FIGURE 5.8 Distribution of default risk before and after the 2005 Hartz IV reforms

Unfortunately, we do not have data on declined mortgage applications, but we have data on homeownership rates that allow us to shed some light on the fortunes of the unemployed compared to the employed (or poor vs. rich) before and after the reform. We do so in three steps. First, we track and compare homeownership rates of the employed versus the unemployed over time. The data show a sharp drop in homeownership among the unemployed that coincides with the cuts of unemployment benefits.

Second, to gauge the effects of reforms on relinquishing ownership, we track homeownership rates by employment status for those that were homeowners before the reform. The data indicate that for this subsample, ownership rates did not differently drop among either the unemployed or employed. We infer from this that the unemployed rarely relinquished housing assets and that the drop in homeownership rates for the unemployed must be due to lower rates of home acquisition after the reform, presumably because of more difficult access to credit. It may seem surprising that the reform is not associated with more widespread sell-off among the unemployed, but as we noted, the Hartz IV reforms gave people incentives to hold onto their housing wealth, which is exempt from the requirement to spend down personal savings before drawing benefits ("Schonvermögen"). Those who were already homeowners before the reform were undoubtedly also in a stronger financial situation than those who were not, and therefore less likely to default. The point for our purposes is simply that the drop in homeownership among the unemployed must be because people are less likely to obtain mortgages after the reform.

Third, among the employed, we find that homeownership rates among the poor and the rich diverged after the reform. That is especially true for those who were not already owners before the reform. Since the poor are at much higher risk of becoming unemployed, the obvious explanation is that mortgage lenders increasingly avoided bad risks after the reform.

The following four tables display the evidence just summarized. Each table shows the difference in homeownership between two groups, before and after the reform ("difference-in-difference"). The first is a comparison of homeownership rates by employment status (Table 5.2). The most authoritative data for this information is the "Sample Survey of Income and Expenditure" (EVS), which is based on about 60,000 respondents and conducted every 5 years (we have data for 1993, 1998, 2003, 2008, 2013, and 2018). We do not have access to the micro-level data, but the Federal Statistical Office publishes – or provided us with – aggregate data on homeownership[16] for all households and for the unemployed. This allows us to compare homeownership rates among the "unemployed" (treated group) versus the "employed"[17] (control group), before and after 2005. Table 5.2 display the results of a difference-in-difference test of this comparison. The results show that homeownership rates among the employed did not significantly change, while they sharply declined among the unemployed. The difference-in-difference estimate is about –12.7 percentage points for homeownership and statistically significant.[18]

The German Socio-Economic Panel (GSOEP) (Liebig et al. 2019) is another source that allows us to track homeownership rates among the

---

[16] Data are published for (i) "households with house or land property" and (ii) "households with land property," among other breakdowns. We report as "homeownership" item (i) minus (ii).

[17] The "unemployed" are households where the main earner is unemployed. The "employed" are defined as "all households" minus the "unemployed." For presentational ease, we refer to this group as the "employed" even though it is technically the group of "not unemployed" households.

[18] We re-estimated the models in Table 5.2 but added control variables, namely the unemployment rate and/or (linear of factorial) time. The difference-in-difference estimate remains statistically significant.

TABLE 5.2 *Homeownership (EVS)*

Homeownership	Pre-2005	Post-2005	Difference
Employed	0.423	0.455	0.0316 (0.023)
Unemployed	0.222	0.126	−0.0959** (0.023)
Difference	0.201** (0.023)	0.329** (0.023)	−0.127** (0.033)

Note: Standard errors in parentheses. $N = 12$.[19]
*$p < 0.05$ and **$p < 0.01$

unemployed versus the employed.[20] The EVS and the GSOEP use somewhat different definitions of homeownership[21] and employment status,[22] and they cover different time periods.[23] So, while estimates from the two sources are not directly comparable, we do expect that they reveal similar patterns. Table 5.3, which displays difference-in-difference estimates – comparing the unemployed with the employed before and after 2005 – shows that this is, indeed, the case: homeownership rates dropped markedly among the unemployed, comparing 2000–2004 with 2005–2010, and the difference-in-difference estimate is about −7.5 percentage points.

The second step in our three-pronged approach compares the development of homeownership for the subsample of respondents who already were homeowners before the reform (during 2000–2004), using the

[19] We only have aggregate data and for the years listed above, so the number of observations in Table 5.2 is 12.

[20] Again, strictly speaking, the "not unemployed" since it includes pensioners and other people not in the labor force.

[21] The SOEP provides information on home ownership and how the property has been acquired (inherited vs. purchased). We construct a binary home ownership variable that equals one for homeowners that have purchased their home and zero for those that do not own a home. About 25 percent of home ownership is the result of inheritance, and we drop these cases from the analysis. Substantive results are similar when we include inherited homeowners into the analysis.

[22] Our unit of analysis is the household, but we have person-level information that allows us to code the employment status of the household head and her/his partner. We code unemployment as unemployment of either the head or her/his partner, or both.

[23] The SOEP survey started out in 1984 with a sample that was representative for West Germany. Since then, refreshment samples have been periodically added to keep the survey representative. We make use of all samples that cover the 2000s (samples A to F, with F starting in 2000) and apply cross-sectional weights.

TABLE 5.3 *Homeownership (GSOEP)*

Homeownership	Pre-2005	Post-2005	Difference
Employed	0.402	0.384	–0.0182** (0.005)
Unemployed	0.256	0.162	–0.0936** (0.014)
Difference	0.146** (0.013)	0.221** (0.013)	–0.0754** (0.015)

Note: Standard errors (clustered at household level) in parentheses. $N = 100{,}667$.
$^{*}p < 0.05$ and $^{**}p < 0.01$

GSOEP data. We again use difference-in-difference estimates even though, by construction, there are no differences between the unemployed and employed before the reform since the sample is restricted to those that are homeowners before the reform. Table 5.4 shows that there are no meaningful differences after the reform, either – the estimated difference-in-difference is essentially zero and not statistically significant. This suggests that the unemployed in the GSOEP sample are not disproportionally relinquishing their homes after the reform and that the divergence in ownership rates between the unemployed and employed documented above is driven by the inability of the unemployed to secure mortgage credit after the reform.

It could still be the case, however, that the unemployed simply decide that they cannot afford a mortgage after the reform. That is consistent with the model, but not speaking to the role of lenders. Therefore, in the third step, we compare changes in homeownership among the employed only, comparing rich and poor employed respondents. The Hartz reforms made lower income groups more likely to default – because they are at higher risk of unemployment[24] – and we therefore expect homeownership

---

[24] To distinguish between low and high risks, we divide people by income. Although income is only one factor affecting default risks, those with lower incomes are expected to experience a higher increase in the risk of default after the reform for two reasons. First, they are at higher risk of unemployment – simply because income and unemployment risk are negatively correlated – and the lowering of long-term unemployment benefits makes them worse default risks. Second, private assets (k in our model) become more important when unemployment benefits are lower (lower b can be offset with higher k), and people with lower income generally have fewer private assets. Moreover, by reducing protected assets (other than home equity), the reform made people with lower savings higher default

TABLE 5.4 *Homeownership (GSOEP), conditional on being homeowner pre-reform*

Homeownership	Pre-2005	Post-2005	Difference
Employed	1	0.963	
Unemployed	1	0.968	
Difference	0	0.005	0.005
		(0.012)	(0.012)

Note: Standard errors (clustered at household-level) in parentheses. $N = 39{,}170$. $^*p < 0.05$ and $^{**}p < 0.01$

TABLE 5.5 *Homeownership (GSOEP), rich versus poor employed*

Homeownership	Pre-2005	Post-2005	Difference
Rich	0.577	0.583	0.00590
			(0.009)
Poor	0.249	0.223	– 0.0259**
			(0.008)
Difference	0.328**	0.360**	– 0.0318**
	(0.014)	(0.017)	(0.012)

Note: Standard errors (clustered at household level) in parentheses. $N = 55{,}798$. $^*p < 0.05$ and $^{**}p < 0.01$

rates among the employed poor and the employed rich to diverge after the reform. This is what the data show, with a statistically significant difference-in-difference estimate of about –3.2 percentage points (Table 5.5). As for the unemployed, the effect is mostly due to a relative drop in homeownership among those poor who were not already owners before the reform, suggesting that they faced tighter access to credit after the reform.

Overall, the patterns in both data sets (the EVS and the GSOEP) are consistent with the hypothesis that access to credit worsened for the unemployed as well as those at higher risk of unemployment, after the Hartz reforms lowered unemployment benefits. Different data sources

---

risks. Therefore, we expect that access to mortgage credit becomes more difficult for lower income households after the reform.

and our three-pronged empirical approach support this conclusion, but since we do not have data on mortgage applications (and rejections), we cannot be certain that lending decisions drove the results. Future research will have to (dis)confirm that interpretation.

We would have liked to test the hypothesis that access to, and conditions of, mortgage credit vary as a function of income support generosity, using cross-national data. But because regulatory frameworks of financial markets vary greatly (even within the EU) and because there is very little data, we can only offer a very preliminary test. Table 5.6 shows that the spread of interest rates (the coefficient of variation, the Gini coefficient, and p90/p10 ratios) – a measure for the inequality in access to credit – cross-nationally correlates, in the predicted direction, with two measures of income replacement generosity, one measure of public subsidies for home ownership, and the home ownership rate.

CONCLUSION

The financialization of advanced economies has made ability to access credit markets, and the terms of such access, increasingly important for understanding inequality. Creditworthiness affects who is able to purchase a home, as well as who is able to move between work and family and between work and further education. And the interest rate spread directly affects the dispersion of discretionary income under well-supported assumptions about the relationship between income and risks. Improved credit information strengthens this relationship and empowers lenders to differentiate between high- and low-risk groups, allowing them to raise interest rates for low-income groups or to exclude them from credit markets in the first place. The combination of financialization and Big Data is therefore a double whammy for the poor: Like everyone else, they increasingly depend on borrowing to smooth income and acquire assets, but at the same time, they are increasingly considered bad risks and face less favorable terms of borrowing.

Yet these unequalizing effects are strongly conditioned by the regulatory regime and the welfare state. Where the state assumes some of the risks of lending – for example, by acting as a backstop in mortgage markets – or where the social protection system is generous, the effects of financialization and Big Data are muted. Our evidence from the housing market strongly supports these claims. Since our evidence is based on isolated instances of changes in financial regulation and in unemployment benefits, it is difficult to gauge the broader implications of the massive

TABLE 5.6 *Cross-national correlation matrix*

	(1)	(2)	(3)	(4)	(5)	(6)
(1) CoV of interest rates[a]	1					
(2) Gini of interest rates	0.982*	1				
(3) p90/p10 interest rates	0.861*	0.868*	1			
(4) Income replacement[b] (% of GDP)	–0.453*	–0.400	–0.529*	1		
(5) Income replacement[b] (PPS per capita)	–0.516*	–0.458*	–0.584*	0.792*	1	
(6) Homeownership subsidies[c]	–0.535*	–0.573*	–0.516*	0.640*	0.494	1
(7) Homeownership rate[a]	0.462*	0.430*	0.401*	–0.665*	–0.683*	–0.681*

Note: N = 17 for all variables (BEL, CYP, DEU, ESP, EST, FRA, GRC, HUN, IRL, ITA, LUX, LVA, MLT, NLD, PRT, SVK, and SVN, but N = 12 for variable (6) (no data for BEL, GRC, ITA, SVK, and SVN). $^*p < 0.1$.
Variables are averaged across available years since 1994. Variable (6) refers to around 2015, and variable (7) to around 2010–2014.
Sources: (a) Interest rate and homeownership data are from the Household Finance and Consumption Survey (HFCS), waves 1 and 2. www.ecb.europa.eu/pub/economic-research/research-networks/html/researcher_hfcn.en.html (last accessed June 3, 2021 [https://perma.cc/TA4 R-XWVZ]).
(b) Income replacement = social protection expenditures for sickness/healthcare + disability + survivor + unemployment. Source: http://ec.europa.eu/eurostat/cache/metadata/en/spr_esms.htm (last accessed June 3, 2021 [https://perma.cc/6B3S-T B8 C])/http://appsso.eurostat.ec.europa.eu/nui/show.do?dataset=spr_exp_sum (last accessed June 3, 2021 [https://perma.cc/YRW9-JKHT]).
(c) Average of three measures of public support for homeownership: (i) public spending on grants and financial support to home buyers (PH2.1), (ii) forgone tax revenue due to tax relief for access to homeownership (PH2.2), (iii) spending on housing allowances by type of housing-related costs covered (PH3.1). Source: www.oecd.org/social/affordable-housing-database.htm (last accessed June 3, 2021 [https://perma.cc/YQA3-RFXS]). Some imputation.

shifts toward financialization and individualized data on risk. That said, even in our specific cases, the effects are considerable.

In our US mortgage data, the p90/p10 ratio of interest rates increased from 1.2 in 1999 to 1.4 in 2020. Over the term of a thirty-year mortgage, this translates as over US$31,000 more in interest payments (assuming a typical home purchase price of US$300,000 with 2020 interest rates).[25] To put this amount into perspective, the family median net worth (including residential housing assets minus liabilities) for Americans in 2019 was US$188,000 (whites), US$24,000 (Blacks), and US$36,000 (Latinos) (Bhutta et al. 2020, table 2). Differential interest rates not only affect discretionary income inequality but also are likely to significantly exacerbate wealth inequality (especially if interest rates and/or home prices will rise). Clearly, the continued government backing of mortgages in the USA, as well as the expanding role of Ginnie Mae in financing housing for low-income people, keeps spreads lower than they otherwise would be – a dampening effect of regulation that does not apply to other loan markets, notably consumer debt.

According to our estimates, the Hartz reforms significantly widened the gap between the rich and the poor when it comes to owner-occupied housing. This not only increases inequality in terms of benefits of home-ownership in the short run but is also likely to increase wealth inequality in the long run. Our evidence only scratches the surface, and the cumulative effects on inequality across all lending markets are likely to be large – perhaps even rivaling those of rising wage inequality. Surely, these changes merit much greater attention by comparative political economists.

An important question for future research is whether the improved capacity of markets to differentiate between risk groups will lead to a weakening of the regulatory regime, if not the welfare state, which has in the past facilitated relative equality in access to credit markets. A major difficulty in keeping a progressive coalition together is that the underlying risk distribution is strongly right-skewed, which means that the median in the distribution – who is likely to be politically influential – is someone who would benefit from greater differentiation in access to credit. Is it too pessimistic to suppose that the rising importance of credit, combined with better information about the shape of the distribution, will lead to calls for the state to step back?

---

[25] In Freddie Mac's "Single Family Loan-Level Dataset" with mortgage characteristics set as given previously, the p10 interest rate (r) is 2.75 percent, and the p90 interest rate is 3.875 in 2020. On a US$300,000 home with 20 percent down payment, the total interest paid for a thirty-year mortgage is about US$112,000 ($r = 2.75$) and US$166,000 ($r = 3.875$). If the interest rate ratio were 1.2 (as in 1999) instead of 1.4, the p90 interest rate in 2020 would be 3.23, with total interest paid being approximately US$135,000. The difference in total interest paid between high and low interest rates in these two scenarios is 166,000 − 112,000 = 54,000 (1.4 ratio) and US$135,000 − 112,000 = 23,000 (1.2 ratio). The higher interest rate spread therefore costs the high interest rate mortgage holder 54,000 − 23,000 = 31,000.

APPENDICES

Appendix 5A: The Model

We assume that individual i's time horizon is equal to the term of any loan so that the interest rate on the loan is proportional to the total interest that has to be paid back (in addition to the principal). The loan amount is L_i, and the interest rate is r_i, where the money borrowed is used to pay for housing, daycare, and other services or time off work for education and retraining that are part of an anticipated career trajectory. There is also a risk, p_i, of "catastrophic" loss of income, and the non-loan private fund available for consumption in this case is k_i, which is income from selling assets, bringing forward long-term pension savings, or the like. The (von Neumann–Morgenstern) expected utility of individual i with income Y_i is now defined as follows:

$$U_i = [\ln\left(Y_i - L_i \cdot (1 + r_i)\right) + a \cdot \ln(L_i)] \cdot (1 - p_i) + \ln(k_i) \cdot p_i \qquad (A1)$$

where a is the demand for credit, which we assume to be common here.

The model uses a log function to capture a standard concave utility function (u'- > 0 and u" < 0) in a simple and tractable manner. Note that if the catastrophic life event is triggered, we have assumed that the individual will be unable to afford to pay back the loan and will default. We will endogenize the default decision below.

From the perspective of the lender, we assume the competitive rate in a market with no default risk is $\bar{r}$. But in determining the interest rate for borrower i, the lender adjusts for i's risk of default. If the lender has full information about i's risk type, and if there are a large number of other borrowers with the same risk profile, the lender will break even when:

$$(1 - p_i) \cdot (1 + r_i) \cdot L_i - p_i \cdot L_i = (1 + \bar{r}) \cdot L_i^{26} \qquad (A2)$$

which implies that:

---

[26] Strictly speaking, this equation applies to groups of borrowers with the same risk profile, not to individuals. So we should use means for each group – 1, 2, 3, …, N – and use the subscripts $i = 1, i = 2, i = 3, …, i = N$. If the equation literally referred to an individual i, the lender could no longer behave in a risk-neutral manner, as we have assumed. But since the meaning is clear, we forgo complicating the notation.

$$r_i = \frac{\bar{r} + 2p_i}{1 - p_i}. \tag{A3}$$

The more likely i is to default, the higher the interest rate charged to that individual.

The optimal loan requested by individual i is found by setting the first-order condition of Eq. (A1) equal to 0, which yields:

$$L_i^* = \frac{1}{2} \cdot \alpha_i \cdot \frac{Y_i}{1 + r_i}. \tag{A4}$$

The lower the interest rate, the greater the demand for credit, which is another standard result.

Discretionary income, D_i, is:

$$D_i = Y_i - L_i \cdot r_i. \tag{A5}$$

Inserting the optimal loan amount (Eq. [A4]) at the break-even interest rate (Eq. [A3]), we find that:

$$
\begin{aligned}
D_i &= Y_i - \frac{1}{2} \cdot \alpha \cdot \frac{Y_i}{1 + \dfrac{\bar{r} + 2p_i}{1 - p_i}} \cdot \frac{\bar{r} + 2p_i}{1 - p_i} \\
&= Y_i \cdot \left(1 - \frac{1}{2} \cdot \alpha \cdot \frac{\bar{r} + 2p_i}{1 + \bar{r} + p_i}\right).
\end{aligned} \tag{A6}
$$

If the lender has no information about risk type, they will have to set an average interest rate that is proportional in equilibrium to the amount of defaulted loans among all borrowers (which is always observed as losses), so the break-even condition is now:

$$\sum((1 - p_i) \cdot L_i) \cdot (1 + \bar{\bar{r}}) - \sum p_i \cdot L_i = \sum(1 + \bar{r}) \cdot L_i = (1 + \bar{r}) \cdot \sum L_i \tag{A7}$$

which implies that:

$$\bar{\bar{r}} = \frac{(1 + \bar{r}) \cdot \overline{L} + \overline{pL}}{(1 - p) \cdot L} - 1, \tag{A8}$$

where $\bar{\bar{r}}$ is the interest rate charged to any borrower.[27]

---

[27] Note that since the individual loan amount depends on income, if p_i is (negatively) related to income, the average loan amount among those who end up in the bad state is not the same as among those who stay in the good state. Hence, $\sum p_i \cdot L_i = \bar{p} \cdot \overline{L}$.

Lenders can learn about individual risks through credit history. With Bayesian updating, the "observed" risk is a weighted function of a prior and the signal. If $p_l^o = [p_{min}^o, p_{max}^o]$ is the observed risk of individual i by lender l, we can write:

$$p_l^o = \iota \cdot p_i^s + (1 - \iota) \cdot \bar{p} \tag{A9}$$

where p_i^s is a noisy signal drawn from a distribution that is centered on the individual's true risk, p_i, and $\bar{p}$ is the mean among all borrowers, which is the prior. The parameter ι is a measure of the "precision" of the signal, which equals the information about i available to the lender. With no information ($\iota = 0$), i only observes the population mean, $p_i^o = \bar{p}$, and the range is therefore 0. At the other extreme, with complete information, $p_i^o = p_i$, the range equals the difference between those with the lowest and highest risk.

In the next iteration of the model, "catastrophic" loss of income does not necessarily lead to default. Instead, we assume that if assets that can be used in the bad state are at or below a certain threshold, T_i, the borrower will default; otherwise, they will not:

$$\text{If } \begin{Bmatrix} k_i \leq T_i \text{ then default} \\ k_i > T_i \text{ then do not default} \end{Bmatrix}. \tag{A10}$$

If the lender cannot observe either risk of income loss, p_i, or individual thresholds, T_i, we find the break-even common (average) interest rate to be:

$$(1+\bar{r}) \cdot \sum(1-p_i) \cdot L_i + (1+\bar{r}) \cdot \sum p_i \cdot p_{(k_i > T_i)} \cdot L_i - \sum p_i \cdot p_{(k_i < T_i)} \cdot L_i = (1+\bar{r}) \cdot \sum L_i$$

$$\bar{r} = \frac{(1+\bar{r}) \cdot \sum L_i + \sum p_i \cdot p_{(k_i < T_i)} \cdot L_i}{\sum(1-p_i) \cdot L_i + \sum p_i \cdot (1 - p_{(k_i > T_i)}) \cdot L_i} - 1$$

$$\bar{r} = \frac{(1+\bar{r}) \cdot \overline{L} + \overline{p} \cdot p_{(k < T)} \cdot L}{(1-p) \cdot L + p \cdot (1 - p_{(k < T)}) \cdot L} - 1. \tag{A11}$$

The expected repayment on the left-hand side is the probability of being in the good state times the (certain) repayment (first term), plus the probability of being in the bad state and getting paid (second term) and not getting paid (third term).

If the lender knows p_i and k_i, but not individual subjective thresholds for defaults, the break-even interest rate offered to each individual is:

$$(1 - p_i) \cdot (1 + r_i) \cdot L_i + p_i \cdot p_{(k_i > T)} \cdot (1 + r_i) \cdot L_i - p_i \cdot p_{(k_i < T)} \cdot L_i = (1 + \bar{r}) \cdot L_i$$

$$r_i = \frac{1 + \bar{r} + p_i \cdot p_{(k_i < T)}}{1 - p_i + p_i \cdot p_{(k_i > T)}} - 1$$

$$r_i = \frac{\bar{r} + 2 \cdot p_i \cdot p_{(k_i < T)}}{1 - p_i \cdot p_{(k_i < T)}}. \tag{A12}$$

Note that if everyone defaults after falling into the bad state, the result converges to Eq. (A3), where higher risk exposure means a higher interest rate. But those who are likely to service their debt in the bad state will be rewarded with a lower interest rate and that makes differences in k_i a source of inequality, even in the good state.

When the state transfers income to those in the bad state, we assume that the benefit, b_i, is paid for by a flat-rate tax on all income earners (i.e., those in the good state). Specifically, the benefit is:

$$b_i = b = \frac{t \cdot \sum Y_i}{n} = \frac{t \cdot \bar{y}}{n/N} = t \cdot \frac{\bar{y}}{\bar{p}}, \tag{A13}$$

where n is the number of people in that bad state, N is the total population, and $\bar{p}$ is the mean probability of falling into the bad state.

Appendix 5B: The Effect of a Flat-Rate Benefit on the Distribution of Default Risks

Figure 5A.1 compares the entire distribution of income in the bad state, k_i, with the distribution of default thresholds, T_i. The k_i-distribution before government transfers is the dashed curve, while the distribution after government transfers is the dotted curve. The effect is to raise the income of everyone in the bad state by the amount b.

As public transfers shift the income distribution $(k_i + b)$ to the right, the probability of those in the bottom decile servicing their debt increases. In the example in Figure 5A.1, the combined dark and very dark area under the T_i distribution is the share of the bottom decile of the distribution who do not default (because they are above the threshold). In the example, this share is about 60 percent of those in the bottom decile for the $k_i + b$ distribution, compared with about 20 percent for the k_i distribution. At the high end of the k_i distribution, on the other hand, the effect of the subsidy is to only slightly reduce the default from about 10 percent to

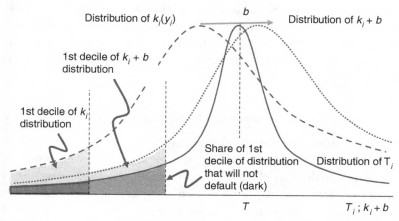

FIGURE 5A.1 The effect of public spending on the location of the distribution of income in the bad state relative to T_i

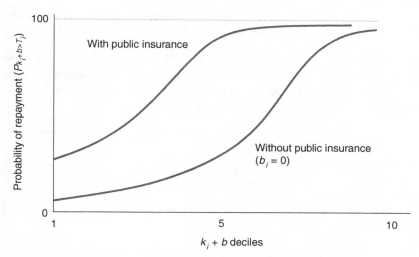

FIGURE 5A.2 The relationship between income in the bad state and the probability of repayment

about 5 percent (because we are now at the "thin" tail of the T_i distribution). Using this logic, Figure 5A.2 shows the relationship between income deciles and the probability of not defaulting, contingent on whether the state redistributes resources to those in the bad state or not.

We can see that the variance of the distribution with public insurance is lower than without. In our example, if we measure the variance as d9/d1 ratios, it falls from about 4 (80 in the top decile and 20 in the bottom) to about 1.5 (90 in the top and 60 in the bottom).

Appendix 5C: The Relationship between Income and Default Risk

The assumption that default risk is negatively related to income can be tested with various existing survey data. For example, the European Quality of Life Survey includes the following set of questions: "Has your household been in arrears at any time during the past 12 months, that is, unable to pay as scheduled any of the following? [Q60]":

- Rent or mortgage payments for accommodation [Q60a]
- Utility bills, such as electricity, water, gas [Q60b]
- Payments related to consumer loans, including credit card overdrafts (to buy electrical appliances, a car, furniture, etc.) [Q60 c]

This allows us to explore the relationship between being behind in paying the rent/mortgage, utility bills, and consumer loans, on the one hand, and income, on the other. As expected, there is generally a clear income gradient to being in arrears (see Figure 5A.3).

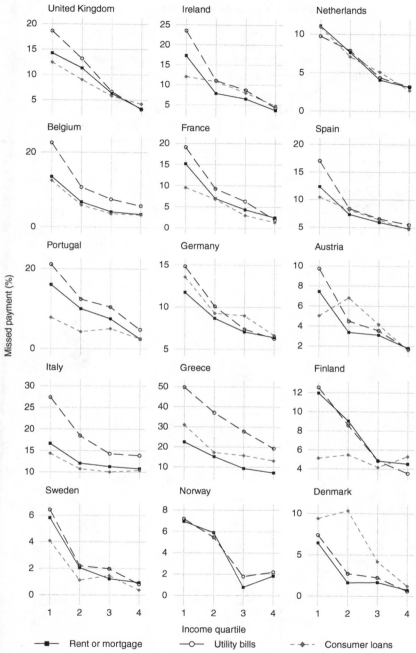

FIGURE 5A.3 The relationship between income and being in arrears
Note: Values are averaged across all available years. Y-axis varies by country.
Source: European Quality of Life Survey Integrated Data File, 2003–2016 (http://
doi.org/10.5255/UKDA-SN-7348-3, last accessed June 3, 2021 [https://perma.cc/
2JLS-CAHT]). Averages across all available years.

Appendix 5D: Regression Discontinuity Results

This appendix presents a variety of robustness checks. In particular:

- Table 5A.1 Different bandwidth selection procedures
- Table 5A.2 Different kernel functions
- Table 5A.3 Covariate adjusted estimates
- Table 5A.4 Different specification of the running variable I
- Table 5A.5 Different specification of the running variable II
- Table 5A.6 Sensitivity to observations near the cutoff (donut hole approach)
- Table 5A.7 Placebo outcomes
- Table 5A.8 Placebo cutoffs
- Table 5A.9 Mass points

TABLE 5A.1 *Different bandwidth selection procedures*

	(1)	(2)	(3)	(4)	(5)	(6)	(7)	(8)	(9)	(10)
BW type	mserd	msetwo	msesum	msecomb1	msecomb2	cerrd	certwo	cersum	cercomb1	cercomb2
RD estimate	1.003***	1.233***	0.762***	1.003***	1.003***	1.146***	1.274***	0.888***	1.146***	1.146***
	(0.0976)	(0.104)	(0.0887)	(0.0976)	(0.0976)	(0.108)	(0.0994)	(0.0908)	(0.108)	(0.108)
Robust 95% CI	[0.901; 1.283]	[1.113; 1.556]	[0.685; 1.012]	[0.901; 1.283]	[0.901; 1.283]	[0.984; 1.428]	[1.133; 1.548]	[0.776; 1.117]	[0.984; 1.428]	[0.984; 1.428]
Kernel					Triangular					
Poly. (p)					1					
Bias (q)					2					
N	5,025	5,025	5,025	5,025	5,025	5,025	5,025	5,025	5,025	5,025
N (l)	2,147	2,147	2,147	2,147	2,147	2,147	2,147	2,147	2,147	2,147
N (r)	2,878	2,878	2,878	2,878	2,878	2,878	2,878	2,878	2,878	2,878
Eff. N (l)	340	320	460	340	340	280	260	380	280	280
Eff. N (r)	360	220	480	360	360	300	200	400	300	300
BW est. (l)	17.15	16.33	23.48	17.15	17.15	14.26	13.58	19.53	14.26	14.26
BW est. (r)	17.15	10.85	23.48	17.15	17.15	14.26	9.03	19.53	14.26	14.26
BW bias (l)	28.13	16.67	29.80	28.13	28.13	28.13	16.67	29.80	28.13	28.13
BW bias (r)	28.13	20.21	29.80	28.13	28.13	28.13	20.21	29.80	28.13	28.13

Note: Standard errors in parentheses (clustered at the FICO-2d level). Estimates adjusted for mass points in the running variable. * $p < 0.05$, ** $p < 0.01$, *** $p < 0.001$

- mserd: one common MSE-optimal bandwidth selector for the RD treatment effect estimator
- msetwo: two different MSE-optimal bandwidth selectors (below and above the cutoff) for the RD treatment effect estimator
- msesum: one common MSE-optimal bandwidth selector for the sum of regression estimates (as opposed to difference thereof)
- msecomb1: for min (mserd, msesum)
- msecomb2: for median (msetwo, mserd, msesum), for each side of the cutoff separately
- cerrd: one common CER-optimal bandwidth selector for the RD treatment effect estimator
- certwo: two different CER-optimal bandwidth selectors (below and above the cutoff) for the RD treatment effect estimator
- cersum: one common CER-optimal bandwidth selector for the sum of regression estimates (as opposed to difference thereof)
- cercomb1: for min (cerrd, cersum)
- cercomb2: for median (certwo, cerrd, cersum), for each side of the cutoff separately

TABLE 5A.2 *Different kernel functions*

	(1)	(2)	(3)
Kernel function	Triangular	Epanechnikov	Uniform
RD estimate	1.003***	1.245***	1.290***
	(0.0976)	(0.100)	(0.0945)
Robust 95% CI	[0.901; 1.283]	[1.148; 1.572]	[1.195; 1.6]
BW type	mserd	mserd	mserd
Kernel	Triangular	Epanechnikov	Uniform
Order Loc. Poly. (p)	1	1	1
Order bias (q)	2	2	2
N	5,025	5,025	5,025
N (l)	2,147	2,147	2,147
N (r)	2,878	2,878	2,878
Eff. N (l)	340	160	120
Eff. N (r)	360	180	140
BW est. (l)	17.15	8.93	6.91
BW est. (r)	17.15	8.93	6.91
BW bias (l)	28.13	18.54	16.65
BW bias (r)	28.13	18.54	16.65

Note: Standard errors in parentheses (clustered at the FICO-2d level)
$^{*}p < 0.05$, $^{**}p < 0.01$, and $^{***}p < 0.001$
Estimates adjusted for mass points in the running variable.

TABLE 5A.3 Covariate adjusted estimates

	(1)	(2)	(3)	(4)	(5)
Covariate(s)	None	Month dummies	Lagged DV	Average interest rate	Month dummies + lagged DV + average interest rate
RD estimate	1.003***	1.510***	0.962***	1.313***	0.656***
	(0.0976)	(0.107)	(0.0844)	(0.0998)	(0.0349)
Robust 95% CI	[0.901; 1.283]	[1.442; 1.888]	[0.809; 1.154]	[1.249; 1.664]	[0.618; 0.824]
BW type	mserd	mserd	mserd	mserd	mserd
Kernel	Triangular	Triangular	Triangular	Triangular	Triangular
Order Loc. Poly. (p)	1	1	1	1	1
Order bias (q)	2	2	2	2	2
N	5,025	5,025	5,001	5,025	5,001
N (l)	2,147	2,147	2,125	2,147	2,125
N (r)	2,878	2,878	2,876	2,878	2,876
Eff. N (l)	340	220	120	240	280
Eff. N (r)	360	240	140	260	300
BW est. (l)	17.15	11.98	7.00	12.82	14.01
BW est. (r)	17.15	11.98	7.00	12.82	14.01
BW bias (l)	28.13	23.36	15.08	23.99	26.68
BW bias (r)	28.13	23.36	15.08	23.99	26.68

Note: Standard errors in parentheses (clustered at the FICO-2d level)

* $p < 0.05$, ** $p < 0.01$, and *** $p < 0.001$

Estimates adjusted for mass points in the running variable.

Covariate-adjusted estimates. Additional covariates included: 0 (model 1), 11 (model 2), 1 (models 3 and 4), and 13 (model 5)

TABLE 5A.4 *Different specification of the running variable I*

	(1)	(2)	(3)	(4)	(5)
Unit of running variable	Month	Quarter	Trimester	Biannual	Annual
RD estimate	1.003*** (0.0976)	1.228*** (0.101)	1.178*** (0.103)	0.933*** (0.0918)	0.704*** (0.104)
Robust 95% CI	[0.901; 1.283]	[1.062; 1.496]	[1.046; 1.471]	[0.92; 1.293]	[0.334; 0.753]
BW type	mserd	mserd	mserd	mserd	mserd
Kernel	Triangular	Triangular	Triangular	Triangular	Triangular
Order Loc. Poly. (p)	1	1	1	1	1
Order bias (q)	2	2	2	2	2
N	5,025	5,025	5,025	5,025	5,025
N (l)	2,147	2,147	2,147	2,147	2,147
N (r)	2,878	2,878	2,878	2,878	2,878
Eff. N (l)	340	180	160	240	960
Eff. N (r)	360	240	240	360	1,198
BW est. (l)	17.15	3.16	2.83	2.72	4.14
BW est. (r)	17.15	3.16	2.83	2.72	4.14
BW bias (l)	28.13	4.24	3.68	4.13	4.42
BW bias (r)	28.13	4.24	3.68	4.13	4.42

Note: Standard errors in parentheses (clustered at the FICO-2d level)
$^*p < 0.05$, $^{**}p < 0.01$, and $^{***}p < 0.001$
Estimates adjusted for mass points in the running variable.
The data is at the month-year-FICO-2d level (as in the previous analyses), but the running variable is recoded to quarters, trimesters, half years, and years. Note that this changes the interpretation of the bandwidth estimates.

TABLE 5A.5 *Different specification of the running variable II*

	(1)	(2)	(3)	(4)	(5)
Unit of measurement of outcome and running variable	Month	Quarter	Trimester	Biannual	Annual
RD estimate	1.003***	2.128***	1.401***	0.514***	0.658***
	(0.0976)	(0.0504)	(0.0689)	(0.0707)	(0.0843)
Robust 95% CI	[0.901; 1.283]	[2.212; 2.551]	[1.309; 1.618]	[0.273; 0.535]	[0.205; 0.54]
BW type	mserd	mserd	mserd	mserd	mserd
Kernel	Triangular	Triangular	Triangular	Triangular	Triangular
Order Loc. Poly. (p)	1	1	1	1	1
Order bias (q)	2	2	2	2	2
N	5,025	1,680	1,260	840	420
N (l)	2,147	720	540	360	180
N (r)	2,878	960	720	480	240
Eff. N (l)	340	40	40	80	40
Eff. N (r)	360	60	60	100	60
BW est. (l)	17.15	2.09	2.05	4.10	2.56
BW est. (r)	17.15	2.09	2.05	4.10	2.56
BW bias (l)	28.13	4.44	4.89	4.21	3.76
BW bias (r)	28.13	4.44	4.89	4.21	3.76

Note: Standard errors in parentheses (clustered at the FICO-2d level, but not in model 3 due to non-convergence)
* $p < 0.05$, ** $p < 0.01$, *** $p < 0.001$
Estimates adjusted for mass points in the running variable.
The data set is constructed at the year-month, year-quarter, year-trimester, year-biannual, and year-level (all at FICO-2d). Note that this changes the overall number of observations (N).

TABLE 5A.6 *Sensitivity to observations near the cutoff (donut hole approach)*

	(1)	(2)	(3)	(4)
Donut hole (months)	0	+/−1 = 2 months	+/−2 = 4 months	+/−3 = 6 months
RD estimate	1.003*** (0.0976)	0.895*** (0.0897)	1.020*** (0.0485)	1.208*** (0.101)
Robust 95% CI	[0.901; 1.283]	[0.833; 1.16]	[1.158; 1.387]	[1.29; 1.882]
BW type	mserd	mserd	mserd	mserd
Kernel	Triangular	Triangular	Triangular	Triangular
Order Loc. Poly. (p)	1	1	1	1
Order bias (q)	2	2	2	2
N	5,025	5,005	4,965	4,925
N (l)	2,147	2,147	2,127	2,107
N (r)	2,878	2,858	2,838	2,818
Eff. N (l)	340	400	140	100
Eff. N (r)	360	400	140	100
BW est. (l)	17.15	20.12	8.73	7.98
BW est. (r)	17.15	20.12	8.73	7.98
BW bias (l)	28.13	29.79	17.34	17.43
BW bias (r)	28.13	29.79	17.34	17.43

Note: Standard errors in parentheses (clustered at the FICO-2d level)
*$p < 0.05$, **$p < 0.01$, and ***$p < 0.001$
Estimates adjusted for mass points in the running variable.
Excluded are 0 (model 1), 1 (model 2), 2 (model 3), or 3 (model 4) months to the left and right of the cutoff.

TABLE 5A.7 *Placebo outcomes*

	(1)	(2)	(3)	(4)
Outcome	Gini of interest rates	Loan-to-value	Avg. interest rate	Avg. FICO score
RD estimate	1.003*** (0.0976)	−1.344 (0.895)	−0.144** (0.0514)	−0.348 (18.74)
Robust 95% CI	[0.901; 1.283]	[−2.819; 0.573]	[−0.161; 0.051]	[−37.038; 36.343]
BW type	mserd	mserd	mserd	mserd
Kernel	Triangular	Triangular	Triangular	Triangular
Order Loc. Poly. (p)	1	1	1	1
Order bias (q)	2	2	2	2
N	5,025	5,025	5,025	5,025
N (l)	2,147	2,147	2,147	2,147
N (r)	2,878	2,878	2,878	2,878
Eff. N (l)	340	760	40	2,147
Eff. N (r)	360	779	60	2,858
BW est. (l)	17.15	38.45	2.91	143.00
BW est. (r)	17.15	38.45	2.91	143.00
BW bias (l)	28.13	24.96	5.17	31.27
BW bias (r)	28.13	24.96	5.17	31.27

Note: Standard errors in parentheses (clustered at the FICO-2d level)
*$p < 0.05$, **$p < 0.01$, and ***$p < 0.001$
Estimates adjusted for mass points in the running variable.
Columns (2) to (4) are placebo outcomes. Note that the robust 95% CI in model (3) includes 0.

TABLE 5A.8 *Placebo cutoffs*

	(1)	(2)	(3)	(4)	(5)
Cutoff	1-2008	6-2007	1-2007	6-2006	1-2006
RD estimate	1.003*** (0.0976)	0.0419 (0.0372)	0.181*** (0.0499)	−0.097*** (0.0217)	0.114*** (0.0290)
Robust 95% CI	[0.901; 1.283]	[0.029; 0.217]	[0.012; 0.219]	[−0.123; −0.018]	[0.049; 0.167]
BW type	mserd	mserd	mserd	mserd	mserd
Kernel	Triangular	Triangular	Triangular	Triangular	Triangular
Order Loc. Poly. (p)	1	1	1	1	1
Order bias (q)	2	2	2	2	2
N	5,025	2,147	2,147	2,147	2,147
N (l)	2,147	2,027	1,907	1,787	1,667
N (r)	2,878	120	240	360	480
Eff. N (l)	340	80	100	120	220
Eff. N (r)	360	100	120	140	240
BW est. (l)	17.15	4.98	5.41	6.55	11.19
BW est. (r)	17.15	4.98	5.41	6.55	11.19
BW bias (l)	28.13	10.26	10.86	6.81	9.19
BW bias (r)	28.13	10.26	10.86	6.81	9.19

Note: Standard errors in parentheses (clustered at the FICO-2d level)
*$p < 0.05$, **$p < 0.01$, and ***$p < 0.001$
Estimates adjusted for mass points in the running variable.
The placebo cutoffs are every six months prior to the discontinuity (1-2008), up to 1-2006. Only observations to the left of the discontinuity are part of the sample, to avoid contamination. Note the small size of the coefficients in models (2) to (5).

Credit Markets

TABLE 5A.9 *Mass points*

	(1)	(2)
Masspoints	Adjusted	Ignored
RD estimate	1.003***	1.228***
	(0.0976)	(0.102)
Robust 95% CI	[0.901; 1.283]	[1.103; 1.525]
BW type	mserd	mserd
Kernel	Triangular	Triangular
Order Loc. Poly. (p)	1	1
Order bias (q)	2	2
N	5,025	5,025
N (l)	2,147	2,147
N (r)	2,878	2,878
Eff. N (l)	340	180
Eff. N (r)	360	200
BW est. (l)	17.15	9.56
BW est. (r)	17.15	9.56
BW bias (l)	28.13	22.32
BW bias (r)	28.13	22.32

Note: Standard errors in parentheses (clustered at the FICO-2d level)
$^{*}p < 0.05$, $^{**}p < 0.01$, and $^{***}p < 0.001$
Model 1: Estimates adjusted for mass points in the running variable
Model 2: Estimates not adjusted for mass points in the running variable

6

Labor Market Risks

The focus in this chapter is on insurance against labor market risks. Such insurance comes in a variety of forms (Estevez-Abé, Iversen, and Soskice 2001): (i) employment protection, (ii) wage protection for workers with different skills and at different tenure levels, and (iii) unemployment protection. In CMEs, the first two are shaped by collective bargaining between employers' associations, on the one hand, and unions and professional associations (with the state in a supporting role), on the other, while in liberal market economies (LMEs), they are left mostly to the market. In LMEs, instead, the main protection against risks is through the acquisition of general skills that are portable across jobs. In both LMEs and CMEs, employment and wage protection are therefore mostly channeled through private or collective contracting where the state plays a secondary and mostly supportive role (through collective agreement "extension laws," educational spending, and employment regulations).[1]

Unemployment protection, however, is different because it has been provided almost exclusively through the state, and it comes closest in nature to the other forms of social insurance we have discussed in this book. As in the cases of health insurance, old-age insurance, and credit, the redistributive effects depend on the size of the risk pool, on benefit generosity, and on the specific financing arrangements (especially whether it is based on general taxation or contributions). This chapter will focus on unemployment insurance and will highlight how information interacts with, and reinforces, the growing segmentation of labor markets by education, occupation, and location.

---

[1] The main exceptions are the "income policies" of the 1970s, and arguably also employment and income guarantees during the pandemic.

In the previous chapters, we considered the importance of information – the level, shareability, and distribution – for the feasibility of markets, the possibility of dividing risk pools, and demand for public insurance. We address some of these topics in this chapter as well, but we also focus on another key question about information: How do people learn about their risks, and how do they translate this knowledge into political preferences? Unemployment insurance clearly illustrates this logic because there are both private and collective aspects to being informed about risks and policies, which combine with the other types of labor market protection to shape the politics of unemployment insurance.

INFORMATION ABOUT RISK

There are often strong private incentives to be informed about risks. The risk of unemployment affects optimal savings behavior, decisions about borrowing, the purchase of consumer durables and private property, and even family planning. This is true of many risks in health and finance as well, and the decision to purchase insurance (when available in the market) relies directly on an assessment of risk. Indeed, this "need to know" is an important source of asymmetric information in insurance markets, since individuals may learn things that insurers cannot observe.

Of course, information is never complete. Especially during the early phases of the rise of social insurance, understanding of both risks and actuarial science was quite poor. We have argued that in the presence of such "generalized ignorance" or uncertainty, markets will be underdeveloped, and estimates of risk will be biased toward the mean. If individual workers have no information about their own risk of unemployment, their best guess is that their own risk is the same as everyone else's (which is captured by the overall unemployment rate). We have argued that uncertainty is therefore a source of solidarity and support for all-encompassing public risk pools.

Specifically, in Chapter 2, we showed that individual acquisition of information can be modeled as a Bayesian updating game where an individual's perceived or "observed" risk, p_i^o, is a combination of a prior and a signal:

$$p_i^o = \alpha \cdot p_i^s + (1 - \alpha) \cdot p^{prior} \text{(similar to Eq. 7, Chapter 2),} \quad (1)$$

where p_i^s is a noisy signal drawn from a distribution that is centered on the individual's true risk (p_i), p^{prior} is a prior about the risk, and α is a measure of the "precision" of the signal, which in our model equals the private information available to i. In the simplest formulation, with no private information ($a = 0$), i only observes the population mean – the national unemployment rate – which serves as the prior. In this situation, everybody's perceived risk, p_i^o, is the same, namely, the national unemployment rate.

However, it is probably more reasonable to assume that people have *some* private information and more fine-grained priors than the national mean. If so, perceived risk (p_i^o) differs between individuals. This is how information leads to differentiation in demand for insurance, and this is how more information polarizes public opinion (we will go into more specific detail about this later).

To allow for the realistic possibility of more fine-grained priors, we rewrite Eq. (1) as follows:

$$p_i^o = a \cdot p_i^s + (1 - a) \cdot p_i^{ref}, \qquad (2)$$

where p_i^{ref} is the average unemployment in i's relevant reference group, which is distinct from (and more fine-grained than) the national unemployment rate.

It is difficult, or even impossible, to observe individual signals (p_i^s). Although they may include incidental exposure to, say, unemployed neighbors, it often comprises information sought out deliberately because people have an individual incentive to know and plan for the possibility of becoming unemployed. Consumption as well as saving behavior depend on expectations about future income streams and also determine the purchase of insurance when available (Hendren 2017). Moreover, people have private information about their own character (e.g., how willing are they to work harder if required to do so), their relationship to superiors, and even subtle changes in work organization, technology, or demand that affect their job. In addition, people learn about unemployment risks from unions, professional associations, networks of coworkers, media, and official statistics. Over time, such information becomes part of the prior for the next phase of updating, unless there is an interruption, such as change in occupation. We treat readily available information about education, occupation, and location as part of the prior – and public information – while subjective unemployment risks that are not accounted for by the prior are assumed to be part of the signal and treated as private information.

With respect to the priors (p_i^{ref}), we conjecture that they are increasingly predictive of actual risk experiences. There are two reasons for this. First, these days, high-quality, detailed information about unemployment by education, occupation, and location (or other observables, such as industry, gender, or age) is freely available from public sources and can be accessed by anyone with an internet connection. Most countries have been collecting this information for a long time. What has changed over time is the accessibility and timeliness of this information. Today, everyone has timely information about the risk profile of their reference group at their fingertips, and for most, it would be part of their prior. Indeed, potential insurers would also have access to this information. We think it is also likely that the information contained in labor force statistics has got better and has definitely been recorded more frequently over time, though we suspect that these improvements mostly occurred decades ago – before our empirical application below (which starts in the mid-1980s).

The second reason why priors are increasingly predictive of actual risk experiences is that observables are increasingly predictive of actual risk experiences. We believe that there are two main drivers for the rise in the predictability of observables. One is simply that as we just argued, information is getting better over time: Labor market statistics have improved in accuracy and detail and are shared on an almost daily basis by local media, (un)employment offices, trade publications, and so on. The other driver is the growing segmentation of labor markets, which is broadly related to the transition from a Fordist industrial economy to a more decentralized knowledge-intensive, service-centered economy. However, in the past, skilled and semi-skilled workers often worked side by side in the same plants and industries, many in large vertically integrated companies that spanned several sectors and often included both urban and more rural areas; there is now sharp segregation of skilled and semi-skilled labor markets, as well as a growing differentiation by occupation and geography (advanced companies are concentrated in the urban centers with few backward linkages to small towns and rural areas). This shift has changed the nature of risks from being fairly homogenous across groups, if discontinuous in time, to very heterogeneous across groups, if (perhaps) more stable in time. This labor market segmentation is further cemented by employment protection legislation – as argued by Rueda and others (Lindbeck and Snower 1989; Rueda 2005, 2006, 2007) – and the increasing sorting and skill segregation at the firm level (Song et al. 2019).

The implication is a growing bifurcation of risks that becomes increasingly tied to observables such as education, occupation, and location. If this is true, observables should account for more and more of the variance, while there is little scope for the individual to learn about risks that are unobserved by others, notably insurance companies. In the old economy, unemployment risks would have been harder to predict based on observables, and whatever information was available would have been largely private (based on local, firm-specific, and individual factors). This is our first hypothesis.

H1: Total information on labor market risks has increased over time, while private information has declined.

In our theoretical model, spending preferences are proportional to risks, and since information about risks bifurcates perceptions about risks, information should also polarize political preferences. This is our second hypothesis (as developed in Chapter 2 and previously in this chapter).

H2: Information and polarization covary.

Yet this presupposes an aspect that is not captured by the above logic, namely the ability and incentives of individuals to translate economic interests into political preferences. This is a nontrivial step because, unlike information about risks, the benefits of political knowledge are not private but collective. As we have argued, knowing risks enables people to make better financial decisions, but government-provided social insurance, including unemployment insurance, is a public good that is unaffected by the vote choice of any single individual.

Specifically, the level of unemployment insurance is not affected by which party someone votes for, unlike the decision to buy private insurance. On aggregate, individual decisions obviously matter for outcomes in a democracy, but for the individual, it is perfectly reasonable to be "rationally ignorant" about public policies (Downs 1957). As in the case of workers not knowing their risks, rationally ignorant voters may then reasonably assume that their interests are best represented by the middle position in the political space (Iversen and Soskice 2015b).[2]

Most voters are not completely ignorant about politics, however, and there are various potential reasons for why that is – all closely related to the classic paradox of why people turn out to vote even though a single vote has an infinitesimal effect on the outcome of an election (Aldrich 1993). One solution to this puzzle is that nationally organized groups,

---

[2] The precise reason why voters should prefer a centrist candidate, party, or policy position if they are uninformed cannot, however, be exactly the same as when they assume average risks because there is no such thing as an actuarially accurate policy position. Nevertheless, under reasonable assumptions, the center is the preferred position of "loss-averse" voters who try to avoid making big mistakes if they are ill-informed. The result follows from spatial voting under uncertainty where voters minimize the expected difference (loss) between their vote and their (unobserved) interests (Iversen and Soskice 2015b).

who *do* have a tangible stake in the policy outcome, use their resources to incentivize their members to vote for a particular policy or party. Most obviously, political parties have an interest in the outcome of elections, and unions, professional associations, and employers' associations all have an interest in public policies such as unemployment protection. Any of these collective actors signaling a particular policy position may in turn sway members to adopt the same position, given that members can reasonably assume that the organized group charged with representing their economic interests understands the issues better than they do.

Yet, quite apart from the tricky methodological issue of how to separate the effects of membership from the causes of membership, nationally organized formal organizations have been in decline since at least the 1970s. Membership in political parties and unions has fallen sharply, and few people today are members of any political mass organization. Instead, political information (and misinformation) mostly flows through informal social networks, whether they are organized by neighborhoods, the workplace, or online groups. Social networks form powerful incentive structures because they generate expectations about "appropriate" behavior, policy views, and knowledge about politics among their members. Networks are thus natural sites for political preference formation, and they help link interests and political preferences for one key reason: socioeconomic homophily. This refers to the thoroughly documented fact in sociology that informal social networks are made up of people with similar socioeconomic characteristics (Jackson 2010; McPherson, Smith-Lovin, and Cook 2001).

Homophily is important for our argument because when politics becomes a recurrent theme of group discussion, people quickly learn facts and internalize political views that broadly map onto their underlying interests. This corresponds to a relatively precise signal in the Bayesian updating model above. Some learning is about facts, such as the risk of unemployment, which help individuals make good economic decisions, but much acquisition of political information is a reflection of social incentives: getting the approval of peers, avoiding their disapproval, and building up standing within the group. For these reasons, people may acquire costly information about politics, even when such information cannot be used to change political outcomes. We therefore expect political discussion in social networks to have the effect of strengthening the link between both objective and subjective indicators of risks and political preferences. This is our third hypothesis.

H3: Political discussion in social networks strengthens the link between risk and political preferences.

We have argued throughout the book that an increase in shared information nurtures an appetite for segmentation and privatization (the *first argument* in Chapter 2). There are good reasons to believe that information about
labor market risks has increased, as discussed previously (and as shown later
for the case of Germany). However, for reasons unrelated to information,
unemployment insurance is not a likely candidate for privatization. Yet the
institutional features of the Swedish unemployment insurance system in
principle allow for segmentation of premiums and benefits, and indeed, a
reform of the system by a conservative government in 2006 led to segmentation in practice. This (short-lived) reform is an example of what happens
when a solidaristic public system is replaced with a segmented, quasi-private
insurance system in the presence of distinct and easily identifiable risk
profiles. We describe these reforms and their consequences below.

LABOR MARKET RISK AND POLITICAL PREFERENCES

The first hypothesis states that information about labor market risks has
increased over time, while private information has decreased. We cannot
observe private information (p_i^s), but we have data for p_i^o in the form of
subjective unemployment worries, and we also have data on observables, of
course, such as education, occupation, and location. In particular, we rely on
the German Socio-Economic Panel (SOEP), as in the previous chapter.
Because the data set is in panel format and because it records employment
status for every month of the year, we can track actual (un)employment
experiences of individuals over time. Therefore, we can code whether or not
(and when and for how long) a person lost their job in the months after
responding to the subjective unemployment risk item. More concretely, we
estimate the following model:

$$u_{i,t+1} = \beta_1 \cdot p_{i,t}^o + \sum \beta_j \cdot p_{i,j,t}^{ref} + \varepsilon_{i,t}$$

$$u_{i,t+1} = \beta_1 \cdot [p_i^s + \sum \beta_j \cdot p_{i,j,t}^{ref}] + \sum \beta_j \cdot p_{i,j,t}^{ref} + \varepsilon_{i,t}, \qquad (3)$$

$$u_{i,t+1} = \beta_1 \cdot p_i^s + \sum \beta_j (1 + \beta_1) \cdot p_{i,j,t}^{ref} + \varepsilon_{i,t}$$

where $u_{i,t+1}$ is a binary variable that equals 1 for unemployment in the
next period ($t + 1$) and zero otherwise, and β_1 is a measure of private
information that captures information not accounted for by observables.
We will regress unemployment in the next period on subjective unemployment risk in the current period and a set of observables (p_i^{ref}). We will use

R-squared (McFadden's pseudo-R-squared, since we will be using logistic regression) as a measure of total information. Our hypothesis is that R-squared rises over time, while β_1 decreases (or at least does not increase).[3]

Our dependent variable $u_{i,t+1}$, that is, unemployment in the next period, can be measured in different ways. We focus on the first or first two years after the subjective unemployment risk item was asked and code the following events as "unemployed in the next period":

- Will report unemployment in at least one month within the next twelve months
- Will report unemployment in at least one month within the next twenty-four months
- *Will report unemployment in at least six months within the next twelve months*
- Will report unemployment in at least six months within the next twenty-four months
- Will report unemployment in at least twelve months within the next twenty-four months

Since voluntary and/or very temporary unemployment is typically not a source of serious hardship, we focus our presentation on the third operationalization (italicized): future unemployment experience is defined as being out of a job for at least six months within the twelve months after answering the subjective risk survey item, though results are comparable across these different dependent variables.[4]

The SOEP data contain three subjective unemployment risk items that have been asked repeatedly over time:

- "How likely is it that you will experience the following career changes within the next two years? In the next two years: Will you lose your job? Please estimate the probability of such a change taking place on a scale from 0 to 100, where 0 means such a change will definitely not take place, and 100 means it definitely will take place." The answer categories are as follows: 0 – "this will definitely not

---

[3] A corollary of H1 is that subjective and observable measures of risk become more correlated over time. What people know is increasingly captured by what everyone knows (or easily could know). In other words: $corr(p^o_{i,t}, \sum_j \beta_j \cdot p^{ref}_{i,j,t})$ rises over time.

[4] Labor force status is collected retrospectively. For example, a respondent interviewed in January 2017 will provide labor force information for the previous twelve months (January–December 2016). Moreover, our dependent variable is "unemployment within the next twelve months" (or even twenty-four months). Therefore, even though we use all available years 1984–2018, the last estimate of McFadden's pseudo-R2 we have is for 2016.

happen" and 10, 20, …, 90 to 100 – "this definitely will happen" (Variable plb0433_v2, available for select years 1999–2018).

- "What do your future employment prospects look like? How probable is it in the next two years … that you will look for a new job." The answer categories are "unlikely," "probably not," "probably," and "certain" (Variable plb0433_v1, available for select years 1985–1998).

- "How concerned are you about the following issues? Your job security [if you are employed]." The answer categories are "not concerned at all," "somewhat concerned," and "very concerned" (Variable plh0042, available for all years 1984–2018).

The first of these items comes closest to a subjective probability assessment and would therefore be our preferred choice. Unfortunately, it is only available nine times and only for recent years (1999–2018). Because testing our hypothesis requires long time series, we opt for the third item since it covers the largest number of years.[5]

With respect to the observables, we include education, occupation, location, age (in years), gender, and migration background.[6] Our sample is restricted to those currently employed and aged eighteen to sixty-five. We estimate the same model for every year, and we distinguish between East, West, and combined Germany.

In all three samples – East Germany, West Germany, and combined Germany – the explained variance (as measured by the McFadden pseudo R-squared) increases over time (see Figure 6.1). The increase is particularly steep in East Germany, where the predicted pseudo-R2 nearly doubles within the observed time period, but the linear fit lines statistically significantly increase in all three panels. We interpret these patterns as evidence consistent with the conjecture that labor market risks have become more predictable over time. While we are mostly interested in the trend, we note that the pseudo-R2 levels are relatively high, at least in more recent years, since according to their inventor, McFadden pseudo-R2 values of "0.2 to 0.4 … represent an excellent fit" (McFadden 1977, 307).

---

[5] The correlation between the first and third items is about 0.5.
[6] Education is measured at six 1997 ISCED levels; occupation is measured at the ISCO two-digit level; location is measured by the sixteen German Länder, and the migration status variable distinguishes no/direct/indirect migration background. We also include two technical variables: "pop" and "psample" (for "sample membership" and "sample member," respectively).

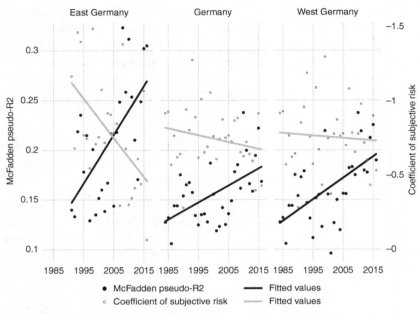

FIGURE 6.1 Total information and private information over time
Note: The dependent variable is a dummy variable for becoming unemployed for at least six months in the next twelve months. The explanatory variables are subjective risk perceptions and a set of control variables. The "McFadden pseudo-R2" fit lines statistically significantly increase in all three panels (*$p < 0.05$). The "coefficient of subjective risk" is trending down in all panels but only statistically significantly so in the first panel (East Germany).
Source: SOEP 1984–2018.

The subjective risk coefficient (the gray hollow circles in Figure 6.1) is generally statistically significant. This is consistent with existing scholarship that shows that subjective perceptions about risk are accurate in the sense that they can be "predicted" with the occurrence of that risk in the future (Campbell et al. 2007; Dominitz and Manski 1997a, 1997b; Green 2011; Green et al. 2001; Hacker, Rehm, and Schlesinger 2013; Hendren 2013; Kassenboehmer and Schatz 2017; Rehm 2016; Stephens Jr. 2004). However, in contrast to our measure of overall explained variance, the size of the subjective risk coefficient decreases over time. Once again, the patterns are clearest in East Germany (left panel) – where the decline is statistically significant – but the linear fit lines slope downward in all three panels. To assess the importance of private signals versus priors more directly, we can decompose the overall explained variance (the McFadden pseudo-R2, shown in Figure 6.1) into the share attributable to the sub-jective risk variable and the share attributable to observables, by means of a Shapley decomposition of the overall McFadden pseudo-R2. The Shapley decomposition has desirable properties[7] (Huettner and Sunder 2012; Young 1985). A variable's – or group of variables' – Shapley value is derived by averaging the marginal contribution to pseudo-R2 of that variable, or group of variables, across all permutations of models. We therefore reestimate our model for all possible combinations of right-hand-side variables. Because we are interested in just two groups of explanatory variables (signals vs. priors), there are only four permutations.

The top row of Figure 6.2 shows the share of pseudo-R2 attributable to observables, while the bottom row shows the share of pseudo-R2 attrib-utable to private signals. By construction, these two shares sum to 1 for every year. The patterns are clear: The share of explained variance is higher for the observables, and it increases over time.

Overall, then, the evidence from Germany suggests that public infor-mation about labor market risks has increased over time, while the importance of private information has not (in most specifications, we find that it has actually decreased). This is consistent with our first hypothesis.

Our second hypothesis states that information and polarization cov-ary. More concretely, if people have more information, they can align their political preferences more closely with their personal expected risk exposure. In the previous test, we derived a measure of the overall infor-mation with respect to labor market risks in Germany (McFadden's pseudo-R2) over the last few decades. Here, we will use the same measure and explore its correlation with a measure of attitude polarization on public (unemployment) benefit generosity.

Ideally, we would like to measure attitude polarization based on the SOEP data set that we used in the previous test. Unfortunately, that data set does not capture attitudes on public unemployment benefit generosity, at least not frequently enough.[8] To our knowledge, the most frequently

---

[7] These are (1) efficiency (the goodness of fit of the full model is decomposed among the regressors); (2) monotonicity (an increase in R-squared must not decrease the value); and (3) equal treatment (perfect substitutes in terms of the goodness of fit receive the same value) (Huettner and Sunder 2012).

[8] Variable plh0019 is the most plausible item but is only available for years 1997, 2004, and 2017 (we only have data on the McFadden pseudo-R2 up to 2016): "In addition to the

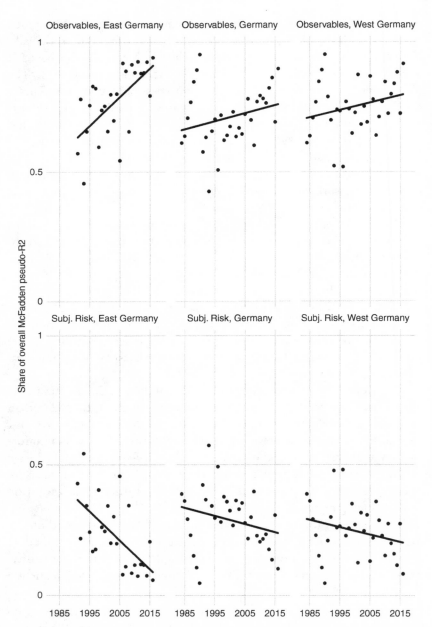

FIGURE 6.2 Total information and private information over time (Shapley decomposition)
Note: Shown is the share of explained variance (McFadden's pseudo-R2, from Figure 6.1) attributable to observables (top row) and subjective risk (bottom row), based on Shapley decompositions.
Source: SOEP 1984–2018.

available item covering attitudes on public (unemployment) benefit generosity in Germany is the following survey question in the German General Social Survey (ALLBUS, 1980–2018) (GESIS-Leibniz-Institut Für Sozialwissenschaften 2020):

- [iw04] "The state must ensure that people can make a decent living, even in illness, hardship, unemployment, and old age." Reversed answer categories are as follows: 1 – completely disagree, 2 – tend to disagree, 3 – tend to agree, and 4 – completely agree (our translation).

This item is available for the following years: 1984, 1991, 1994, 2000, 2004, 2010, and 2014. For the previous test, we estimated McFadden's pseudo-R2 for East and West Germany separately. We therefore measure attitude polarization in East and West Germany separately as well. Hence, we have thirteen observations to correlate McFadden's pseudo-R2 with attitude polarization (seven observations from West Germany 1984–2014, and six observations from East Germany 1991–2014). Obviously, with so few observations, we can do little more than conduct plausibility probes.

In our theoretical model, more accurate information polarizes attitudes by decreasing support for public benefits among those with low risk and increasing support among those with high risk. (In our formulation, the dividing line between high and low risk is the mean risk.) We cannot reliably classify respondents into these categories in the German General Social Survey (ALLBUS) and therefore measure attitude polarization simply based on the coefficient of variation among the employed aged eighteen to sixty-five (the same way we restrict the sample in the SOEP analysis).

In Germany, support for decent government benefits in times of need – including unemployment – is generally high (the scale of the variable ranges from 1 to 4, and the mean values are between 3.1 and 3.7), and the coefficient of variation is typically modest (ranging from 0.129 to 0.252). But does it covary with overall information on labor market risks? To explore this, we regress our measure of polarization (the coefficient of variation on the ALLBUS item listed above) on the McFadden pseudo-R2s from the previous test. Because we pool observations from East and West Germany, we include

state, private individuals such as free-market companies, organizations, associations, or individual citizens are responsible for a large number of social tasks in our society today. Who, in your opinion, should be responsible for the following areas?" Answer categories are as follows: (1) only the state, (2) mostly the state, (3) the state and private forces, (4) mostly private forces, and (5) only private forces.

an indicator variable for the two Germanys, and we also control for the overall (East and West German) unemployment rate.

Figure 6.3 shows the partial correlation between overall labor market information (measured by McFadden's pseudo-R2, as previously shown) and attitude polarization, after taking into account the control variables. Since we only have a very small number of observations, robustness is of concern, and we therefore show five panels, one for each of the five dependent variables we use to retrieve MacFadden's pseudo-R2. The full estimations, as well as results from robust regressions, are shown in Tables 6A.1 and 6A.2.

The figure reveals a clear positive and robust correlation between overall information and attitude polarization: When people have more information about labor market risks, preferences regarding (unemployment) benefit generosity are more polarized. Consistent with our hypothesis, conflict does seem to increase with information. (But given the data challenges, we caution against interpreting this finding as more than a plausibility probe.)

Our third hypothesis is about the alignment of interests and attitudes. So far, we have assumed that people's risk exposure translates into policy preferences. This is a standard assumption in the literature, but as discussed previously, it is not without its problems. We therefore derived a third hypothesis, namely, that political discussion mediates the impact of risk exposure on political preferences: Respondents engaged in more political discussion learn from others and are incentivized to seek relevant information, which in combination enable people to better align their political preferences with their (economic) interests (as assumed in the theoretical model).

Neither the SOEP nor the ALLBUS data allow us to test this hypothesis, so we have to rely on yet another data source in this chapter. This time, we opt to make use of the European Social Survey (ESS), which contains an item on redistribution preferences that has been employed in many studies:

- "Using this card, please say to what extent you agree or disagree with each of the following statements. The government should take measures to reduce differences in income levels." Answer categories are as follows: 1 – agree strongly, 2 – agree, 3 – neither agree nor disagree, 4 – disagree, and 5 – disagree strongly.

We recode the item into a binary variable equaling one for respondents that "agree" or "strongly agree" that governments should take measures to reduce differences in income levels, and zero otherwise. This aids our

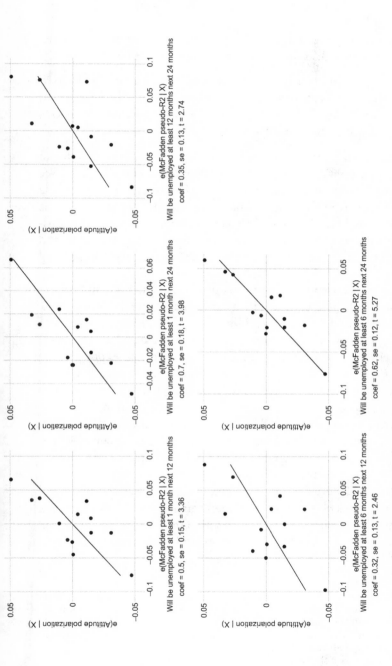

FIGURE 6.3 Total information and attitude polarization

Note: Shown is the partial correlation between information about labor market risks (as measured by McFadden's pseudo-R2) and attitude polarization. The panels differ by which dependent variable is used to retrieve McFadden's pseudo-R2, as indicated at the horizontal axis titles. Attitude polarization is the coefficient of variation on a survey item inquiring about unemployment benefit generosity ("The state must ensure that people can make a decent living, even in illness, hardship, unemployment, and old age"). The control variables ("X") are a dummy for West versus East Germany, as well as the unemployment rate. Table 6A.1 contains the full regression results.

Source: SOEP 1984–2018 for McFadden's pseudo-R2 (see Figure 6.1) and ALLBUS 1980–2018 for attitude polarization.

presentation because we can display substantive effects in terms of predicted probabilities.

The first, and only the first, round of the ESS contains a variable on the frequency of political discussion (European Social Survey 2003):

- "How often would you say you discuss politics and current affairs?" Reversed answer categories are as follows: 7 – every day, 6 – several times a week, 5 – once a week, 4 – several times a month, 3 – once a month, 2 – less often, and 1 – never.

We conjecture that people regularly engaged in political discussion can better align their political preferences with their (economic) interests. We are primarily interested in whether this applies to risk exposure and support for redistributive policies, but since we think our hypothesis should hold more broadly, we will also explore whether political discussion mediates the relationship between redistribution attitudes and income, as well as the relationship between redistribution attitudes and ideology.

We measure risk exposure by means of occupational unemployment rates (at the ISCO one-digit level), as in some of our previous work (Cusack, Iversen, and Rehm 2006; Rehm 2009).[9] We estimate a series of logit models with pro-redistribution attitudes as the dependent variable and the interaction between political discussion and risk exposure – or alternatively the interaction between political discussion and income or the interaction between political discussion and ideology (as measured by left-right self-placement), respectively – as explanatory variables of interest. Of course, our models include a set of control variables (education, gender, age, union membership, employment status, unemployment experience, and country dummies). Table 6A.3 contains the estimations, and Figure 6.4 displays the correlations of interest.

The top row of Figure 6.4 shows the relationship between occupational unemployment rates on the horizontal axes (ranging from 1 to 20, which is slightly less than their range in the estimation sample) and the predicted probabilities of being supportive of redistribution on the vertical axis. There are seven panels, one for each category of the political discussion

---

[9] The occupational unemployment rates (OURs) are calculated from aggregate data based on the European Union Labor Force Survey (EU-LFS). The EU-LFS is available at http://ec .europa.eu/eurostat/data/database (last accessed June 7, 2021 [https://perma.cc/GN47-Q PHT]). We rely on series "Employment by sex, occupation and educational attainment level (1,000) (lfsa_egised)" and "Previous occupations of the unemployed, by sex (1,000) (lfsa_ugpis)" to construct the OURs.

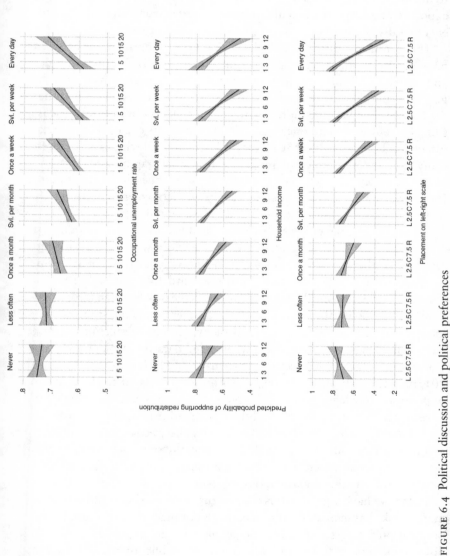

FIGURE 6.4 Political discussion and political preferences

Note: Shown are predicted probabilities of supporting redistribution as a function of risk exposure (top row), income (middle row), and ideology (bottom row), for different levels of political discussion. Based on models (3), (4), and (5) in Table 6A.3.

Source: European Social Survey 2002.

variable, ranging from "never" on the left to "every day" on the right. We find that there is no correlation between risk exposure and support for redistribution among respondents that "never" discuss politics or do so "less often than once a month." But the theoretically expected positive correlation emerges among respondents that have political discussions "once a month" and strengthens significantly as a function of more frequent political discussion. As a result, the relationship between risk exposure and support for redistribution is quite strong among respondents that discuss politics "several times per week" or even "every day."

The second and third rows of Figure 6.4 show the correlations between pro-redistribution attitudes and income and pro-redistribution attitudes and left-right self-placement, respectively. These correlations should be negative, and they mostly are. More interestingly, however, we find that the correlations become more negative as a function of political discussion. Therefore, we find once again that respondents engaged in political discussion hold attitudes that are more closely aligned with their (theoretically expected economic) interests: The attitudinal gap between rich and poor respondents is much larger among those engaged in frequent political discussion, and among such respondents, ideology also more closely maps onto redistribution attitudes in ways we would expect.

Unfortunately, the political discussion item is only available in the first wave of the ESS, and we therefore cannot explore whether our findings replicate in other waves. The first wave does however provide some preliminary evidence that is consistent with our third hypothesis. We find it encouraging that political discussion mediates the link between (economic) interests and political attitudes for three different markers of (economic) interest – risk exposure, income, and ideology. The basic result, information has a polarizing effect, also holds when using data on ideology from the Comparative Study of Electoral Systems (CSES) (Iversen and Soskice 2015b), and political discussion is also positively related to the measure of political knowledge in the CSES. Nevertheless, it would be desirable to have better data on people's (political discussion) networks in order to study how they strengthen (or weaken) the link between economic interests and political attitudes (Alt et al. 2021). Generally speaking, we think it is plausible to assume that networks are an important, and often reliable, source of information regarding risk exposure.

So far, we have argued in this chapter that information regarding labor market risks has increased over time, that labor market risks translate into political preferences, especially for people who are exposed to political discussion, and that information polarizes public opinion on social insurance and ultimately fuels demand for segmentation of the public system. We have found some evidence consistent with this reasoning, though we had to rely on a variety of data sources to test our hypotheses. In the next section, we turn to a case study that we believe illustrates the mechanisms by which better information enables the segmentation of unemployment risk pools and leads to more partisan division.

SEGMENTATION OF UNEMPLOYMENT INSURANCE IN SWEDEN

As noted previously, unemployment insurance has historically been mainly a government responsibility. Yet developments in Sweden – the most unlikely of cases – are a good illustration of how information can upend that history. Until the 1990s, Sweden had one of the most generous unemployment insurance systems in the world, with lenient eligibility requirements and a 90 percent replacement rate (Davidsson and Marx 2013). The system was largely tax-financed, and the modest fees that were paid directly to the unemployment insurance funds (UIFs) were leveled out through an equalization fund, rendering the system highly solidaristic (Holmlund and Lundborg 1999). At the same time, the administration of the UIFs was delegated to unions (known as a "Ghent" system), which boosted unions' efforts to organize workers (Clasen and Viebrock 2008; Ebbinghaus, Göbel, and Koos 2011; Rothstein 1992). As a result, almost every Swede was a member of a union and its affiliated UIF (even though the two types of membership were formally separated in most cases).

However, this system was significantly overhauled, first under the center-right Bildt government during the economic crisis of the early 1990s, when replacement rates and benefit ceilings were reduced and eligibility requirements tightened, and then again in a series of more fundamental reforms from 2006 to 2008 under another center-right government, this one led by Fredrik Reinfeldt. With the latter reforms, benefits were cut further, but the key change was to shift a greater share of the financing burden from the state to the UIFs, with fees varying according to actuarial principles based on the unemployment rate in each UIF, while the obligation to pay into the equalization fund was lifted (Clasen and Viebrock 2008). This burden-shifting was used to partly finance an across-the-board tax cut (Kjellberg 2009). The reforms were partially reversed in 2014, but they offer revealing insights into the politics of social insurance and the logic of fragmenting insurance pools.

The most obvious consequence of the reforms was the emergence of sharp differences in insurance fees (see Figure 6.5). Because Swedish

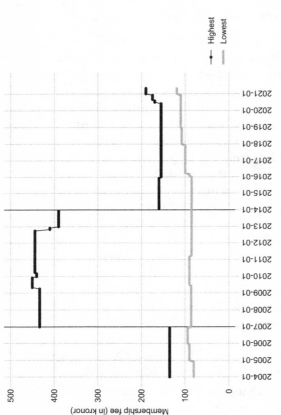

FIGURE 6.5 Membership fees for UIFs with highest and lowest fees

Note: Shown are the highest and lowest membership fees (in Swedish kronor per month) for each time point, among the following forty unions: Akademikernas, Alfa, Byggnadsarbetarnas, Elektrikernas, Farmacitjänstemännens, Fastighets, Finans- och Försäkringsbranschens, Försäkringstjänstemännens, GS, Grafiskas, HTFs, Hammarbetarnas, Handelsanställdas, Hotell- och Restauranganställdas, IF Metalls, Industrifackets, Journalisternas, Kommunalarbetarnas, Ledarnas, Livsmedelsarbetarnas, Lärarnas, Musikernas, Målarnas, Pappersindustriarbetarnas, SIFs, STs, SeA, Sekos, Skogs- o träfackets, Skogs- och Lantbrukstjänstemännens, Småföretagarnas, Svensk Handels Arbetslöshetskassa, Sveriges Entreprenörers, Sveriges arbetares, Sveriges fiskares, Säljarnas, Teaterverksammas, Transportarbetarnas, Unionens, and Vision.

Source: This graph is a replication of a figure available at www.iaf.se/statistikdatabasen/arsstatistik/medlemsavgifter-2020/ (last accessed June 7, 2021 [https://perma.cc/P2U7-UXBH]). Data are from https://externastat.iaf.se/report.aspx?ID=115 (last accessed June 7, 2021 [https://perma.cc/J9Z7-M79 U]; highest and lowest membership fees are based on the variables "Medlemsavgift" and "Medlemsavgift ej arbetslös").

unions are segregated by occupation and socioeconomic status and because unions serve as gatekeepers for entry into the UIFs based on detailed information about workers' education and current and past employment, differences in occupational unemployment rates directly translate into differences in fees (Kjellberg and Ibsen 2016). Decades of deindustrialization and skill-biased technological change has segregated labor markets by education and occupation, and this shift has been accompanied by starkly different unemployment risks. The divergence in UIF membership fees can be seen in Figure 6.5, which plots the lowest and highest monthly fee of several dozen funds. Before January 2007, there was very little differentiation in fees. With the reforms, some funds had to increase their fees significantly, while others could keep them low. With the partial rollback of the reforms in 2014, fees converged again.

The reforms were accompanied by another, parallel, development: a massive increase in the number of supplementary insurance plans offered by unions in partnership with private insurance companies. These private top-up plans fill the sometimes large gap in replacement rates for higher-income workers. The private component of the system has been enabled by a combination of the "voluntary" character of the Ghent system, high segregation of unions by occupation, and a growing divergence of risk by occupation. UIFs represent (increasingly) distinct risk pools with clearly demarcated boundaries, not unlike some of the more successful mutual aid societies at the turn of the previous century but with much better data about workers. In 2009, the unemployment rate among hotel and restaurant workers, for example, was 9 percent, while it was only 2 percent, on average, for the Swedish Confederation of Professional Associations (Saco) (Kjellberg 2009, 492).[10]

It is thus the fact that unions are organizing increasingly homogeneous risk pools, combined with their power to exclude workers who do not "belong" in the pool that render the system actuarially sustainable. The relationship between this and information may not be immediately obvious, but it is related in the sense that private providers need to have the information to separate good from bad risks – a standard precondition for insurance markets to work. To become a member of a UIF, workers not only have to declare their occupation but also have to demonstrate that they have the formal qualifications required for a particular trade. As gatekeepers, Swedish UIFs have thus enabled the emergence of private

---

[10] The Saco represents more than half a million white-collar members (teachers, architects, economists, lawyers, engineers, doctors, scientists, etc.) of professional associations.

markets in unemployment insurance, offered by private insurance companies, by providing reliable information about individual unemployment risks. It may be seen as a historical "coincidence" that Swedish UIFs are differentiated by skills and risks, and that risks have been magnified by skill-biased technological change, but it is the data-driven power to differentiate risk pools that fuels the economics of segmentation. The Ghent system of UIFs being tied to unions, which enables the enforcement of such differentiation, is also a good illustration of how information about risk can facilitate the emergence of insurance markets because the UIFs were underwritten by private insurers. On average, contributions were increased by about a third as a result of the reforms (ignoring tax savings), but that cost was borne almost exclusively by funds with high unemployment levels (where the increase was as high as 59 percent). Predictably, UIF membership plummeted among high-risk blue-collar unions, which in turn reduced average insurance fees (see Figure 6.6), while exposing many uninsured workers to the risk of poverty (Kjellberg 2009; OECD 2015a).

The Swedish case also speaks to the *politics* of private insurance. There is little doubt that the bourgeois government, which had been elected on the promise to reduce unemployment, wanted to weaken unions and force them to accept lower wage increases (Kjellberg and Ibsen 2016). Because workers in Ghent systems tend to choose their union and UIF membership at the same time, it also had a desired effect on unionization. Union density rates dropped from 77 percent in 2006 to 71 percent in 2008, with losses concentrated among low-income, high-risk Trade Union Confederation (LO) unions. But the politics is not fully captured as one of union power.

To understand how the reform was politically possible despite the traditional strength of Swedish unions, we need to consider the distributive consequences across unions. The professional white-collar confederations, Saco and Swedish Confederation of Professional Employees (TCO),[11] cover mainly low-risk workers, and their UIF plans are inexpensive despite a generous 80 percent replacement rate when voluntary top-ups are included (OECD 2015a). It is reasonable to assume that those covered by private plans have been net beneficiaries, after factoring in the tax cut, and if we add to their ranks older workers whose jobs are virtually guaranteed by the Law on Employment Protection (Kjellberg 2009), the total number of workers who gained may well exceed half of the Swedish labor force.

---

[11] The Swedish Confederation of Professional Employees (TCO) represents more than a million white-collar employees.

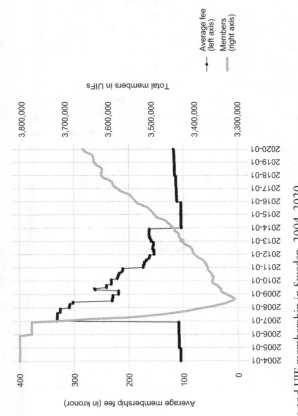

FIGURE 6.6 Average fees and UIF membership in Sweden, 2004–2020

Note: Shown are the average membership fees of UIFs (weighted by the number of fund members), in Swedish kronor per month (left axis). The overall number of members of UIFs is shown on the right axis. The unions included are: Akademikernas, Alfa, Byggnadsarbetarnas, Elektrikernas, Farmacitjänstemännens, Fastighets, Finans- och Försäkringsbranschens, GS, Grafiskas, HTFs, Hamnarbetarnas, Handelsanställdas, Hotell- och Restauranganställdas, IF Metalls, Industrifackets, Journalisternas, Kommunalarbetarnas, Ledarnas, Livsmedelsarbetarnas, Lärarnas, Musikernas, Målarnas, Pappersindustriarbetarnas, SIFs, STs, SeA, Sekos, Skogs- o träfackets, Skogs- och Lantbrukstjänstemännens, Småföretagarnas, Svensk Handels Arbetslöshetskassa, Sveriges Entreprenörers, Sveriges arbetares, Sveriges fiskares, Säljarnas, Teaterverksammas, Transportarbetarnas, Unionens, and Vision.

Source: This graph is a replication of a figure published by the IAF (Inspektionen för arbetslöshetsförsäkringen (IAF) 2016, 21). Membership data are from https://externastat.iaf.se/report.aspx?ID=111 (last accessed June 7, 2021 [https://perma.cc/2RKT-7PSB]) and membership fee data are from https://externastat.iaf.se/report.aspx?ID=115 (last accessed June 7, 2021 [https://perma.cc/J9Z7-M79 UJ]).

181

The reform did not have the intended effect on wage restraint, however, and the high unemployment rate did not come down as promised by the government (Kjellberg and Ibsen 2016). At the same time, because of the exodus of members from the UIFs with the most vulnerable workers, a large group of uninsured workers ended up on social assistance (Kjellberg 2009). This had an unanticipated negative effect on public finances, and rather than picking another fight with LO before the upcoming election by cutting social benefits or making UIF membership compulsory (a long-standing demand by employers and the Conservatives), the government reached a "Job Pact" with the unions in 2014 that restored the old contribution rates and significantly cut fees for high-unemployment unions (see Figure 6.5 above). The old solidaristic cross-subsidization system was at least partially revived.

The reversal was not a return to the status quo ante, however. Cuts to replacement rates and benefit ceilings, which began in the early 1990s, were maintained and only partially restored under the new SAP government (Gordon 2019). Eligibility requirements have also been tightened to the point where less than 50 percent of unemployed receive regular unemployment benefits. Most importantly, the expansion of supplementary insurance among TCO and SACO members has not been reversed. The number of private insurance holders rose from less than 200,000 in 2002 to 1.7 million in 2010 (Davidsson 2013); in 2014, supplementary private insurance covered 40 percent of the labor force (Høgedahl and Kongshøj 2017). Indeed, TCO has used access to private top-up insurance as a membership recruitment tool, and its membership has increased as a result (Gordon 2019). This can be seen as a "Ghent effect," but unlike the workings of the historical Ghent system, it now creates a wedge between low-unemployment white-collar unions and higher-unemployment LO (blue-collar) unions.

With the rising share of privately insured professionals, the public system is increasingly becoming a redistributive system as opposed to a common pool insurance system. This institutional bifurcation of the unemployment insurance system is reflected in increasingly divided voting behavior. LO members still disproportionally support the SAP, but rising numbers are voting for either the radical-left Left Party or the radical-right Sweden Democrats. At the same time, Saco and private unions in TCO increasingly vote for center-right parties (Arndt and Rennwald 2016). Arndt (2018) also documents that private-sector white-collar union members across the Scandinavian countries are much less supportive of redistribution, and far more supportive of privatization, than LO union members. It is perhaps an indication of weaker social networks that nonunionized workers are much more likely to vote for the Sweden Democrats, and much less likely to vote for SAP, than unionized workers – even after controlling for a range of observables (Arndt and Rennwald 2016).

SAP's loss of support to the Sweden Democrats is also illustrative of the importance of the interaction between information and the bifurcation of risk. As Gordon notes, "Sweden has one of the highest differences between migrant- and native-born unemployment rates in the rich democracies" (2019, 962). Segregation in unemployment risks based on a very visible trait like immigration status reduces the insurance motive to support generous unemployment benefits among the native majority (Alt and Iversen 2017), and it has exacerbated insider-outsider divisions in the social-democratic coalition (Lindvall and Rueda 2014). In sum, Sweden is a striking example of a solidaristic unemployment insurance program shifting to a system in which insurance is tied more closely to unemployment risks. Other solidaristic programs are showing similar fractures. In Denmark, union-based UIFs with low-risk members, especially academics, are offering supplementary insurance that brings replacement rates to over 80 percent (from the current level of about 50 percent) at very low prices. UIFs with high-risk members, on the other hand, offer individualized plans that are order of magnitudes more expensive, and in fact rarely taken up (Nørgaard and Olsen 2020). The public insurance system still redistributes from low-risk, high-income to high-risk, low-income, but the continuous drop in the replacement rate (from a little under 60 percent in 1994 to 48 percent in 2020) has made it less redistributive over time, and good risks now have an exit option that undermines their incentive to support the public system.

CONCLUSION

In Chapter 2, our third argument states that information shapes political attitudes. There are two fundamental reasons for this, at least in the case of insurance against social risks. First, when people are uninformed about where they are in the risk distribution, they can do no better than assuming that their risks are identical to those of others, which, in the case of unemployment risks, is the national unemployment rate. There would be little reason to expect partisan division. Yet such division is often intense. In Sweden, the topic of unemployment benefits was one of the most hotly contested issues in the 1990s, and the issue continues to spark conflict (Davidsson and Marx 2013, 515). An obvious source of such conflict is simply that workers are increasingly informed of their risks. In this chapter, we have shown, using panel data, that future unemployment can be better predicted over time, and most of this information is accounted for

by easily observable indicators of unemployment by education, occupation, and location. It is also of relevance here that labor markets have
become more segmented and therefore more predictable.

Yet information about risks is only a necessary condition for polarization
in policy preferences. Voters must translate such information into support for
political parties that will advance their interests. This requires a different logic
because, whereas people have a strong private incentive to know about their
labor market risks in order to make good private financial decisions, there is
little reason for individuals to know about politics. In 2006, the center-right
"Alliance for Sweden" campaigned on restoring full employment. Should an
LO member with high unemployment risk therefore vote for one of the
alliance parties? Probably not – the government ended up cutting benefits
for LO members, raising the cost of their insurance, and did nothing to reduce
unemployment – but having such knowledge is a public good. Building on
existing work, we have argued that acquiring political information depends
on participation in social networks where political discussion is common.
Indeed, polarization in political preferences is much more pronounced among
those who are in political discussion networks than those who are not. Not
only does such network participation increase exposure to political information, but it also gives people a social incentive to be informed.

Lastly, this chapter has drawn attention to a surprising development, at
least to us: the (partial) shift toward a privatized unemployment benefit
system in Sweden. Unemployment insurance is conventionally treated as a
classic case of market failure because common shocks imply correlated risks,
and insurers need to be able to make actuarial calculations with determinis-
tically expected payoffs. Yet, for a period of time, the Swedish unemployment
benefit system has been fragmented into distinct insurance pools backed by
private insurers, and it continues to have a large private component in the
form of supplementary insurance. This is also increasingly true in the Danish
case. Somewhat paradoxically, such quasi-privatization has been facilitated
by the historically close ties between the UIFs and unions (the Ghent system)
because this enables strict policing of who can get into what insurance pool
based on increasingly salient information about occupation and education.

A fully privatized unemployment insurance system remains a chimera,
however, because, if this were the case, a major economic crisis could lead
to widespread UIF insolvencies. In this situation, the government would
come under tremendous political pressure to step in to guarantee benefits.
This points to an obvious moral hazard problem because insurers may not
charge enough to build up the necessary reserves for large economic
downturns, in anticipation of being bailed out. Low-risk workers may

therefore benefit doubly from a quasi-private system. They will enjoy lower insurance rates because they are in favorable risk pools, and the government will indirectly subsidize these rates by serving as a payer of last resort.

APPENDIX

TABLE 6A.1 *Total information and attitude polarization (OLS regression)*

	(1)	(2)	(3)	(4)	(5)
	Dependent variable: attitude polarization (Coefficient of variation on "the state must ensure that people can make a decent living, even in illness, hardship, unemployment, and old age")				
McFadden	0.504**	0.705**	0.346*	0.324*	0.618**
pseudo-R2	(0.150)	(0.177)	(0.127)	(0.132)	(0.117)
West	0.097**	0.108**	0.100**	0.090**	0.125**
Germany	(0.021)	(0.020)	(0.024)	(0.024)	(0.018)
Unemployment	0.006*	0.006*	0.008*	0.005+	0.008**
rate	(0.002)	(0.002)	(0.003)	(0.003)	(0.002)
Constant	0.028	0.004	0.007	0.045	−0.037
	(0.046)	(0.044)	(0.059)	(0.053)	(0.041)
N	13	13	13	13	13
Adj. R2	0.743	0.791	0.685	0.655	0.859

Note: Models vary by different dependent variables for estimating McFadden's pseudo-R2:
(1) Unemployed >1 month next 12 months; (2) unemployed >1 month next 24 months; (3) unemployed >12 months next 24 months; (4) unemployed >6 months next 12 months; and (5) unemployed >6 months next 24 months.
The dependent variable is the coefficient of variation on a survey item inquiring about unemployment benefit generosity ("The state must ensure that people can make a decent living, even in illness, hardship, unemployment, and old age").
+ $p < 0.10$, * $p < 0.05$, and ** $p < 0.01$
Sources: SOEP 1984–2018 for McFadden's pseudo-R2 and ALLBUS 1980–2018 for attitude polarization.

TABLE 6A.2 *Total information and attitude polarization (robust regression)*

	(1)	(2)	(3)	(4)	(5)
	Dependent variable: attitude polarization (Coefficient of variation on "the state must ensure that people can make a decent living, even in illness, hardship, unemployment and old age")				
McFadden	0.513*	0.708**	0.366*	0.330+	0.621**
pseudo-R2	(0.170)	(0.209)	(0.143)	(0.147)	(0.128)
West	0.098**	0.109**	0.105**	0.091**	0.126**
Germany	(0.023)	(0.023)	(0.027)	(0.026)	(0.019)
Unemployment	0.006*	0.006*	0.008*	0.005+	0.008**
rate	(0.002)	(0.002)	(0.003)	(0.003)	(0.002)
Constant	0.027	0.004	−0.001	0.042	−0.037
	(0.051)	(0.052)	(0.067)	(0.059)	(0.044)
N	13	13	13	13	13
Adj. R2	0.698	0.734	0.652	0.604	0.837

Note: This is the same as Table 6A.1, except that the estimations are based on robust regressions (Li 1985), which eliminates outliers (Cook's distance >1) and weighs observations.
Sources: SOEP 1984–2018 for McFadden's pseudo-R2 and ALLBUS 1980–2018 for attitude polarization.

TABLE 6A.3 *Political discussion and political preferences (European Social Survey)*

	(1)	(2)	(3)	(4)	(5)
	Pro-redistribution attitudes				
Pol. discussion			−0.041	0.109	0.268**
			(0.028)	(0.073)	(0.052)
Occupational UR	0.014*	0.011+	−0.012	0.015**	0.012+
(OUR)	(0.006)	(0.006)	(0.014)	(0.006)	(0.007)
OUR * Pol.			0.007*		
Discussion			(0.003)		
Income	−0.107**	−0.106**	−0.107**	−0.045	−0.105**
	(0.015)	(0.014)	(0.015)	(0.042)	(0.014)
Income # Pol.				−0.014	
discussion				(0.010)	

(continued)

TABLE 6A.3 *(continued)*

	(1)	(2)	(3)	(4)	(5)
	Pro-redistribution attitudes				
Left-right		−0.155**			0.099+
		(0.033)			(0.054)
Left-right # Pol. discussion					−0.053**
					(0.010)
Age	0.003+	0.004+	0.003	0.003	0.004
	(0.002)	(0.002)	(0.002)	(0.002)	(0.002)
Female	0.320**	0.280**	0.327**	0.323**	0.286**
	(0.076)	(0.083)	(0.073)	(0.076)	(0.083)
Educ: Upper secondary	0.086	0.130	0.077	0.061	0.134
	(0.151)	(0.185)	(0.150)	(0.156)	(0.183)
Educ: Postsecondary	−0.186	−0.126	−0.198	−0.215	−0.116
	(0.161)	(0.220)	(0.164)	(0.176)	(0.219)
Educ: Tertiary	−0.093	−0.077	−0.093	−0.107	−0.087
	(0.252)	(0.305)	(0.255)	(0.264)	(0.309)
Educ: Lower secondary	−0.356*	−0.356+	−0.358*	−0.380*	−0.362*
	(0.144)	(0.183)	(0.151)	(0.154)	(0.176)
Union member	0.273**	0.207*	0.270**	0.269**	0.198*
	(0.083)	(0.086)	(0.084)	(0.084)	(0.082)
Dummy for employed	−0.044	−0.038	−0.048	−0.050	−0.032
	(0.103)	(0.087)	(0.102)	(0.102)	(0.084)
Dummy for self-employed	−0.372**	−0.322**	−0.377**	−0.377**	−0.321**
	(0.091)	(0.086)	(0.093)	(0.093)	(0.093)
Ever unemployed 3 + months	0.274**	0.283**	0.283**	0.276**	0.280**
	(0.038)	(0.046)	(0.036)	(0.039)	(0.051)
Constant	1.098**	1.832**	1.277**	0.659**	0.548
	(0.181)	(0.238)	(0.233)	(0.177)	(0.380)
N	14878	13823	14828	14828	13788
Pseudo R2	0.087	0.101	0.087	0.087	0.106

Note: Includes country fixed effects. Ages 18–65. Coefficients above standard errors (clustered at the ISCO-1d level).
$+ p < 0.10$, $*p < 0.05$, and $**p < 0.01$
Source: European Social Survey 2002.

7

Conclusion

By all accounts, most advanced democracies have seen a rise in market income inequality over the past four to five decades (Huber and Stephens 2001; OECD 2018a). This rise is commonly attributed to (i) the decline of the working class (Gingrich and Häusermann 2015; Huber and Stephens 2001; Korpi 1983; Stephens 1979) and unions (Ahlquist 2017, 2019; Ahlquist and Levi 2013; Brady, Baker, and Finnigan 2013; Macdonald 2019; Mosimann and Pontusson 2017; Wallerstein and Western 2000), (ii) skill-biased technological change (Autor, Katz, and Kearney 2006; Goldin and Katz 2009), (iii) globalization (Hellwig 2014; Hoeller, Joumard, and Koske 2013), (iv) deindustrialization (Iversen and Cusack 2000; Iversen and Wren 1998), or (v) growing labor market segmentation (by ethnicity or skill) (King and Rueda 2008; Rueda 2007). In this book, we argued that the massive increase in data about risks is another, complementary, driver of inequality. Because data enables the fragmentation of all-encompassing risk pools into smaller ones, it strikes at the very heart of the solidaristic welfare state. We think it is plausible that the long-run impact of the information revolution on income inequality will rival other widely recognized drivers of inequality in magnitude. Moreover, it undoubtedly reinforces the trend.

Insuring against risks of all sorts is the main function of the welfare state, and it has been a major source of redistribution (Hacker and Rehm 2022). Even if voters support social programs ex ante as a form of insurance, the people receiving benefits are those who have lost income because of unemployment, illness, old age, and so on. Bradley et al. (2003) find that the level of taxes and transfers is a strong independent predictor of redistribution (measured as the reduction in inequality from before taxes and transfers to after taxes and transfers) after controlling for a range of variables that are predicted, in the literature, to affect redistribution. Much of this effect is likely due to the leveling effects of social insurance. More directly, it can be shown that the insurance value of services, such as public healthcare, notably reduces inequality when added to income (Elkjær and Iversen 2020). Such redistribution is politically feasible, at least in part, because voters are risk-averse, and because a majority has an interest in social insurance. This majority can be very large when people are uncertain about where they are in the risk distribution.

In the early twentieth century, rapid industrialization and urbanization – accompanied by a massive shift of workers from mostly agricultural occupations into the industrializing urban centers – caused pervasive uncertainty, and this uncertainty, in turn, spurred people across economic classes to support a greater role of the state in social protection. Before Keynesian ideas took hold, economic recessions added to the uncertainty by sometimes spilling over into major economic crises, as was true with the Great Depression. The post-WWII period has been more macro-economically stable, but the Great Recession and the COVID-19 pandemic are reminders that modern societies can still be exposed to shocks that can raise uncertainty and potentially boost political support for the welfare state.

The postwar period has also witnessed notable changes in the economic structure caused by deindustrialization, globalization, and the ICT revolution. Throughout these upheavals, people, insurers, and financial institutions have learned more and more about the risks these developments bring about, and the explosion in the availability of data about such risks has facilitated this learning process. The increasing bifurcation of workers into secure and insecure positions (Alt and Iversen 2017; King and Rueda 2008; Rueda 2007) and the decline in class mobility (OECD 2018a) have further expedited the process. We argued that information about risk has, in turn, become a major driver of marketization and segmentation of insurance and hence also of inequality. In the following sections, we will briefly recap the theory and evidence presented in this book before highlighting a few potential areas for future research.

A BRIEF SYNOPSIS OF THE ARGUMENT

Imagine that we could divide people into groups that reflect their true underlying risk. If individuals and insurers were fully informed about who belonged to which group, it would, in principle, be straightforward to calculate actuarially fair insurance rates for each group, and if people are risk-averse and concerned about their future well-being, everyone would buy insurance if they could. In the case of insurance against income loss, each individual would choose a level of insurance that would leave them with identical income in the good and bad states, adjusted for discounting of the future.

Historically, information has been highly incomplete, however, and this has been a source of both widespread market failure and state intervention. In the classic Akerlof scenario of asymmetric information (1970) – with the used car market as an illustrative example – buyers cannot distinguish good from bad cars. If sellers offer their car at the mean price, buyers will fear buying a bad car (a "lemon") and will thus be few in number, while sellers with above-average cars would pull their cars from the market, setting in motion a process that would end in a market for lemons only.

Analogously, if insurers cannot distinguish good from bad risks and therefore charge an average premium across all risk groups, those at high risk will opt in, while those with low risk will opt out (and self-insure through personal savings and wealth). In Akerlof's model, this again results in a market for bad risks, although more realistic insurance models imply markets that are underdeveloped and mostly limited to easily identifiable risks.

Mutual aid societies (MASs) provided partial solutions to market failure by organizing workers by craft or occupation and restricting entry into each MAS based on certified skills. But when trying to insure large groups in the industrializing economy, MASs encountered a double bind: exit of low risks into private insurance or self-insurance and entry of bad risks from among a vastly expanding industrial working class. To stay relevant, MASs had to greatly broaden their appeal, but the logic of MASs was based on membership entry control and exclusion. The exclusionary logic of MASs rendered them mostly irrelevant in the big push to mobilize the masses of newly enfranchised groups.

In addition to the problem of low, asymmetric information, markets could not cope with intergenerational transfers, which emerged as a pressing concern at the dawn of democracy. From a theoretical perspective, the problem is that future younger generations cannot credibly commit to transfers to current young generations, a dilemma we referred to as a time-inconsistency problem in social insurance. Markets fail because any cross-generational transfer would cause young people to exit an insurance scheme that offered such transfers, instead opting into a policy that only offered benefits to current generations (thus approximating actuarially fair insurance for all insurance holders at any given moment in time). Instead, the time-inconsistency problem was solved by long-standing democratic parties using intraparty and intergenerational bargains to offer reliable party platforms credibly promising future benefits. The power of the state to tax effectively cut off the exit option, and most voters saw PAYG transfer systems as desirable intergenerational insurance schemes for risks concentrated at the end of life.

The initial solution to both types of market failures therefore resulted in compulsory public insurance, which incorporated very diverse risks in all-encompassing pools – not always a single national pool as in Scandinavia but much larger pools than the underlying risk distribution would imply for market-based, actuarially fair insurance – and these encompassing schemes were highly redistributive (even in Bismarckian welfare states). By compelling good risks into the common pool(s), state-mediated insurance did much to equalize life chances well into the second half of the twentieth century because risks tend to decline in income and taxes, and contributions are proportional to income, not risks. Uncertainty about the position in the risk distribution – in part, as noted above, because of a rapidly changing economy and, in part, because of high occupational mobility – helped expand support for the welfare state as it created a rational basis for the perception among broad swaths of the electorate that they were in the same boat. As succinctly summarized in a recent book by Rachel Friedman (2020), the modern welfare state fuses prudential calculations of self-interest with collectivist notions of our responsibility to each other as members of a larger national community.

Yet information about risks has exploded in the past three to four decades as insurers and major tech companies accumulate and analyse data at an unprecedented rate. Information about credit and health history, occupational exposure to unemployment, demographic risks, and increasingly genetic information and individual data recorded by trackers are upending life, health, unemployment, car, and other related insurance markets, as well as consumer credit markets, by enabling insurers to create increasingly individualized risk profiles and narrow risk pools. Much of this information can now be credibly shared with insurers through a large infrastructure of independent labs, genetic testing companies, trackers with smartphone apps, as well as cloud-based data sharing. Big Data, combined with credible means to share them, render private insurance markets feasible in a way that they never were in the past.

As we argued previously, this shift is reinforced by a parallel move that is difficult to separate from information: the increasing segmentation of labor, housing, and health markets by education, occupation, and location. Those with university degrees (and an increasing number with postgraduate degrees) are usually in competitive labor markets and often move around a great deal, but they are rarely in direct competition with those who have only secondary or lower education. By most accounts, cross-class and intergenerational mobility have declined in the knowledge economy compared to the industrial economy – something that is evident both across educational levels and across geographical space – and this alters people's calculations about risks and the need for insurance. This is particularly evident for unemployment insurance where risks are increasingly concentrated in the lower third of the skill distribution and in "left-behind" communities in small towns and rural areas. As workers share information about this new reality, preferences over the level of public insurance diverge. As we saw in the striking case of Swedish unemployment insurance, long a beacon of solidarity, the unemployment insurance system itself can segment when unemployment insurance funds (UIFs) are controlled by unions who effectively police entry based on occupation and education (not unlike early MASs). The situation is very similar when it comes to the differentiation of health and credit risks.

The divergence in preferences over public spending should not be taken to mean that those with high education and income are unconcerned about insurance. While a few may have enough personal wealth to forgo insurance altogether, standard treatments assume that insurance is a normal good with demand increasing with income. When public insurance is the only game in town, this condition can sometimes have the surprising consequence of increasing demand for public spending among the well-off. But a negative relationship between income and risk generally outweighs the income effect and ensures "normal" class preferences. In the case of unemployment, this relationship is strongly negative, and so is demand. For public spending on health insurance, by contrast, demand increases with income, and this is also true for "superior" public goods, such as higher education and environmental protection. It is always true, however, that those with higher income have an interest in private options because markets do not imply any subsidization of those with lower incomes. Marketization therefore tends to exacerbate class divisions (Busemeyer and Iversen 2020).

EMPIRICAL ILLUSTRATIONS

Our empirical applications are from the health (Chapter 4), credit (Chapter 5), and labor market domains (Chapter 6). In this section, we briefly return to each of these domains in succession.

Life and Health Insurance

The information logic is easiest to show in situations when private markets are left more or less to their own devices. Life insurance is a case in point. Profits in the life insurance business depend on making accurate predictions about life expectancy, but life insurance faces the same problem of adverse selection as other insurance markets. The first life insurance company evolved out of a mutual aid society that provided Scottish presbyterian ministers with widows insurance. Entry was limited to those with a title-granting graduate-level seminary education in theology, and no one became a seminarian just to get access to insurance. This effective gatekeeping eliminated adverse selection.

Commercial insurers cannot use such exclusionary criteria to select their customers, but they can increasingly distinguish groups of potential buyers with different risk profiles and hence also different life expectancies. The proliferation of diagnostic testing – including, notably, genetic tests as these can provide increasingly accurate predictions about life expectancy – is an important case in point. We find that better diagnostic capabilities facilitate the expansion of life insurance markets, and such expansion goes hand in hand with greater segmentation of insurance and hence greater price and benefit differentiation (see Chapter 4).

Because the medical information required for risk assessments is very similar in health insurance, here, too, the potential for market-driven differentiation increases with information. In the American private health insurance system, for example, private plans have become more tailored to employers with different risk profiles among their employees. Similarly, across Europe, we are observing the proliferation of supplementary private health insurance, mostly catering to employers or individuals with lower risks and higher incomes. Even in a quintessentially "social democratic" welfare state like Denmark, more than 2 million Danes now have some supplementary insurance.

That said, there are limitations to private provision, which can also be illustrated by the American case. While public opinion is split over the desirability of private insurance, there is broad cross-class support for two major government programs: Medicare and Medicaid. Medicare covers those over the age of sixty-five, which is the cohort with the greatest need for healthcare. This presents a classic case of what we referred to as the time-inconsistency problem in social insurance: insurers would like to offer coverage to the younger and middle-aged, which they will mostly tap into when they are old, yet insurers cannot do so in a credible way because today's young and middle-aged policyholders have no way of securing a commitment from tomorrow's young and middle-aged individuals to finance their own care when they grow old. Instead, as we have argued, the long time horizon of political parties made commitments to PAYG systems believable to voters, and they were thus supported by majorities given that private markets could not do the same.

A similar logic applies to insurance against poverty, which cannot be provided through markets either. For example, it is estimated that about a third of all Americans who reach the age of sixty-five will end up in a long-term care facility, and most of their bills will be paid by Medicaid as people spend down their savings.[1] If you are not rich and do not expect to die young, Medicaid may be your best bet of securing long-term care if you end up needing it. Even though Medicaid targets the poor, it also provides insurance to those members of the middle class who are at risk of becoming poor (Busemeyer and Iversen 2020). It is therefore not surprising that the program enjoys broad support, contrary to the widely held expectation that benefits targeting the poor are politically vulnerable (see Korpi and Palme (1998) for the classic statement).

Most large-scale public insurance systems that emerged during the Golden Age of welfare state expansion were PAYG or intended to alleviate poverty. Gradually, however, old-age pensions have been supplemented by "funded" systems, which are either individual (e.g., IRAs in the USA) or collectively bargained (as was the case for many occupational pension schemes in Europe). This shift was facilitated by, and in turn further stimulated, a large expansion of the financial sector (Bonoli and Palier 2007), itself partly fueled by improved information as discussed in Chapter 5. Life insurance has always essentially been a funded system where the expected payout to each insurance holder is typically less than what they pay into the system. Once full funding renders the time-inconsistency problem moot, and without other impediments to the

---

[1] Kaiser Family Foundation (www.kff.org/infographic/medicaids-role-in-nursing-home-care, last accessed June 7, 2021 [https://perma.cc/TK6G-FGZV]).

market formation, information then determines the potential for private markets and the extent of cost-benefit differentiation.

Funded systems are still the exception in health insurance, but they do exist. As discussed, Germany is one of two advanced industrialized countries with a significant private health insurance market, providing some 11 percent of the population with primary health insurance coverage. Premiums are tied to health risks and are calculated so that they cover expected health costs over the customer's lifetime. In this system, younger insurance holders save up for the higher expenses they expect when they get older.

The USA is the other advanced industrial country with a significant private health insurance market. Since 2004, people have been able to set up HSAs, but the annual maximum contributions are low (in 2021, US$3,600 per year for a single). These accounts appeal largely to young, healthy individuals who do not mind being covered under a high deductible (but low premium) health plan. HSAs do not play a particularly large role – there are about 30 million accounts[2] – but they serve as a proof of concept.

When markets are not feasible and risks are not highly concentrated among low-income groups, we sometimes observe that those with higher incomes prefer more spending. As noted above, this paradoxical pattern is explained by the fact that insurance is a normal good. In many countries, the response to "excess demand" among the well-off has been to allow people to buy private top-up insurance. Many do so, and an important question is whether this will gradually lead to a bifurcation of health insurance, in which the state provides a basic minimum, while private insurers and clinics offer access to high-end procedures and comfortable accommodation without long waiting lists, catering mainly to the middle and upper-middle classes. Not surprisingly, this has become a partisan issue with the center-right promoting private options through tax credits and regulatory accommodation, and the center-left seeking to improve the public system via taxes and regulatory roadblocks for private markets.

Yet greater access to private alternatives is not the only way markets matter. "Choice," "internal markets," "competition," and "agency autonomy" are some of the buzzwords of the new public management literature (Lane 2000), and they reflect a novel political reality where those politicians who want to defend the role of the state in public

---

[2] Source: www.devenir.com/hsa-investment-assets-soar-to-23-8-billion-up-52-in-2020/ (last accessed June 7, 2021 [https://perma.cc/7HGY-F4QY]).

insurance and public goods provision often support solutions that cater to the tastes of the middle and upper-middle classes by imitating market mechanisms in the public system. The importance of having a choice over, say, doctors and hospitals (with corresponding competition between providers over users and resources) is widely accepted on both the left and right, but such choice always disproportionately benefits those who have the required information, time, and cognitive resources to take advantage of that choice, notably those who have a good education and who are embedded in well-connected social networks. The rest, which overlaps to a significant extent with Akerlof's "lemons," are left with the lowest-performing providers and sometimes the longest lines. In this sense, the private market casts a shadow over the public system, and one of the main drivers behind growing public segmentation has therefore indirectly been the data revolution.

In focusing on the distributive consequences of information, we do not want to ignore the importance of information for efficiency. In terms of the consequences of more and better information and taking health insurance as an example, we agree with the simple idea that information is a necessary condition for effective treatment. From both an individual and public health perspective, more testing can only be a good thing. But effective testing also facilitates market formation and segmentation of insurance by risk groups, and this is significantly increasing inequality. Simply put, uncertainty promotes solidarity, while information facilitates segmentation. It is this largely overlooked consequence of information that we have drawn attention to in this book, even as we accept the importance of information in effective treatment and in the efficient use of resources.

Credit Markets

In the financial sector – for example, in equity trading – even small advantages in information can have huge monetary consequences, and it is therefore not surprising that more and better information is quickly exploited, including in consumer credit markets. In these markets, more information allows creditors to identify default risk more accurately and cheaply. As a consequence, better default risks – who tend to be richer – can access credit at lower interest rates, while worse default risks – who tend to be poorer – are charged higher rates or are excluded from access to credit altogether. So more information results in higher inequality in *discretionary income* (income after debt servicing).

In most countries, average mortgage interest rates have declined considerably in the last few decades, which has offset the unequalizing effect of more information. However, even small differences in mortgage interest rates cumulate to become considerable inequalities, as we have shown in Chapter 5. Moreover, there is no guarantee that low mortgage interest rates are here to stay, and average interest rates for consumer credit – most importantly credit cards – are much higher and have not declined nearly as much, if at all. Combined with the increase in household debt (as documented in Figure 5.1), we believe that the impact of information on income inequality, through the debt channel we identify in Chapter 5, will likely be substantial.

Institutions continue to matter, including in credit markets. Governments regulate mortgage markets and often implement policies that subsidize homeownership and access to credit for higher default risks – in ways that do not square with existing social policy typologies. For example, in the USA – usually seen as an example of a stingy residual welfare state – heavy regulation of mortgage markets has historically produced considerable risk redistribution by essentially requiring quasi-public financial institutions – notably Fannie May and Freddie Mac – to buy up mortgages with little concern for underlying risks. Politically, this is made sustainable by bringing together a strange alliance of private lenders, builders, progressive politicians, and even "ownership society" conservatives. In contrast, in Denmark – usually seen as an example of a generous social democratic welfare state – mortgage markets are largely left to market forces.[3]

Government policies also indirectly shape access to credit because welfare state generosity influences default risks. In countries that replace a higher percentage of wages in the event of unemployment, sickness, or disability, banks do not have to worry as much about arrears and default. For example, when people without wealth become unemployed in the USA, they often cannot pay their monthly mortgages and end up defaulting. In Denmark, defaulting on a mortgage is exceedingly rare because

---

[3] Hicks (2015) has argued more generally that governments in relatively egalitarian countries sometimes push for privatization because, in these countries, markets result in smaller increases in inequality while promising potential gains in welfare or voter satisfaction. Hicks's focus is on private education, but it jibes well with our finding that mortgage markets embedded in systems with strong unemployment protection result in less differentiation in interest rates. In private health and other insurance markets, however, risks are less contingent on the (post-fisc) income distribution, and the argument is therefore less applicable in these domains.

unemployment benefits are sufficiently generous to allow people to continue servicing their debt. There is as much information available to Danish lenders as there is to American ones, but the information is less consequential for setting interest rates in Denmark than it is in the USA.

The German combination of generous unemployment benefits and private mortgage institutions once functioned in a similar manner to the Danish system, but as we demonstrated in Chapter 5, the Hartz reforms, which saw a reduction in unemployment benefits, has increased inequality in access to credit, even among the employed, and has probably contributed to the increasing socioeconomic stratification of homeownership. Because many countries have retrenched unemployment benefits, the developments in Germany may be representative of other countries as well.

Labor Market Risks

Unemployment risk often varies by easily observable traits, such as occupation, education, and location. We have argued that this is increasingly the case, due to skill-biased technological change and increasing labor market segmentation, and data from Germany are consistent with this conjecture. Outright privatization of unemployment insurance is unlikely for various reasons (two of which are correlated risks and moral hazard), though segmentation is theoretically feasible, at least in the Ghent systems, as developments in Sweden and Denmark show. Privatization or segmentation may be blocked (politically or otherwise), but increasing predictability of risk should polarize public opinion on benefit generosity, as we have shown is the case in Germany.

In Sweden, the organization of unions and UIFs along occupational lines facilitated the transition to a quasi-private unemployment insurance system (see Chapter 6). Unemployment risk in Sweden is stratified by occupation. Therefore, when reforms tied unemployment insurance contributions to unemployment risk, inequality in rates and contributions increased dramatically, and many workers lost insurance because they could no longer afford it.

It is tempting to conjecture that growing differentiation of risks by education and occupation coupled with more information about these risks will lead to privatization. But while public consensus is breaking down and political efforts at privatizing social insurance are real, when most social insurance is in the public domain and paid through taxes, privatization often entails a "double-payment" problem that entrenches support for public provision. Once again, the institutional variation we have observed does not neatly correspond with standard typologies such as Esping-Andersen's (1990) "worlds of welfare" or Hall and Soskice's (2001) "varieties of capitalism." While large public spending does tend to create double-payment problems and while cost-benefit differentiation in Bismarckian systems may alleviate some of the pressure for privatization, the Swedish case of UIFs runs counter to expectation, and Bismarckian systems have not proven immune to change either (Hinrichs 2010). There seems to be a common trend away from the solidaristic "Golden Age" social insurance state. The educated middle- and upper-middle classes increasingly want more for less because they see that they are not a great burden on the system, yet have high expectations about the quality of benefits.

THE FUTURE POLITICS OF SOCIAL INSURANCE

Despite the growing feasibility of private markets and marked trends toward privatization in some policy domains, social insurance in most advanced democracies remains predominantly public. In policy terms, this can be explained by a combination of nondiscrimination regulations and compulsory taxation. Specifically, where insurers are forced to admit people with preexisting conditions and/or where information about risks cannot be used to decide who to admit, it is hard for profit-maximizing private firms to reach more than a small segment of potential buyers without the help of major public subsidies. As in the low-information case, adverse selection will be a problem that deters good risks from joining insurance plans. In terms of tax policy, if the state declines to accommodate private options through either tax deductions or tax credits, the double-payment problem will strictly limit the number of people who are able and willing to pay the price for private alternatives.

Yet, even when *policies* constrain private markets, the *politics* of social protection is being fundamentally transformed. When asymmetric information and time inconsistency undermine markets and MASs, support for public provision will tend to be widespread – especially when there is high uncertainty about current and future location in the risk distribution, and preferences therefore gravitate toward the center. But when information is plentiful, the politics shifts because markets become more economically feasible and because the preference distribution will diverge from the center. Many more voters than before will see their interests aligned with greater differentiation in insurance. If such preferences are not catered for through privatization, public opinion will polarize, and pressure will build to allow more choice and competition in the public system. This invariably gives those with greater educational, cognitive, and financial resources an advantage.

Partisanship over social insurance is likely to continue to loom large in the new world of high information and "shadow" private markets. The political left and right have, of course, always represented different segments of the income-risk distribution, but differences in constituency preferences are – if anything – growing starker as people become more informed about risks and as markets become more feasible. There may also be a feedback loop from partisanship to the distribution of preferences. In political systems that favor the political left – whether through electoral systems, the strength of the union movement, or the media landscape – policies that limit markets (as described previously) and promote interclass mobility will tend to homogenize the risk pool and facilitate cross-class compromise (Alt and Iversen 2017; Rehm 2016). In this important sense, policies shape politics (Mettler and Soss 2004).

Ultimately, whether social insurance is kept in the public sphere or transitioned to private markets comes down to the formation of sustainable majorities, and such majorities invariably require the support of the middle class. If we think of the middle class as being at the center of the joint distribution of income and risk, what makes the outcome of the tussle between public and private solutions hard to predict is the fact that the median in both distributions is to the left of the mean: in terms of income, the median is usually relatively poor, while in terms of risk, the median is usually relatively secure. The middle therefore tends to benefit from fiscal redistribution, which is implied by most tax-and-transfer systems, yet it also benefits from lower risk redistribution. When private insurance was effectively ruled out by market failure, this resulted in a convergence of interests in redistribution and insurance, using state compulsion in both cases. What is new is that preferences for redistribution and insurance are diverging for large portions of the electorate.

One of our main goals of this book is to develop a theoretical argument that draws attention to the causes of this shift in politics and to provide evidence and illustrations from a range of different social insurance contexts and related policy domains. Where appropriate, we have highlighted the differences in national institutions and how they impact distributive outcomes, but over time, we tend to see parallel changes across institutional contexts: Bismarckian systems started out with more differentiation, but unemployment benefits have been cut and the contribution component strengthened, just as in the Nordic countries; pension systems have everywhere shifted from PAYG to market-mediated funded systems, and while the scope of voluntary private health insurance varies, Bismarckian countries are no less prone to market reform than Nordic or liberal ones. Parties still matter, and institutional differences persist, but distinct institutional configurations have seen parallel changes. Everywhere these changes have worked to divide large solidaristic risk pools into smaller ones with greater differentiation in costs and benefits and a gradually increasing role for private markets. The common force of change behind these trends, we conjecture, is the information revolution.

FUTURE WORK

We have argued that the information revolution has an important impact on shaping welfare state politics and that it increases (income and risk) inequality. We believe that the information revolution threatens social solidarity. We hope that others share our interest in the topic and that they find the theoretical and empirical endeavors we present in this book inspiring. But we are well aware that we have only taken a few steps on the way to understanding the role of the information revolution in the politics of social protection. There are still many related topics to explore, and we briefly highlight a few of them here.

First, a central challenge in all empirical applications in this book was how to measure information. Measuring aspects of information – such as its quantity, quality, shareability, and symmetry – is a very difficult problem, and we anticipate that readers will find some of our proposed solutions more convincing than others. Following the empirical implications of theoretical models (EITM) approach, we have tried to align our empirical explorations closely with our theoretical models, and our statistical tests rely (to our knowledge) on the best available data. Measurement of information is a wide-open field, and we hope that our efforts will stimulate interest, foster debate, and spark innovation.

Second, our theoretical framework assumes that the information asymmetries are such that individuals know more than (insurance) companies or the state. This is a standard assumption, and it strikes us as very reasonable in many instances. However, as (Big Tech) companies guzzle up more and more information about more and more individuals, linking them across many domains and mining them for patterns, the information asymmetries may not just grow smaller and disappear – as we assume – but eventually reverse. Our intuition is that this would increase the "cream skimming" of insurance companies: Their risk classification would be excellent; they could identify bad risks with high accuracy; and they would not need to worry as much about adverse selection. But "reversed asymmetric information" – for lack of a better term – is not a case we cover in our theoretical models. It might become one in need of systematic analysis in the future.

Third, closely related to the increasingly proactive role of tech companies in differentiating good from bad risks is the potential for racial, gender, and other forms of overt or subtle discrimination. We have assumed that insurers are profit maximizers and that assumption alone yields the unequalizing effects of information that we have documented. But tech and insurance companies have the power, whether intentionally applied or not, to divide people beyond legitimate differentiation on risks. There is a long, shameful history of "redlining" in American mortgage lending, and recently, AI algorithms have been shown to be racially biased across many domains (Lee, Resnick, and Barton 2019; Sweeney 2013). Links to criminal records, for example, may be used as a way to screen out groups of applicants for, say, a bank loan or as a tool to target higher-interest credit cards. Nondiscrimination and civil rights laws prohibit such practices, but the implementation of this legislation is difficult and lagging behind the application of discriminatory algorithms and data mining.

Fourth, following on from the previous point, we have no doubt that the regulation of information will become an increasingly important and politically contentious topic. Loosely speaking, we think of information as "being able to accurately engage in risk classification," which is a function of data. Who owns data, who should own data, who decides who can access it, and even what data *is* are all open and contested questions that deserve serious attention from many perspectives (Arrieta-Ibarra et al. 2018; Lane 2020; Prewitt 2021). Despite the many unanswered questions, there is much legislative activity with respect to data protection, such as the recent GDPR in the EU or the California Consumer Privacy Act (Cortez 2020). Most legislation is national – with the major exception of the GDPR – but the nature of the problem probably requires some supranational regulation as well. Data know no boundaries, and it is unlikely that they can be effectively protected and managed by national regulations.

Finally, we would like to draw attention to a broad theoretical challenge. We have argued that heterogeneous electorates tend to accept solidaristic, state-sponsored solutions to social risks when such risks are uncertain and poorly understood. More information, on the other hand, tends to break up all-encompassing risk pools into smaller and more homogenous ones, to the detriment of equality and a sense of common cause. This stands in contrast to existing accounts that see reciprocity and solidarity emerging out of small homogenous groups where people know each other well. In game theory, cooperation is easier to achieve in small groups than in large ones, and sociological network theory implies that small homogenous groups can more easily arrive at a common understanding of interests. In his seminal work on social capital in Italy, Putnam (1993) reached a similar conclusion and so did Olson (1993), from a very different perspective.

We do not dispute that trust and cooperation are more likely to emerge in small homogenous groups. Indeed, we have used this logic to explain preference formation. But it is not conducive to cross-class solidarity and redistribution unless incorporated into large national risk pools. The distinction is related to Putnam's concern that trust and solidarity with others in one's group may not always produce "generalized trust." In later work, he distinguishes between "bonding social capital," and "bridging social capital" (Putnam 2000). The former comes close to the kind of inward-looking social organization we saw with mutual aid societies at the turn of the previous century. Bridging social capital, on the other hand, comes closer to the solidarism that we argued characterized the early stages of welfare state development. We believe it is far more likely that notions of national solidarity emerged through "anonymous" democratic electoral channels than repeated interaction in small homogenous groups. But the relationship between these dynamics deserves further theoretical development.

References

Acharya, Viral V., Matthew Richardson, Stijn van Nieuwerburgh, and Lawrence J. White. 2011. *Guaranteed to Fail: Fannie Mae, Freddie Mac, and the Debacle of Mortgage Finance*. Princeton University Press.

Ahlquist, John S. 2017. "Labor Unions, Political Representation, and Economic Inequality." *Annual Review of Political Science* 20(1): 409–32.

—— 2019. "Work and Workers in International Markets." In *Oxford Handbook of International Political Economy*, eds. Jon Pevehouse and Leonard Seabrook. Oxford University Press.

Ahlquist, John S. and Ben W. Ansell. 2017. "Taking Credit: Redistribution and Borrowing in an Age of Economic Polarization." *World Politics* 69(4): 640–75.

Ahlquist, John S., John R. Hamman, and Bradley M. Jones. 2017. "Dependency Status and Demand for Social Insurance: Evidence from Experiments and Surveys." *Political Science Research and Methods* 5(1): 31–53.

Ahlquist, John S. and Margaret Levi. 2013. *In the Interest of Others: Organizations and Social Activism*. Princeton University Press.

Akerlof, George A. 1970. "The Market for 'Lemons': Quality Uncertainty and the Market Mechanism." *The Quarterly Journal of Economics* 84(3): 488–500.

Aldrich, John. 1993. "Rational Choice and Turnout." *American Journal of Political Science* 37(1): 246–78.

—— 1995. *Why Parties? The Origin and Transformation of Political Parties in America*. Chicago University Press.

Alesina, Alberto and Paola Giuliano. 2011. "Preferences for Redistribution." In *Handbook of Social Economics*, eds. Jess Benhabib, Alberto Bisin, and Matthew O. Jackson. North-Holland, 93–131.

Alexandersen, Nina et al. 2016. "The Development of Voluntary Private Health Insurance in the Nordic Countries." *Nordic Journal of Health Economics* 4 (1): 68–83.

Alt, James et al. 2021. "Diffusing Political Concerns: How Unemployment Information Passed between Social Ties Influences Danish Voters." *The Journal of Politics*.

Alt, James and Torben Iversen. 2017. "Inequality, Labor Market Segmentation, and Preferences for Redistribution." *American Journal of Political Science* 61 (1): 21–36.

Andersson, Lars Fredrik and Liselotte Eriksson. 2017. "Sickness Absence in Compulsory and Voluntary Health Insurance: The Case of Sweden at the Turn of the Twentieth Century." *Scandinavian Economic History Review* 65 (1): 6–27.

Ansell, Ben. 2014. "The Political Economy of Ownership: Housing Markets and the Welfare State." *American Political Science Review* 108(2): 383–402.

Aoki, Masahiko. 1988. *Information, Incentives and Bargaining in the Japanese Economy: A Microtheory of the Japanese Economy.* Cambridge University Press.

Arent, Stefan and Wolfgang Nagl. 2013. "Unemployment Compensation and Wages: Evidence from the German Hartz Reforms." *Jahrbücher für Nationalökonomie und Statistik/Journal of Economics and Statistics* 233 (4): 450–66.

Armingeon, Klaus et al. 2020. *Comparative Political Data Set 1960–2018.* Institute of Political Science, University of Berne.

Arndt, Christoph. 2018. "White-Collar Unions and Attitudes towards Income Inequality, Redistribution, and State–Market Relations." *European Sociological Review* 34(6): 675–93.

Arndt, Christoph and Line Rennwald. 2016. "Union Members at the Polls in Diverse Trade Union Landscapes." *European Journal of Political Research* 55(4): 702–22.

Arrieta-Ibarra, Imanol et al. 2018. "Should We Treat Data as Labor? Moving beyond 'Free'." *AEA Papers and Proceedings* 108: 38–42.

Autor, David H., Lawrence F. Katz, and Melissa S. Kearney. 2006. "The Polarization of the U.S. Labor Market." *The American Economic Review* 96(2): 189–94.

Balasubramanian, Ramnath, Ari Chester, and Nick Milinkovich. 2020. "Rewriting the Rules: Digital and AI-Powered Underwriting in Life Insurance." *Our Insights (McKinsey).* www.mckinsey.com/industries/finan cial-services/our-insights/rewriting-the-rules-digital-and-ai-powered-under writing-in-life-insurance# (September 2).

Baldwin, Peter. 1990. *The Politics of Social Solidarity: Class Bases of the European Welfare State, 1875–1975.* Cambridge University Press.

Barber, Benjamin, Pablo Beramendi, and Erik Wibbels. 2013. "The Behavioral Foundations of Social Politics: Evidence from Surveys and a Laboratory Democracy." *Comparative Political Studies* 46(10): 1155–89.

Barr, Nicholas. 2001. *The Welfare State as Piggy Bank: Information, Risk, Uncertainty, and the Role of the State.* Oxford University Press.

2012. *Economics of the Welfare State.* 5th ed. Oxford University Press.

Beck, Nathaniel and Jonathan N. Katz. 1995. "What to Do (and Not to Do) with Time-Series Cross-Section Data." *American Political Science Review* 89(3): 634–47.

Beito, David T. 1990. "Mutual Aid for Social Welfare: The Case of American Fraternal Societies." *Critical Review* 4(4): 709–36.

2000. *From Mutual Aid to the Welfare State: Fraternal Societies and Social Services, 1890–1967.* University of North Carolina Press.

Bélisle-Pipon, Jean-Christophe, Effy Vayena, Robert C. Green, and I. Glenn Cohen. 2019. "Genetic Testing, Insurance Discrimination and Medical Research: What the United States Can Learn from Peer Countries." *Nature Medicine* 25(8): 1198–204.

Bendz, Anna. 2017. "Empowering the People: Public Responses to Welfare Policy Change." *Social Policy & Administration* 51(1): 1–19.

Beramendi, Pablo. 2007. "Inequality and the Territorial Fragmentation of Solidarity." *International Organization* 61(4): 783–820.

2012. *The Political Geography of Inequality.* Cambridge University Press.

Besley, Timothy, John Hall, and Ian Preston. 1999. "The Demand for Private Health Insurance: Do Waiting Lists Matter?" *Journal of Public Economics* 72 (2): 155–81.

Bhutta, Neil et al. 2020. "Changes in US Family Finances from 2016 to 2019: Evidence from the Survey of Consumer Finances." *Federal Reserve Bulletin* 106(5): 1–42.

Blackwell, Timothy and Sebastian Kohl. 2018. "The Origins of National Housing Finance Systems: A Comparative Investigation into Historical Variations in Mortgage Finance Regimes." *Review of International Political Economy* 25 (1): 49–74.

2019. "Historicizing Housing Typologies: Beyond Welfare State Regimes and Varieties of Residential Capitalism." *Housing Studies* 34(2): 298–318.

Boadway, Robin and Michael Keen. 2000. "Redistribution." In *Handbook of Income Distribution,* eds. Anthony Atkinson and François Bourguignon. Elsevier, 679–789.

Bonoli, Giuliano and Bruno Palier. 2007. "When Past Reforms Open New Opportunities: Comparing Old-Age Insurance Reforms in Bismarckian Welfare Systems." *Social Policy & Administration* 41(6): 555–73.

Brackenridge, R. D. C. and Arthur E. Brown. 2006. "A Historical Survey of the Development of Life Assurance." In *Brackenridge's Medical Selection of Life Risks,* eds. R. D. C. Brackenridge, Richard S. Croxson, and Ross MacKenzie. Springer, 3–19.

Bradley, David et al. 2003. "Distribution and Redistribution in Postindustrial Democracies." *World Politics* 55(2): 193–228.

Brady, David, Regina S. Baker, and Ryan Finnigan. 2013. "When Unionization Disappears: State-Level Unionization and Working Poverty in the United States." *American Sociological Review* 78(5): 872–96.

Busemeyer, Marius R. 2012. "Inequality and the Political Economy of Education: An Analysis of Individual Preferences in OECD Countries." *Journal of European Social Policy* 22(3): 219–40.

Busemeyer, Marius R. and Torben Iversen. 2014. "The Politics of Opting out: Explaining Educational Financing and Popular Support for Public Spending." *Socio-Economic Review* 12(2): 299–328.

2020. "The Welfare State with Private Alternatives: The Transformation of Popular Support for Social Insurance." *The Journal of Politics* 82(2): 671–86.

Calonico, Sebastian, Matias D. Cattaneo, Max H. Farrell, and Rocio Titiunik. 2017. "Rdrobust: Software for Regression-Discontinuity Designs." *The Stata Journal* 17(2): 372–404.

Campbell, David, Alan Carruth, Andrew Dickerson, and Francis Green. 2007. "Job Insecurity and Wages." *The Economic Journal* 117(518): 544–66.

Catlin, Aaron C. and Cathy A. Cowan. 2015. "History of Health Spending in the United States, 1960-2013." *Rockville, MD: Centers for Medicare & Medicaid Services.*

Clasen, Jochen and Elke Viebrock. 2008. "Voluntary Unemployment Insurance and Trade Union Membership: Investigating the Connections in Denmark and Sweden." *Journal of Social Policy* 37(3): 433–51.

Cohen, Lizabeth. 1999. *Making a New Deal: Industrial Workers in Chicago, 1919–1939.* Cambridge University Press.

Coletti, Margaret H. and Howard L. Bleich. 2001. "Medical Subject Headings Used to Search the Biomedical Literature." *Journal of the American Medical Informatics Association: JAMIA* 8(4): 317–23.

Conde-Ruiz, J. Ignacio and Paola Profeta. 2007. "The Redistributive Design of Social Security Systems." *The Economic Journal* 117(520): 686–712.

Corman, Juliane and David Levin. 2016. "Support for Government Provision of Health Care and the Patient Protection and Affordable Care Act." *Public Opinion Quarterly* 80(1): 114–79.

Cortez, Elif Kiesow. 2020. *Data Protection Around the World: Privacy Laws in Action.* Springer Nature.

Costa-Font, Joan and Valentina Zigante. 2016. "The Choice Agenda in European Health Systems: The Role of Middle-Class Demands." *Public Money & Management* 36(6): 409–16.

Cousins, Mel. 2005. *European Welfare States: Comparative Perspectives.* SAGE.

Cusack, Thomas, Torben Iversen, and Philipp Rehm. 2006. "Risks at Work: The Demand and Supply Sides of Government Redistribution." *Oxford Review Economic Policy* 22(3): 365–89.

Davidsson, Johan Bo. 2013. *The Limits to Solidarity. Unions and the Rise of Private Unemployment Insurance in Sweden.* Brussels: Presentation for ProWelfare Conference. www.ose.be/files/conferenceProwelfare051213/Davidsson_2013_slides_Prowelfare_05122013.pdf (June 17, 2016).

Davidsson, Johan Bo and Paul Marx. 2013. "Losing the Issue, Losing the Vote: Issue Competition and the Reform of Unemployment Insurance in Germany and Sweden." *Political Studies* 61(3): 505–22.

DeFusco, Anthony A. and Andrew Paciorek. 2017. "The Interest Rate Elasticity of Mortgage Demand: Evidence from Bunching at the Conforming Loan Limit." *American Economic Journal: Economic Policy* 9(1): 210–40.

Dey, Nilanjan, Amira S. Ashour, Simon James Fong, and Chintan Bhatt. 2019. *Wearable and Implantable Medical Devices: Applications and Challenges.* Academic Press.

Dickson, Eric S. and Kenneth A. Shepsle. 2001. "Working and Shirking: Equilibrium in Public-Goods Games with Overlapping Generations of Players." *The Journal of Law, Economics, and Organization* 17(2): 285–318.

Dimick, Matthew, David Rueda, and Daniel Stegmueller. 2016. "The Altruistic Rich? Inequality and Other-Regarding Preferences for Redistribution." *Quarterly Journal of Political Science* 11(4): 385–439.

Dominitz, Jeff and Charles F. Manski. 1997a. "Perceptions of Economic Insecurity: Evidence from the Survey of Economic Expectations." *Public Opinion Quarterly* 61(2): 261–87.

1997b. "Using Expectations Data to Study Subjective Income Expectations." *Journal of the American Statistical Association* 92(439): 855–67.

Dow, J. B. 1971. "Early Actuarial Work in Eighteenth-Century Scotland." *Transactions of the Faculty of Actuaries* 33(240): 193–229.

Downs, Anthony. 1957. *An Economic Theory of Democracy.* Harper.

Dunlop, A. Ian. 1992. *The Scottish Ministers' Widows' Fund, 1743-1993.* Saint Andrew Press.

Duverger, Maurice. 1954. *Political Parties, Their Organization and Activity in the Modern State.* John Wiley & Sons.

Ebbinghaus, Bernhard, Claudia Göbel, and Sebastian Koos. 2011. "Social Capital, 'Ghent' and Workplace Contexts Matter: Comparing Union Membership in Europe." *European Journal of Industrial Relations* 17(2): 107–24.

Eichengreen, Barry. 2008. "Origins and Responses to the Current Crisis." *CESifo Forum* 9(4): 6–11.

Elkjær, Mads Andreas and Torben Iversen. 2020. "The Political Representation of Economic Interests: Subversion of Democracy or Middle-Class Supremacy?" *World Politics* 72(2): 254–90.

Esping-Andersen, Gosta. 1990. *The Three Worlds of Welfare Capitalism.* Princeton University Press.

Estevez-Abé, Margarita, Torben Iversen, and David Soskice. 2001. "Social Protection and the Formation of Skills: A Reinterpretation of the Welfare State." In *Varieties of Capitalism: The Institutional Foundations of Comparative Advantage*, eds. Peter A. Hall and David Soskice. Oxford University Press, 145–83.

European Social Survey. 2003. "European Social Survey (ESS), Round 1-2002. Data File Edition 6.6." *NSD - Norwegian Centre for Research Data, Norway – Data Archive and distributor of ESS data for ESS ERIC.*

Fabbri, Daniele and Chiara Monfardini. 2016. "Opt Out or Top Up? Voluntary Health Care Insurance and the Public vs. Private Substitution." *Oxford Bulletin of Economics and Statistics* 78(1): 75–93.

Fernandez, Rodrigo and Manuel B. Aalbers. 2016. "Financialization and Housing: Between Globalization and Varieties of Capitalism." *Competition & Change* 20(2): 71–88.

Foote, Christopher, Lara Loewenstein, and Paul Willen. 2019. *Technological Innovation in Mortgage Underwriting and the Growth in Credit: 1985–2015.* Federal Reserve Bank of Boston. Federal Reserve Bank of Boston Research Department Working Papers. www.bostonfed.org/publications/research-depart

ment-working-paper/2019/technological-innovation-in-mortgage-underwrit
ing-and-the-growth-in-credit-1985-2015.aspx.

Foubister, Thomas, Sarah Thomson, Elias Mossialos, and Alistair McGuire.
2006. *Private Medical Insurance in the United Kingdom*. World Health
Organization on behalf of the European Observatory on Health Systems
and Policies. https://apps.who.int/iris/bitstream/handle/10665/326537/9289
022884-eng.pdf.

Friedman, Rachel Z. 2020. *Probable Justice: Risk, Insurance, and the Welfare
State*. University of Chicago Press.

Garritzmann, Julian L., Marius R. Busemeyer, and Erik Neimanns. 2018. "Public
Demand for Social Investment: New Supporting Coalitions for Welfare State
Reform in Western Europe?" *Journal of European Public Policy* 25(6): 844–
61.

Gelman, Andrew and Guido Imbens. 2019. "Why High-Order Polynomials
Should Not Be Used in Regression Discontinuity Designs." *Journal of
Business & Economic Statistics* 37(3): 447–56.

GESIS-Leibniz-Institut Für Sozialwissenschaften. 2020. "German General Social
Survey (ALLBUS) - Cumulation 1980-2018." https://dbk.gesis.org/dbksearch/
sdesc2.asp?no=5276&db=e&doi=10.4232/1.13483 (May 13, 2021).

Gingrich, Jane. 2011. *Making Markets in the Welfare State: The Politics of
Varying Market Reforms*. Cambridge University Press.

Gingrich, Jane and Silja Häusermann. 2015. "The Decline of the Working-Class
Vote, the Reconfiguration of the Welfare Support Coalition and
Consequences for the Welfare State." *Journal of European Social Policy* 25
(1): 50–75.

Glenn, Brian J. 2001. "Understanding Mutual Benefit Societies, 1860-1960."
Journal of Health Politics, Policy and Law 26(3): 638–51.

Goering, John and Ron Wienk. 2018. *Mortgage Lending, Racial Discrimination
and Federal Policy*. Routledge.

Goldin, Claudia and Lawrence F. Katz. 2009. *The Race between Education and
Technology*. Harvard University Press.

Goodman, Laurie S., Brian Landy, Roger Ashworth, and Lidan Yang. 2014.
"A Look at Freddie Mac's Loan-Level Credit Performance Data." *The
Journal of Structured Finance* 19(4): 52–61.

Gordon, Joshua C. 2019. "The Perils of Vanguardism." *Socio-Economic Review*
17(4): 947–68.

Gordon, Robert J. 2016. *The Rise and Fall of American Growth. The U.S.
Standard of Living Since the Civil War*. Princeton University Press.

Gottlieb, Daniel. 2007. "Asymmetric Information in Late 19th Century
Cooperative Insurance Societies." *Explorations in Economic History* 44(2):
270–92.

Green, Francis. 2011. "Unpacking the Misery Multiplier: How Employability
Modifies the Impacts of Unemployment and Job Insecurity on Life
Satisfaction and Mental Health." *Journal of Health Economics* 30(2): 265–
76.

Green, Francis, Andrew Dickerson, Alan Carruth, and David Campbell. 2001. *An
Analysis of Subjective Views of Job Insecurity*. School of Economics,

University of Kent. Studies in Economics. https://econpapers.repec.org/paper/ukcukcedp/0108.htm (May 17, 2021).

Grogan, Colleen M. and Sunggeun (Ethan) Park. 2017. "The Politics of Medicaid: Most Americans Are Connected to the Program, Support Its Expansion, and Do Not View It as Stigmatizing." *The Milbank Quarterly* 95(4): 749–82.

Gross, David B. and Nicholas S. Souleles. 2002. "Do Liquidity Constraints and Interest Rates Matter for Consumer Behavior? Evidence from Credit Card Data." *The Quarterly Journal of Economics* 117(1): 149–85.

Grossman, Gene and Elhanan Helpman. 1998. "Intergenerational Redistribution with Short-lived Governments." *The Economic Journal* 108(450): 1299–329.

Hacker, Jacob S. 2002. *The Divided Welfare State: The Battle over Public and Private Social Benefits in the United States*. Cambridge University Press.

2004. "Privatizing Risk without Privatizing the Welfare State: The Hidden Politics of Social Policy Retrenchment in the United States." *American Political Science Review* 98(2): 243–60.

Hacker, Jacob S., Paul Pierson, and Kathleen Thelen. 2015. "Drift and Conversion: Hidden Faces of Institutional Change." In *Advances in Comparative-Historical Analysis*, eds. James Mahoney and Kathleen Thelen. Cambridge University Press, 180–208.

Hacker, Jacob S. and Philipp Rehm. 2022. "Reducing Risk as well as Inequality: Assessing the Welfare State's Insurance Effects." *British Journal of Political Science*. 52(1): 456–66.

Hacker, Jacob S., Philipp Rehm, and Mark Schlesinger. 2013. "The Insecure American: Economic Experiences and Policy Attitudes amid the Great Recession." *Perspectives on Politics* 11(1): 23–49.

Hall, Peter and David Soskice. 2001. *Varieties of Capitalism: The Institutional Foundations of Comparative Advantage*. Oxford University Press.

Hall, Robert E. 1988. "Intertemporal Substitution in Consumption." *Journal of Political Economy* 96(2): 339–57.

Harbord, Kristi. 2019. "Genetic Data Privacy Solutions in the GDPR." *Texas A&M Law Review* 7(1): 269–97.

Hariri, Jacob Gerner, Amalie Sofie Jensen, and David Dreyer Lassen. 2020. "Middle Class Without a Net: Savings, Financial Fragility, and Preferences Over Social Insurance." *Comparative Political Studies* 53(6): 892–922.

Hariri, Jacob Gerner, Amalie Sofie Jensen, David Dreyer Lassen, and Andreas Wiedemann. 2017. *Household Balance Sheets and Social Policy Preferences: New Survey Evidence*. Social Science Research Network. SSRN Scholarly Paper. https://papers.ssrn.com/abstract=3048318 (February 18, 2019).

Harsanyi, John. 1953. "Cardinal Utility in Welfare Economics and in the Theory of Risk- Taking." *Journal of Political Economy* 61 (5): 434–35.

Häusermann, Silja, Thomas Kurer, and Hanna Schwander. 2015. "High-Skilled Outsiders? Labor Market Vulnerability, Education and Welfare State Preferences." *Socio-Economic Review* 13(2): 235–58.

Hausman, Catherine and David S. Rapson. 2018. "Regression Discontinuity in Time: Considerations for Empirical Applications." *Annual Review of Resource Economics* 10(1): 533–52.

Hellwig, Timothy. 2014. "Balancing Demands: The World Economy and the Composition of Policy Preferences." *The Journal of Politics* 76(1): 1–14.

Hemerijck, Anton. 2018. "Social Investment as a Policy Paradigm." *Journal of European Public Policy* 25(6): 810–27.

Hendren, Nathaniel. 2013. "Private Information and Insurance Rejections." *Econometrica* 81(5): 1713–62.

2017. "Knowledge of Future Job Loss and Implications for Unemployment Insurance." *American Economic Review* 107(7): 1778–823.

Hicks, Timothy. 2013. "Partisan Strategy and Path Dependence: The Post-War Emergence of Health Systems in the UK and Sweden." *Comparative Politics* 45(2): 207–26.

2015. "Inequality, Marketisation and the Left: Schools Policy in England and Sweden." *European Journal of Political Research* 54(2): 326–42.

2016. "Acting Right? Privatization, Encompassing Interests, and the Left." *Political Science Research and Methods* 4(2): 427–48.

Hinrichs, Karl. 2010. "A Social Insurance State Withers Away. Welfare State Reforms in Germany – Or: Attempts to Turn Around in a Cul-de-Sac." In *A Long Goodbye to Bismarck? The Politics of Welfare Reform in Continental Europe*, ed. Bruno Palier. Amsterdam University Press, 45–72.

Hoeller, Peter, Isabelle Joumard, and Isabell Koske. 2013. *Income Inequality in OECD Countries: What Are the Drivers and Policy Options?* World Scientific.

Høgedahl, Laust and Kristian Kongshøj. 2017. "New Trajectories of Unionization in the Nordic Ghent Countries: Changing Labour Market and Welfare Institutions." *European Journal of Industrial Relations* 23(4): 365–80.

Holmlund, Bertil and Per Lundborg. 1999. "Wage Bargaining, Union Membership, and the Organization of Unemployment Insurance." *Labour Economics* 6(3): 397–415.

Hørkilde, Mads. 2020. "Eksperter er bekymrede over ny sundhedsforsikring til ældre." *Politiken*. https://politiken.dk/indland/art7997109/Eksperter-er-bekymrede-over-ny-sundhedsforsikring-til-%C3%A6ldre (April 30, 2021).

Howard, Christopher. 1997. *The Hidden Welfare State: Tax Expenditures and Social Policy in the United States*. Princeton University Press.

Huber, Evelyne and John D. Stephens. 2001. "Welfare State and Production Regimes in the Era of Retrenchment." In *The New Politics of the Welfare State*, ed. Paul Pierson. Oxford University Press, 107–45.

Huettner, Frank and Marco Sunder. 2012. "Axiomatic Arguments for Decomposing Goodness of Fit According to Shapley and Owen Values." *Electronic Journal of Statistics* 6: 1239–50.

Inspektionen för arbetslöshetsförsäkringen (IAF). 2016. "Arbetslöshetskassornas Medlemsutveckling." 29. www.iaf.se/granskning/rapporter/2016/arbetsloshetskassornas-medlemsutveckling/.

Iversen, Torben and Thomas Cusack. 2000. "The Causes of Welfare State Expansion. Deindustrialization or Globalization?" *World Politics* 52(3): 313–49.

Iversen, Torben and Philipp Rehm. 2022. "Information and Financialization: Credit Markets as a New Source of Inequality." *Comparative Political Studies.*

Iversen, Torben and David Soskice. 2015a. "Democratic Limits to Redistribution: Inclusionary versus Exclusionary Coalitions in the Knowledge Economy." *World Politics* 67(2): 185–225.

2015b. "Information, Inequality, and Mass Polarization Ideology in Advanced Democracies." *Comparative Political Studies* 48(13): 1781–813.

2019. *Democracy and Prosperity. Reinventing Capitalism through a Turbulent Century.* Princeton University Press.

Iversen, Torben, and John D. Stephens. 2008. "Partisan Politics, the Welfare State, and Three Worlds of Human Capital Formation." *Comparative Political Studies* 41(4–5): 600–37.

Iversen, Torben, and Anne Wren. 1998. "Equality, Employment, and Budgetary Restraint. The Trilemma of the Service Economy." *World Politics* 50(4): 507–46.

Jackson, Matthew O. 2010. *Social and Economic Networks.* Princeton University Press.

Kaiser, Tobias. 2018. "Schonvermögen: Darf Ein Hartz-IV-Empfänger Reich Sein?" *Die Welt.* www.welt.de/wirtschaft/article184579080/Schonvermoeg en-Darf-ein-Hartz-IV-Empfaenger-reich-sein.html (August 28, 2021).

Kalyvas, Stathis N. and Kees van Kersbergen. 2010. "Christian Democracy." *Annual Review of Political Science* 13(1): 183–209.

Kassenboehmer, Sonja C. and Sonja G. Schatz. 2017. "Re-Employment Expectations and Realisations: Prediction Errors and Behavioural Responses." *Labour Economics* 44: 161–76.

Kaufman, Jason Andrew. 2002. *For the Common Good? American Civic Life and the Golden Age of Fraternity.* Oxford University Press.

King, Desmond and David Rueda. 2008. "Cheap Labor: The New Politics of 'Bread and Roses' in Industrial Democracies." *Perspectives on Politics* 6(2): 279–97.

Kjellberg, Anders. 2009. "The Swedish Ghent System and Trade Unions under Pressure." *Transfer: European Review of Labour and Research* 15(3–4): 481–504.

Kjellberg, Anders and Christian Lyhne Ibsen. 2016. "Attacks on Union Organizing: Reversible and Irreversible Changes to the Ghent-Systems in Sweden and Denmark." In *Den Danske Model Set Udefra - Komparative Perspektiver På Dansk Arbejdsmarkedsregulering : Et Festskrif t Til Professor Emeritus Jesper Due Og Og Professor Emeritus Jørgen Steen Madsen,* eds. T. P. Larsen and A Ilsøe. Jurist-og Økonomforbundets Forlag, 279–302.

Korpi, Walter. 1983. *The Democratic Class Struggle.* Routledge.

Korpi, Walter and Joakim Palme. 1998. "The Paradox of Redistribution and Strategies of Equality: Welfare State Institutions, Inequality, and Poverty in the Western Countries." *American Sociological Review* 63 (5): 661–87.

Kotlikoff, Laurence J., Torsten Persson, and Lars E. O. Svensson. 1988. "Social Contracts as Assets: A Possible Solution to the Time-Consistency Problem." *The American Economic Review* 78(4): 662–77.

Kullberg, Linn, Paula Blomqvist, and Ulrika Winblad. 2019. "Health Insurance for the Healthy? Voluntary Health Insurance in Sweden." *Health Policy* 123 (8): 737–46.

Ladd, Helen F. 1998. "Evidence on Discrimination in Mortgage Lending." *Journal of Economic Perspectives* 12(2): 41–62.

Lane, Jan-Erik. 2000. *New Public Management: An Introduction.* Taylor & Francis.

Lane, Julia. 2020. *Democratizing Our Data: A Manifesto.* MIT Press.

Lee, Nicol Turner, Paul Resnick, and Genie Barton. 2019. *Algorithmic Bias Detection and Mitigation: Best Practices and Policies to Reduce Consumer Harms.* Brookings Institute. www.brookings.edu/research/algorithmic-bias-det ection-and-mitigation-best-practices-and-policies-to-reduce-consumer-harms/.

Leeuwen, Marco H. D. Van. 2016. *Mutual Insurance 1550-2015: From Guild Welfare and Friendly Societies to Contemporary Micro-Insurers.* Springer.

LeGrand, Julian. 2009. *The Other Invisible Hand: Delivering Public Services through Choice and Competition.* Princeton University Press.

Li, Guoying. 1985. "Robust Regression." In *Exploring Data Tables, Trends, and Shapes,* eds. David Caster Hoaglin, Frederick Mosteller, and John Wilder Tukey. Wiley Online Library, 281–340.

Liebig, Stefan et al. 2019. "Socio-Economic Panel (SOEP), Data from 1984-2017 Sozio-Oekonomisches Panel (SOEP), Daten Der Jahre 1984-2017." www .diw.de/doi/soep.v34 (November 10, 2020).

Lindbeck, Assar and Dennis J. Snower. 1989. *The Insider-Outsider Theory of Employment and Unemployment.* MIT Press.

Lindvall, Johannes and David Rueda. 2014. "The Insider-Outsider Dilemma." *British Journal of Political Science* 44(2): 460–75.

Lipset, Seymour Martin and Stein Rokkan. 1967. *Party Systems and Voter Alignments: Cross-National Perspectives.* Free Press.

Macdonald, David. 2019. "Labor Unions and Support for Redistribution in an Era of Inequality." *Social Science Quarterly* 100(4): 1197–1214.

Mahoney, James and Kathleen Thelen. 2010. "A Theory of Gradual Institutional Change." In *Explaining Institutional Change: Ambiguity, Agency, and Power,* eds. James Mahoney and Kathleen Thelen. Cambridge University Press, 1–37.

Mares, Isabela. 2003. *The Politics of Social Risk. Business and Welfare State Development.* Cambridge University Press.

Margalit, Yotam. 2013. "Explaining Social Policy Preferences: Evidence from the Great Recession." *American Political Science Review* 107(1): 80–103.

McFadden, Daniel. 1977. "Quantitative Methods for Analyzing Travel Behavior of Individuals: Some Recent Developments." In *Behavioural Travel Modelling,* eds. David A. Hensher and Peter R. Stopher. Croom Helm, 279–218.

McPherson, Miller, Lynn Smith-Lovin, and James M Cook. 2001. "Birds of a Feather: Homophily in Social Networks." *Annual Review of Sociology* 27 (1): 415–44.

Mettler, Suzanne. 2011. *The Submerged State: How Invisible Government Policies Undermine American Democracy*. University of Chicago Press.

Mettler, Suzanne and Joe Soss. 2004. "The Consequences of Public Policy for Democratic Citizenship: Bridging Policy Studies and Mass Politics." *Perspectives on Politics* 2(1): 55–73.

Mitchell, Colin et al. 2020. *The GDPR and Genomic Data – the Impact of the GDPR and DPA 2018 on Genomic Healthcare and Research*. PHG Foundation.

Morgan, Kimberly J. and Andrea Louise Campbell. 2011. *The Delegated Welfare State: Medicare, Markets, and the Governance of Social Policy*. Oxford University Press.

Morgan, Kimberly J. and Alexander Reisenbichler. 2021. "Riding the Tiger: Managing Risk in U.S. Housing Finance and Health Insurance Welfare Markets." *Socio-Economic Review*.

Mosimann, Nadja and Jonas Pontusson. 2017. "Solidaristic Unionism and Support for Redistribution in Contemporary Europe." *World Politics* 69 (3): 448–92.

Mossialos, Elias and Sarah Thomson. 2004. *Voluntary Health Insurance in the European Union*. WHO Regional Office for Europe.

Murray, Charles. 2013. *Coming Apart: The State of White America, 1960-2010*. Crown Forum.

Myles, John and Jill Quadagno. 2002. "Political Theories of the Welfare State." *Social Service Review* 76(1): 34–57.

National Institute for Health Care Management. 2012. "The Concentration of Health Care Spending." *NIHCM Foundation Data Brief* July: 1–12.

New York State Department of Financial Services. 2019. "Use of External Consumer Data and Information Sources in Underwriting for Life Insurance." *Insurance Circular Letter* 1. www.dfs.ny.gov/industry_gui dance/circular_letters/cl2019_01 (April 29, 2021).

Nørgaard, Asbjørn Sonne and Nathalie Nyholm Olsen. 2020. *Ulige Adgang Til Lønforsikringer. En Analyse Af Forskelle i Priser Og Vilkår På Tværs Af Faggrupper*. Cevea.

OECD. 2015a. *Back to Work: Sweden. Improving the Re-Employment Prospects of Displaced Workers*. OECD.

2015b. *OECD Insurance Statistics 2014*. OECD.

2017. "Value Added by Activity." www.oecd-ilibrary.org/economics/value-added-by-activity/indicator/english_a8b2bd2b-en (November 17, 2020).

2018a. *A Broken Social Elevator? How to Promote Social Mobility*. OECD. www.oecd-ilibrary.org/social-issues-migration-health/broken-elevator-how-to-promote-social-mobility_9789264301085-en (May 26, 2021).

2018b. "Household Debt." www.oecd-ilibrary.org/economics/household-debt /indicator/english_f03b6469-en (November 16, 2020).

2018c. *OECD Pensions Outlook 2018*. OECD. www.oecd.org/finance/oecd-pensions-outlook-23137649.htm (December 17, 2019).

2019. *Health at a Glance 2019: OECD Indicators.* OECD. www.oecd-ilibrary.org/social-issues-migration-health/health-at-a-glance-2019_4dd50 c09-en (April 30, 2021).

O'Grady, Tom. 2019. "How Do Economic Circumstances Determine Preferences? Evidence from Long-Run Panel Data." *British Journal of Political Science* 49(4): 1381–406.

Olson, Mancur. 1993. "Dictatorship, Democracy, and Development." *American Political Science Review* 87(3): 567–76.

Pagana, Kathleen Deska and Timothy James Pagana. 1992. *Mosby's Diagnostic and Laboratory Test Reference.* 1st ed. Mosby.

Pagana, Kathleen Deska, Timothy J. Pagana, and Theresa Noel Pagana. 2014. *Mosby's Diagnostic and Laboratory Test Reference.* 12th ed. Elsevier.

Palier, Bruno. 2010. *A Long Goodbye to Bismarck? The Politics of Welfare Reforms in Continental Europe.* Amsterdam University Press.

Panczak, Radoslaw et al. 2013. "High Life in the Sky? Mortality by Floor of Residence in Switzerland." *European Journal of Epidemiology* 28(6): 453–62.

Pei, Zhuan, David S. Lee, David Card, and Andrea Weber. 2021. "Local Polynomial Order in Regression Discontinuity Designs." *Journal of Business & Economic Statistics.*

Personalized Medicine Coalition. 2016. "Personalized Medicine by the Numbers." www.personalizedmedicinecoalition.org/Userfiles/PMC-Corpor ate/file/pmc_personalized_medicine_by_the_numbers.pdf.

Pierson, Paul. 2000. "Increasing Returns, Path Dependence, and the Study of Politics." *American Political Science Review* 94(2): 251–67.

Platteau, Jean-Philippe. 1991. *Traditional Systems of Social Security and Hunger Insurance: Past Achievements and Modern Challenges.* Oxford University Press.

Prewitt, Matt. 2021. "A View of the Future of Our Data." *Noema Magazine.* www.noemamag.com/a-view-of-the-future-of-our-data (May 20, 2021).

Przeworski, Adam. 2003. *States and Markets: A Primer in Political Economy.* Cambridge University Press.

Putnam, Robert D. 1993. *Making Democracy Work.* Princeton University Press.
2000. *Bowling Alone: The Collapse and Revival of American Community.* Simon and Schuster.

Quadagno, Jill. 1987. "Theories of the Welfare State." *Annual Review of Sociology* 13(1): 109–28.

Rangel, Antonio. 2003. "Forward and Backward Intergenerational Goods: Why Is Social Security Good for the Environment?" *American Economic Review* 93(3): 813–34.

Rawls, John. 1971. *A Theory of Justice.* Cambridge University Press.

Rehm, Philipp. 2009. "Risks and Redistribution: An Individual-Level Analysis." *Comparative Political Studies* 42(7): 855–81.
2016. *Risk Inequality and Welfare States. Social Policy Preferences, Development, and Dynamics.* Cambridge University Press.
2020. "The Future of Welfare State Politics." *Political Science Research and Methods* 8(2): 386–90.

Rehm, Philipp, Jacob S. Hacker, and Mark Schlesinger. 2012. "Insecure Alliances: Risk, Inequality, and Support for the Welfare State." *American Political Science Review* 106(2): 386–406.

Rosanvallon, Pierre. 2000. *The New Social Question.* Princeton University Press.

Rothgang, Heinz, Mirella Cacace, Lorraine Frisina, and Achim Schmid. 2008. "The Changing Public-Private Mix in OECD Health-Care Systems." In *Welfare State Transformations*, ed. Martin Seeleib-Kaiser. Palgrave Macmillan, 132–46.

Rothschild, Michael and Joseph Stiglitz. 1976. "Equilibrium in Competitive Insurance Markets: An Essay on the Economics of Imperfect Information." *The Quarterly Journal of Economics* 90(4): 629–49.

Rothstein, Bo. 1992. "Labor-Market Institutions and Working-Class Strength." In *Structuring Politics: Historical Institutionalism in Comparative Analysis*, eds. Sven Steinmo, Kathleen Thelen, and Frank Longstreth. Cambridge University Press, 33–56.

Rothstein, Bo and Dietlind Stolle. 2003. "Social Capital, Impartiality and the Welfare State: An Institutional Approach." In *Generating Social Capital. Civil Society and Institutions in Comparative Perspective*, eds. Bo Rothstein and Dietlind Stolle. Palgrave Macmillan, 191–209.

Rueda, David. 2005. "Insider–Outsider Politics in Industrialized Democracies: The Challenge to Social Democratic Parties." *American Political Science Review* 99(1): 61–74.

2006. "Social Democracy and Active Labour-Market Policies: Insiders, Outsiders and the Politics of Employment Protection." *British Journal of Political Science* 36(3): 385–406.

2007. *Social Democracy Inside Out: Partisanship and Labor Market Policy in Advanced Industrialized Democracies.* Oxford University Press.

Rueda, David and Daniel Stegmueller. 2016. "The Externalities of Inequality: Fear of Crime and Preferences for Redistribution in Western Europe." *American Journal of Political Science* 60(2): 472–89.

2019. *Who Wants What? Redistribution Preferences in Comparative Perspective.* Cambridge University Press.

Sahay, Ratna et al. 2015. "Rethinking Financial Deepening: Stability and Growth in Emerging Markets." *International Monetary Fund.* www.imf.org/en/Publications/Staff-Discussion-Notes/Issues/2016/12/31/Rethinking-Financial-Deepening-Stability-and-Growth-in-Emerging-Markets-42868.

Schattschneider, Elmer Eric. 1942. *Party Government.* Farrar and Rinehart.

Scheve, Kenneth and Matthew J. Slaughter. 2004. "Economic Insecurity and the Globalization of Production." *American Journal of Political Science* 48(4): 662–74.

Scheve, Kenneth and David Stasavage. 2006a. "Religion and Preferences for Social Insurance." *Quarterly Journal of Political Science* 1(3): 255–86.

2006b. "The Political Economy of Religion and Social Insurance in the United States, 1910–1939." *Studies in American Political Development* 20(2): 132–59.

2010. "The Conscription of Wealth: Mass Warfare and the Demand for Progressive Taxation." *International Organization* 64(4): 529–61.

2012. "Democracy, War, and Wealth: Lessons from Two Centuries of Inheritance Taxation." *American Political Science Review* 106(1): 81–102.

Schwartz, Herman and Leonard Seabrooke. 2008. "Varieties of Residential Capitalism in the International Political Economy: Old Welfare States and the New Politics of Housing." *Comparative European Politics* 6(3): 237–61.

Shojania, Kaveh, Elizabeth C. Burton, Kathryn M. McDonald, and Lee Goldman. 2003. "Changes in Rates of Autopsy-Detected Diagnostic Errors over Time: A Systematic Review." *JAMA* 289(21): 2849–56.

Siddeley, Leslie. 1992. "The Rise and Fall of Fraternal Insurance Organizations." *Humane Studies Review* 7(2): 13–16.

Singer, Natasha. 2017. "How Big Tech Is Going After Your Health Care." *The New York Times*. www.nytimes.com/2017/12/26/technology/big-tech-health-care.html (December 27, 2017).

Song, Jae et al. 2019. "Firming Up Inequality." *The Quarterly Journal of Economics* 134(1): 1–50.

Soskice, David, Robert H. Bates, and David Epstein. 1992. "Ambition and Constraint: The Stabilizing Role of Institutions." *Journal of Law, Economics and Organization* 8(3): 547–60.

Stegmueller, Daniel. 2013. "Religion and Redistributive Voting in Western Europe." *The Journal of Politics* 75(4): 1064–76.

Stegmueller, Daniel, Peer Scheepers, Sigrid Roßteutscher, and Eelke de Jong. 2012. "Support for Redistribution in Western Europe: Assessing the Role of Religion." *European Sociological Review* 28(4): 482–97.

Stephens, John D. 1979. *The Transition from Capitalism to Socialism*. Macmillan.

Stephens Jr., Melvin. 2004. "Job Loss Expectations, Realizations, and Household Consumption Behavior." *Review of Economics and Statistics* 86(1): 253–69.

Stiglitz, Joseph E. 1982. "Self-Selection and Pareto Efficient Taxation." *Journal of Public Economics* 17(2): 213–40.

Svirydzenka, Katsiaryna. 2016. *Introducing a New Broad-Based Index of Financial Development*. International Monetary Fund.

de Swaan, Abram. 1986. "Workers' and Clients' Mutualism Compared: Perspectives from the Past in the Development of the Welfare State." *Government and Opposition* 21(1): 36–55.

1988. *In Care of the State: Health Care, Education and Welfare in Europe and the USA in the Modern Era*. Oxford University Press.

Sweeney, Latanya. 2013. "Discrimination in Online Ad Delivery." *Communications of the ACM* 56(5): 44–54.

Swenson, Peter A. 2002. *Capitalists against Markets: The Making of Labor Markets and Welfare States in the United States and Sweden*. Oxford University Press.

2018. "Misrepresented Interests: Business, Medicare, and the Making of the American Health Care State." *Studies in American Political Development* 32 (1): 1–23.

Taylor-Gooby, Peter. 1999. "Markets and Motives Trust and Egoism in Welfare Markets." *Journal of Social Policy* 28(1): 97–114.

Thane, Pat. 2012. "The Ben Pimlott Memorial Lecture 2011 The 'Big Society' and the 'Big State': Creative Tension or Crowding Out?" *Twentieth Century British History* 23(3): 408–29.

Thompson, Helen. 2009. "The Political Origins of the Financial Crisis: The Domestic and International Politics of Fannie Mae and Freddie Mac." *The Political Quarterly* 80(1): 17–24.

Thurston, Chloe N. 2018. *At the Boundaries of Homeownership: Credit, Discrimination, and the American State*. Cambridge University Press.

Van Doorslaer, Eddy. 1999. "The Redistributive Effect of Health Care Finance in Twelve OECD Countries." *Journal of Health Economics* 18(3): 291–313.

Van Doorslaer, Eddy and Cristina Masseria. 2004. "Towards High-Performing Health Systems." In *Income-Related Inequality in the Use of Medical Care in 21 OECD Countries*, ed. OECD. OECD, 109–66.

Van Kersbergen, Kees. 1995. *Social Capitalism: A Study of Christian Democracy and the Welfare State*. Routledge.

Van Kersbergen, Kees and Uwe Becker. 2002. "Comparative Politics and the Welfare State." In *Comparative Democratic Politics. A Guide to Contemporary Theory and Research*, ed. Hans Keman. SAGE, 185–212.

Van Kersbergen, Kees and Philip Manow. 2008. "The Welfare State." In *Comparative Politics*, ed. Danièle Caramani. Oxford University Press, 445–72.

VantageScore. 2020. "The Dynamic Relationship Between a Credit Score and Risk." https://vantagescore.com/pdfs/Credit-Scores-and-Risk-Relationship-WP-FINAL_2020-10-29-021228.pdf.

Wagstaff, Adam and Eddy van Doorslaer. 2000. "Equity in Health Care Finance and Delivery." In *Handbook of Health Economics*, eds. Anthony J. Culyer and Joseph P. Newhouse. Elsevier, 1803–62.

Wallerstein, Michael and Bruce Western. 2000. "Unions in Decline? What Has Changed and Why." *Annual Review of Political Science* 3(1): 355–77.

Walter, Stefanie. 2010. "Globalization and the Welfare State: Testing the Microfoundations of the Compensation Hypothesis." *International Studies Quarterly* 54(2): 403–26.

Wibbels, Erik and John S. Ahlquist. 2011. "Development, Trade, and Social Insurance." *International Studies Quarterly* 55(1): 125–49.

Wiedemann, Andreas. 2021. *Indebted Societies: Credit and Welfare in Rich Democracies*. Cambridge University Press.

Wood, James D. G. 2019. "Mortgage Credit: Denmark's Financial Capacity Building Regime." *New Political Economy* 24(6): 833–50.

Young, Professor H. P. 1985. "Monotonic Solutions of Cooperative Games." *International Journal of Game Theory* 14(2): 65–72.

Index

23andMe, 62
401(k) plans, 33, 64

actuarial science: fair premiums and, 2, 17, 68, 72, 89, 99–100, 190–191; historical perspective on, 45, 48–49, 65, 68; labor markets and, 160, 163n2, 177, 179, 184; prices and, 2; private markets and, 72, 81, 83, 89, 99–100; sound principles of, 10; tables for, 45, 49, 65; trackers and, 3
adverse selection: Akerlof on, 6; credit markets and, 112; gatekeeping and, 193; historical perspective on, 13, 45–50, 54, 65, 67; life expectancy and, 45; opting out and, 30, 54, 199; partisanship and, 37; pooled equilibrium and, 40–42; private information and, 40–42; private markets and, 72, 82n17, 83, 88; regulation and, 37–38; risk and, 1–2, 4, 6, 13, 30, 34, 45–46, 49–50, 54, 65, 67, 72, 82, 112, 199, 202; theoretical model and, 30; time inconsistency and, 30, 34
Affordable Care Act (ACA), 11, 50n2, 60–61, 63, 91, 94, 97
Ahlquist, John S., 109
AIA Australia, 79–80
AIDS, 86
Akerlof, George A., 6, 12, 19, 23–25, 27, 29, 190, 196
algorithms, 10, 12, 81, 93, 116n7, 119, 202
"Alliance for Sweden" campaign, 184
Alphabet, 5, 62
Amazon, 5, 62

American National Election Survey (ANES), 97–99
Ansell, Ben W., 109
Apple, 5, 62, 79
Arndt, Christoph, 182–183
artificial intelligence (AI), 5, 27, 62, 81–82, 202
Australia, 80, 90, 102, 107
Austria, 80, 90, 102, 107, 147
autocorrelation, 87
automobiles, 3

bad state, 20–21, 25n9, 40, 41, 112n5, 114, 142n27, 143–145, 190
bankruptcy, 31, 33, 46, 74, 96
banks: default and, 116, 132, 197; Fannie Mae and, 65, 109, 116–117, 121; financial crises and, 14, 61, 65, 116n7; Freddie Mac and, 65, 109, 116–117, 119–130, 140n25, 197; government-sponsored enterprises (GSEs) and, 116–121; loans and, 65, 105, 116, 131–132, 202; mortgages and, 131 (*see also* mortgages); small-town, 105
Barr, Nicholas, 12, 19, 24–25
Bayesianism, 15n1, 26, 56, 113, 143, 160, 164
Besley, Timothy, 93
Beveridge model, 53
Big Data: consequences of, 5; differential risk pools and, 63; financialization and, 138; informed patients and, 22; poor people and, 138; private markets and, 13,

63, 191; uncertainty reduction by, 13; utility and, 119; variety of available data, 108

Big Tech, 81, 201

Bildt government, 11, 177

Bismarckian system, 52–53, 58, 67, 191, 199–201

Blue Cross Blue Shield, 1, 49–50, 60

Boadway, Robin, 19

Bradley, David, 188

budget constraints, 20, 36n20, 42–43

burial insurance, 47–48

Busemeyer, Marius R., 39–40

Bush, George W., 17

Calico, 62

Canada, *90*, 102, *107*

CAT scans, 1

Clareto, 77–78

Clinton, Bill, 116

Code on Genetics, 93

coercion, 15, 25

collective bargaining, 64, 159, 195

commercial banks, 116–117, 131n14

commercial insurance: customer exclusions and, 193; digitalization and, 76; mutual aid societies (MASs) and, 45–50, 54–55, 67; unemployment insurance funds (UIFs) and, 66

Comparative Political Data Set, 102

Comparative Study of Electoral Systems (CSES), 176

COVID-19 pandemic, 61, 74, 77, 86n20, 100, 189

credible information, 28, 38, *39*

credit guarantee schemes (CGSs), 115

credit markets: access to, 105–106; adverse selection and, 112; banks and, 105 (*see also* banks); collective bargaining and, 64, 159, 193; default and, 108–120, 128, 131–136, 141–146, 196–197; democracy and, 105, 117; discretionary income and, 100, 105, 108–115, 118, 138, 140, 142, 196; education and, 7, 33, 110, 115, 138, 141; empirical applications and, 196–198; employment and, 108, 133–135; FICO scores and, 121–130, *149*, *151–158*; flat-rate benefits and, 37, 114–115, 132, 144–146; Germany and, *107*, 131, 135n23, *147*; Gini coefficient and, 121–127, *129*, 138; government-sponsored

enterprises (GSEs) and, 116–121; historical perspective on, 64–65; homeownership and, 108, 116, 131–140; inequality and, 106–115, 118–131, 138, 140, 144, 196–198; information and, 64–65, 112–113; interest rates and, 105, 108, 111–132, 138–144, *152*, *156*; liquidity and, 109; loans and, 118–119 (*see also* loans); middle class and, 106; model for, 110–117, 141–144; mortgages and, 131 (*see also* mortgages); partisanship and, 118; pensions and, 64–65, 114, 131n14, 135n20, 141; Placebo outcomes and, 126–127, 146, *156–157*; poor people and, 115, 133–140, 196; poverty and, 115; redistribution and, 109, 115, 124, 128, 144; reform and, 116–117, 120, 131–137, 140; regression analysis and, 125–126, *127*, 130, 146, *147–158*; regulation and, 14, 109–111, 115–131, 138, 140; rich people and, 133–137, 140, 196; risk and, 105, 108–120, 128–146; savings and loans (S&Ls), 116–117; segmentation and, 40, *159*, 192; Single Family Loan-Level Dataset and, 121; subsidies and, 109, 116, 118, 131n14, 138, *139*, 144; taxes and, 114–115, *139*, 144; transfers and, 109, 114–115, 144; unemployment and, 108–109, 131–138; United States and, *106–107*, 109, 117, 121, 124, 131, 139–140; wealth and, 108, 110, 111n2, 133, 140; welfare and, 105, 108–115, 131–138, 140

credit reports, 76

crime, 21n4

CT scans, 27, 83

deductibles, 17, 50, 195

DeepMind, 62

default: credit markets and, 108–120, 128, 131–136, 141–146, 196–197; flat-rate benefits and, 144–146; historical perspective on, 63; income relationship and, 146; information and, 7; private markets and, 80; theoretical model and, 17

democracy: asymmetric information and, 22–25; credit markets and, 105, 117; future issues, 199; historical perspective on, 51–52, 56, 63–64, 67–68; inequality and, 12, 70, 188; intergenerational transfers and, 190; labor markets and, 163, 183; market failure and, 19–30; mutual aid societies (MASs) and, 16; private markets and, 13, 70, 73, 89, 100; rich people and, 2, 73, 183; social protection and, 2, 56; symmetric information and, 25–29; theoretical model and, 16, 19–20, 30, 32nn15–16, 33; transfers and, 16, 30, 67, 190; uncertainty and, 8; welfare and, 8

Denmark, 8–9, *90*, 92, 102, *107*, 109, 117, *147*, 183, 193, 197–198

Department of Motor Vehicles, 75

destitution, 45, 67

diagnostics, 10, 27, 49, 62, 81, 83–88, 94, 100, 193

digitalization, 76–79

disability, 34, 38, 44, 63, 75, 139, 197

Discovery Limited, 79

discretionary income: credit markets and, 100, 105, 108–115, 118, 138, 140, 142, 196; risk and, 100, 105, 108–115, 138; welfare and, 110–111

discrimination, 2, 5, 35, 38–39, 63, 81, 88, 93–94, 100, 116, 199, 202

"double payment" problem, 9, 13, 37, 39, 68, 89, 92, 94–95, 100, 198–199

education: additional schooling, 107; advantages of, 200; credit markets and, 7, 33, 110, 115, 138, 141; double-payment problem and, 9; employment and, 11, 33, 60, 66, 69, 159, 161–162, 165, 174, 179, 183–184, 192, 197–198; health and, 9, 60, 66, 84, 93, 95–96, 159, 192–193, 197; income and, 9, 11, 17, 33, 60, 64, 69, 92–96, 110, 115, 138, 141, 161, 174, 192, 197; labor markets and, 159, 161–162, 165, 167, 174, 179, 183–184, 198; mutual aid societies (MASs) and, 192; private markets and, 84, 92–95, 96n24; rich people and, 9, 40, 60, 92, 95; risk and, 7, 11, 17, 33, 40, 60, 66, 69, 84, 93, 115, 138, 141, 159, 161–162, 165, 174, 179, 183–184, 192, 197n3, 198; social media and, 196; unemployment and, 11, 60, 66, 159, 161–162, 165, 174, 179, 183–184, 192, 197n3, 198

elasticity, 111

elderly: health and, 2, 7, 18, 29, 34, *96–97*, 99; higher expenses of, 195; insecurity

and, 8, 18; labor markets and, 159, 171, *173*, *185–186*; market feasibility and, 16–18, 30–35; Medicare and, 2, 7, 9, 17, 59–60, *96–99*, 133; mutual aid societies (MASs) and, 44, 47–49, 55; old-age insurance and, 4–5, 13, 31, 159; pensions and, 56 (*see also* pensions); poverty and, 46–47; private markets and, 18, *96–97*; public spending on, 29n13; time inconsistency and, 7, 16–18, 30–35, 47, 56, 89, 96, 193; welfare and, 4, 7–8, 13–14, 18, 33, 53–54, 58, 105, 188, 193, 199

electronic health records (EHRs), 76–79

empirical implications of theoretical models (EITM) approach, 201

Employee Retirement Income Security Act, 50n2, 60–61

employment: credit markets and, 108, 133–135; education and, 11, 33, 60, 66, 69, 159, 161–162, 165, 174, 179, 183–184, 192, 197–198; health insurance and, 2, 4–5, 10, 13, 18, 20, 34–35, 44, 50–51, 55, 58, 60, 66, 159–160, 191–192, 197; historical perspective on, 50, 58, 66, 69n9; homeownership and, 134–137; insiders vs. outsiders and, 66; Job Pact and, 182; labor market risks and, 159, 162, 165, 167, 174n9, 179–181, 184; Law on Employment Protection, 180; mobility and, 49, 66, 68, 189, 191–192, 200; mutual aid societies (MASs) and, 48–49 (*see also* mutual aid societies (MASs); retirement and, 33 (*see also* retirement); sickness pay and, 44, 48; unemployment insurance funds (UIFs) and, 11, 14, 66, 177–184, 192, 198–199

employment protection, 159, 162, 180

Equitable Life Assurance Society, 49

error correction model (ECM), 87, *103*

Esping-Andersen, Gosta, 52, 199

European Observatory on Health Systems and Policies (EOHSP), 93

European Social Survey (ESS), 174, 176, *186–187*

Fair Housing Act, 12, 116n7

Fannie Mae, 65, 109, 116–117, 121

Federal Housing Administration (FHA), 117

FICO score: Gini coefficient and, 121–127, *129*, 138; interest rates and, 121–130; loans and, 121–130, *149*, *151–158*

financial crises, 14, 61, 65, 116n7
financialization, 7, 14, 16, 33, 65, 106–110, 115, 138–139
Finland, *90*, 102, *107*, *147*
Fitbit, 79
flat-rate benefits, 37, 114–115, 132, 144–146
Food and Drug Administration, 62
Foote, Christopher, 120–121, 131
Fordism, 47, 106, 162
fragmentation: information revolution and, 58–67; labor markets and, 50n2; political polarization and, 2; risk pools and, 2, 12, 188; solidarity and, 58–67; unemployment insurance and, 11–12
France, 80, *90*, 102, *107*, *147*
fraternal sciences, 47, 52
Freddie Mac, 65, 109, 116–130, 140n25, 197
Friedman, Rachel, 15n1, 19, 191
funded systems: adverse selection and, 45; information and, 18; intergenerational transfers and, 7; pension systems, 7, 17, 33, *53*, *55*, 58, 64, 193, 201; retirement and, 16, 33, 45, 64, 96; transfers and, 7, 16, 47, 64, 96

GDP, 64, 70, 83, 86n21, 87–91, *104*, *139*
Generali, 80
genetics, 18, 38, 62–63, 81–88, 93–94, 191, 193
German General Social Survey (ALLBUS), 171–172, *173*, *185–186*
German Socio-Economic Panel (GSOEP), 134–137, 165–172
Germany, 195; credit markets and, *107*, 131, 135n23, *147*; Hartz reforms and, 14, 65, 131–137, 140, 198; health insurance and, 17; health savings plans and, 7, 33; labor markets and, 165–172, *173*, *185–186*, 198; private markets and, 80, 89n23, *90*, 91, 96n25, 102; unemployment and, 14, 65, 165, 168–173, *185–186*, 198
Ghent system, 177, 179–180, 182, 184, 198
Gingrich, Jane R., 59
Gini coefficient, 121–127, *129*, 138
Goering, John, 116n7
good state, 20–21, 25n9, 40, *41*, 112n5, 114, 142n27, 143–144
Google, 62, 73

Gordon, Robert, 49
Gottlieb, Daniel, 48, 50n3
government-sponsored enterprises (GSEs), 116–121
GPS, 3
Great Depression, 30, 46, 117, 189
Grogan, Colleen M., 99
group plans, 49–50

Hacker, Jacob, 60
Hall, John, 93
Hariri, Jacob Gerner, 109
Harsanyi, John, 15–16
Hartz IV reforms, 14, 65, 131–137, 140, 198
health: data devices and, 62–63; diagnostics and, 10, 27, 49, 62, 81, 83–88, 94, 100, 193; disease, 10, 44, 62, 67, 79, 84, 86–87, 100–102; education and, 9, 60, 66, 84, 93, 95–96, 159, 192–193, 197; elderly and, 2, 7, 18, 29, 34, 96–97, 99; genetics and, 18, 38, 62–63, 81–88, 93–94, 191, 193; rich people and, 2, 4, 8–9, 58, 60, 91, 95, 193; younger generation and, 4, 6–7, 13, 17–18, 30–31, 48, 56, 67, 86, 92, 96, 101, 193–195
Healthcare NExt, 81
Health Information Technology and Economic and Clinical Health Act, 76
health insurance: Affordable Care Act (ACA), 11, 50n2, 60–61, 63, 91, 94, 97; artificial intelligence (AI) and, 81–82; choice between public/private, 94–99; electronic health records (EHRs), 76–79; empirical applications and, 193–196; employment and, 2, 4–5, 10, 13, 18, 20, 34–35, 44, 50–51, 55, 58, 60, 66, 159–160, 191–192, 197; guaranty associations and, 33; historical perspective on, 44, 49–51, 55, 58, 60–64; illness and, 8, 13–14, 20, 25, 48, 62–63, 75, 96, 108, 110, 171, *173*, *185–186*, 188; information and, 4–8, 11, 13, 60–64, 192–196; laboratories and, 81, 83, 87; labor markets and, 159; medical data and, 75; Medical Information Bureau (MIB) and, 72n4, 75, 78–79; prescription databases and, 75, 77; private markets and, 70–102, *104*, 201; Republican Party and, 94; as second largest insurance, 70; segmentation and, 70; supplementary private, 88–94;

theoretical model and, 17–19, 33–37; trackers and, 76, 79–81, 100; underwriting and, 17, 92–94, 100; voluntary private, 63, 89–93

Health Insurance Portability and Accountability Act (HIPAA), 63n8, 78

health savings plans, 7, 17, 33, 96, 195

HealthVault, 62

Hicks, Timothy, 59, 197n3

high information, 8, 10, 25–27, 38, 56–58, 64, 82n17, 200

Home Mortgage Disclosure Act (HMDA), 120n10

homeownership: credit markets and, 108, 116, 131–140; employment and, 134–137; GSEOP and, 134–137; Hartz IV reforms and, 14; mortgages and, 106 (*see also* mortgages); private markets and, 93; Sample Survey of Income and Expenditure (EVS) and, 134–135, 137; stratified rates of, 198; subsidies and, 131, 138–139, 197; VPHI and, 93; welfare and, 131–138

homophily, 164

housing, 11–12, 115–117, 121, 132–133, 138–141, 192

Human API portal, 77–78

human genome, 62, 81, 83

IBM, 62

Ignacio Conde-Ruiz, J., 53

illness, 8, 13–14, 20, 25, 48, 62–63, 75, 96, 108, 110, 171, *173*, *185–186*, 188

immigrants, 46, 167

individual retirement accounts (IRAs), 47, 64, 193

industrialization, 17, 96n25; deindustrialization and, 12, 30, 179, 188–189; health insurance and, 195; historical perspective on, 44, 49, 51, 56; knowledge economy and, 192; middle class and, 6, 15, 51, 53–54; mutual aid societies (MASs) and, 44, 190; uncertainty and, 189; urbanization and, 189

inequality: credit markets and, 106–115, 118–131, 138, 140, 144, 196–198; democracy and, 12, 70, 188; future issues and, 201; Hartz IV reforms and, 14; historical perspective on, 59–61, 64–65; increased, 2, 7, 14, 16, 19, 33, 59, 61, 64–65, 70–71, 100, 106, 108–113, 118, 128,

130, 138, 140, 188–189, 197–198, 201; information and, 2, 5, 7, 12, 14; labor markets and, 198; mortgages and, 119–131; private markets and, 70–71, 82, 92, 100; reduction of, 92, 112, 118, 138, 188–189, 198; regulation and, 119–131; risk and, 2, 7, 12, 14, 19, 33, 59–61, 65, 82, 92, 100, 108, 111–114, 130, 138, 144, 188–189, 196–198, 201; segmentation and, 59, 61, 188–189, 196; taxes and, 19, 60, 100, 188–189; theoretical model and, 16, 19, 33

information: actuarial science and, 49 (*see also* actuarial science); asymmetric, 2–4, 8, 15, 20–27, 38, *39*, *55*, 56, 63, 74, 82n17, 160, 190, 199, 202; Big Data, 5, 13, 22, 63, 108, 119, 138, 191; credible, 28, 38, *39*; credit markets and, 64–65, 112–113; Department of Motor Vehicles and, 75; diagnostics and, 10, 27, 49, 62, 81–88, 94, 100, 193; division of insurance pools and, 5–10; electronic health records (EHRs) and, 76–79; funded systems and, 18; health insurance and, 4–8, 11, 13, 60–64, 192–196; high, 8, 10, 25–27, 38, 56–58, 64, 82n17, 200; human genome, 62, 81, 83; incomplete, 2, 12, 18, 29, *55*, 66; inequality and, 2, 5, 7, 12, 14, 119–131; laboratories and, 81, 83, 87; labor markets and, 160–165; life insurance and, 4–7, 10, 13, 72–73, 82–88, 101–103, *104*, 193–193; loans and, 112–113, 118–119; low, 8, 10, 14, 18, 25–26, 28, 38, *39*, 56, *57*, 67, 199; market failure and, 6, 9, 19–30, 190; market feasibility and, 16–19, 30–37, 46, 58, 160, 199; Medical Information Bureau (MIB) and, 72n4, 75, 78–79; Moore's Law and, 61–62, 83n18; mortgages and, 119–131; mutual aid societies (MASs) and, 6, 8, 10–13, 199; ownership of, 202; pensions and, 64–65; preferences and, 18–19, 35–37; prescription databases and, 75, 77; privacy and, 10, 26–29, 40–42, 63, 78, 94, 202; regulation and, 2, 14, 18, 38, 63–65, 70, 73, 81, 87–89, 93–94, 100, 110, 117–131, 140, 199, 202; revolution in, 2, 4, 13, 35, *39*, *55*, 58–73, 82, 88, 94, 100, 108, 188, 201; risk and, 1–15, 18–30, 35–37, 160–165; segmentation and, 2, 5–6,

8, 11–14, 16, 18, 58–59, 66–67, 70, 89, 94, 159, 162, 165, 177, 180, 188–189, 192, 196; social insurance and, 2–13, 189–190, 193, 198; social solidarity and, 53–60; symmetric, 20, 25–29, *39, 55*, 82n17; trackers and, 3–4, 29, 79–80, 191; uncertainty and, 16 (*see also* uncertainty); underwriting and, 74–75; unemployment insurance and, 65–67, 183; welfare and, 2–14

information and communication technology (ICT), 4, 8, 119, 131, 189

integration, 2, 5

interest rates: changing, 17; credit markets and, 105, 108, 111–132, 138–144, *152, 156*; Denmark and, 198; equalization of, 65; FICO scores and, 121–130; Gini coefficient and, 121–127, *129*, 138; mortgages, 14, 65, 116–124, 128, 138–140, 197; segmentation and, 52, 58, 70

International Monetary Fund (IMF), 106, *107*

Ireland, *90*, 102, *107, 147*

ISCO, 174

Italy, *90*, 102, *107, 147*, 203

Japan, 58, 66, *90*, 91, 102, *107*

Jawbone, 79

Job Pact, 182

John Hancock Life Insurance, 4, 29, 77–78, 80

Kaiser Family Foundation Poll, 99

Keen, Michael, 19

Korpi, Walter, 53, 193

laboratories, 81, 83, 87

labor markets: actuarial approach and, 160, 163n2, 177, 179, 184; collective bargaining and, 64, 159, 193; democracy and, 163, 183; disability and, 34, 38, 44, 63, 75, 139, 197; education and, 159, 161–162, 165, 167, 174, 179, 183–184, 198; elderly and, 159, 171, *173, 185–186*; empirical applications and, 198–199; employment protection, 159, 162, 180; fragmentation and, 50n2; Germany and, 165–172, *173, 185–186*, 198; Ghent system and, 177, 179–180, 182, 184, 198; health insurance and, 159; inequality and, 198; information and, 160–165;

Law on Employment Protection, 180; market failure and, 184; partisanship and, 177, 183; poor people and, 160, 176; preferences and, 14, 66, 160, 163, 165–177; public system and, 165, 177, 182–183; redistribution and, 172, 174–176, 183, *186–187*; reform and, 165, 177–182, 198; regression analysis and, 166, 172, *173, 185–186*; regulation and, 159; segmentation and, 14, 50, 67, 159, 162, 165, 177, 180, 182, 188, 192, 198; social insurance and, 159–160, 163, 177; subsidies and, 182, 185; Swedish unemployment insurance and, 177–183; taxes and, 159, 177, 180, *181*; uncertainty and, 160, 163n2; unemployment protection, 46, 159, 164, 197n3; unions and, 159, 161, 164, 174, 177–184, 200; United States and, 66; voters and, 163–164, 184; wage protection, 159

Latin America, 66

Law on Employment Protection, 180

layoffs, 110

legal issues: clerical marriage, 44; discrimination, 116; intergenerational contracts and, 31; social media, 81; symmetric information and, 26

Lexis Nexis Risk Classifier, 76

life expectancy: adverse selection and, 45; historical perspective on, 45, 48–51; increased data on, 10, 45; predicting, 18, 193; premiums and, 17; private markets and, 72, 83–87; risk and, 34

life insurance: artificial intelligence (AI) and, 81–82; commercialization of, 45–50, 54–55, 67; credit reports and, 76; Department of Motor Vehicles and, 75; diagnostics and, 10, 27, 49, 62, 81, 83–88, 94, 100, 193; division of insurance pools and, 5, 7; electronic health records (EHRs) and, 76–79; empirical applications and, 193–196; funded plans and, 7, 16–18, 33, 45, 48, 53, 58, 96, 193–195; guaranty associations and, 33; historical perspective on, 44–49, *55, 58*, 63; information and, 4–7, 10, 13, 72–73, 82–88, 101–103, *104*, 193–193; laboratories and, 81, 83, 87; Lexis Nexis Risk Classifier and, 76; market penetration of, 82–88, 101–103, *104*;

Medical Information Bureau (MIB) and, 72n4, 75, 78–79; micro-targeted products and, 73; permanent, 72; prescription databases and, 75, 77; private markets and, 70–94, 100–102, *103–104*; purpose of, 71–72; theoretical model and, 16–17, 29, 33–38; trackers and, 76, 79–81, 100; underwriting and, 71, 73–82, 87–88, 100–101

liquidity, 109

loans: access to, 65, 105–106, 110; bank, 65, 105, 116, 131–132, 202; credit markets and, 118–119; default and, 108 (*see also* default); discretionary income and, 100, 105, 108–115, 118, 138, 140, 142, 196; FICO scores and, 121–130, *149*, *151–158*; flat-rate benefits and, 37, 114–115, 132, 144–146; Gini coefficient and, 121–127, *129*, 138; Hartz reform and, 65, 132; inequality and, 119–131; information and, 112–113, 118–119; interest rates and, 110 (*see also* interest rates); liquidity and, 109; model for, 110–117, 141–144; mortgages, 110 (*see also* mortgages); private markets and, 83; regulation and, 115–131; risk and, 65, 100, 105, 108–109, 111–117, 130, 132, 138, 141–142, 196, 202; Single Family Loan-Level Dataset and, 121; welfare and, 110–111, 113–115, 131–138

loan-to-value ratio, 124, 131, *156*

Loewenstein, Lara, 120–121, 131

low information, 8, 10, 14, 18, 25–26, 28, 38, *39*, 56, *57*, 67, 199

lump sum payments, 33, 35–36, 114

McFadden pseudo R-squared measure, 166–172, *173*, *185–186*

Maclaurin, Colin, 45

market failure: asymmetric information and, 22–25; classic framework for, 19–30; democracy and, 19–30; historical perspective on, 53, *57*, 67; information and, 6, 9, 190; labor markets and, 184; mutual aid societies (MASs) and, 6, 67; private markets and, 94; redistribution and, 6, 12, 67, 191, 200; symmetric information and, 25–29; theoretical model and, 12, 15, 18–20, 29

market feasibility, 160, 199; historical perspective on, 46, 58; information and,

16–18, 30–35; preferences and, 18–19, 35–37; time inconsistency and, 16–18, 30–35

market-mediated funded systems, 201

Medicaid, 8, 10, 60, 68, 96–99, 193

Medical Information Bureau (MIB), 72n4, 75, 78–79

Medical Literature Analysis and Retrieval System Online, 84

Medical Subject Headings (MeSH), 84

Medicare, 2, 7, 9, 17, 59–60, 96–99, 193

Meltzer-Richard model, 114

Microsoft, 5, 62, 81

micro-tracking, 3

middle class: credit markets and, 106; education and, 199; industry and, 6, 15, 51, 53–54; mortgages and, 65, 106; preferences of, 59, 196, 200; private markets and, 69, 71, 92, 97, 200; theoretical model and, 5; universal public system and, 30; voters, 32, 51, 61, 193; welfare and, 6, 8, 13, 15, 54, 68–69, 193–195, 199

Misfit, 79

MLC On Track, 80

mobility, 49, 66, 68, 189, 191–192, 200

Moore's Law, 61–62, 83n18

moral hazard, 10, 45, 48, 184, 198

mortality: artificial intelligence (AI) and, 81–82; Lexis Nexis Risk Classifier and, 76; life expectancy and, 10, 17, 34, 45, 48–51, 72, 83–87, 193; private markets and, 72, 75–76, 79, 81, 84, 86, 101–102

mortgages: credit markets and, 106, 109–140, 146, *147*; FICO scores and, 121–130, *149*, *151–158*; Gini coefficient and, 121–127, *129*, 138; Home Mortgage Disclosure Act (HMDA) and, 120n10; inequality and, 119–131; information and, 119–131; interest rates and, 14, 65, 116–124, 128, 138–140, 197; middle class and, 65, 106; private markets and, 198; redlining and, 11, 116, 202; regulation and, 14, 65, 109, 115, 117–131, 138, 140, 197; risk and, 14, 65, 109, 115–117, 120, 128, 132, 134–138, 197, 202; Single Family Loan-Level Dataset and, 121; underwriting, 120, 207–208

Motor Vehicle Reports, 75

MRI scans, 1, 27, 83

Murray, Charles, 51–52

mutual aid societies (MASs): asymmetric information and, 23, 25, 199; burial insurance, 47–48; commercialization of, 45–50, 54–55, 67; democracy and, 16; destitution and, 45, 67; double bind of, 48, 50, 54, 67, 190; dues to, 46; education and, 192; elderly and, 44, 47–49, 55; Equitable Life Assurance Society, 49; failure of, 12; heyday of, 51; historical perspective on, 10–11, 13, 44–57, 65, 67, 192; immigrants and, 46; increase of, 44; industrialization and, 44; information and, 6, 8, 10–13, 199; limitations of, 6; market failure and, 6, 67; New England Mutual Life Insurance Company, 49; New York Life Insurance Company, 49; as partial solution, 190; protections by, 44; role of, 11; Scottish Presbyterian Widows Fund, 44–46, 49, 83, 193; sickness pay and, 44, 48; solidarity and, 46, 53–58; taxes and, 47; theoretical model and, 15–16, 23, 25, 32; time-inconsistency and, 6–7, 16, 32, 45, 47–48, 54, 56, 199; transfers and, 6, 48, 57–58; unions and, 192; United States and, 44, 46, 49, 55; welfare and, 6, 8, 10, 12–13, 15–16, 25, 48, 51–52, 54, 56; widespread use of, 44

National Human Genome Research Institute, 62
National Laboratory of Medicine, 84
Netherlands, 90, 91, 102, 107, 147
New England Mutual Life Insurance Company, 49
New York Life Insurance Company, 49
New York State Department of Financial Services, 80–81
New Zealand, 90, 102, 107
Norway, 90, 92, 102, 107, 147

Obama, Barack, 76, 81, 90
occupational unemployment rates (OURs), 174n0
OECD Health Statistics, 89, 101
opting out: adverse selection and, 30, 54, 199; Akerlof and, 24; Bismarckian system and, 53; cost of, 19, 29; deterrents against, 9; private markets and, 25; privileged, 15; public system and, 8–9, 15, 19, 24–25, 30, 37, 54, 57, 59, 64, 71,

89n23, 94–96; segmentation and, 8; self-insurance and, 11–12, 20–22, 50n2, 51, 57, 60, 67, 73, 93, 190; theoretical model and, 15, 19, 24–25, 29–30, 37, 41
Oscar Health Insurance, 80

Palme, Joakim, 53, 193
Park, Sunggeun (Ethan), 99
participation, 9, 67, 95, 102, 184
partisanship: adverse selection and, 37; coercion and, 6; Comparative Political Data Set and, 102; credit markets and, 118; historical perspective on, 59; labor markets and, 177, 183; preferences and, 12, 19, 59, 200; private markets and, 71, 92, 94, 97, 101–102, 103–104, 195; regulation and, 37–38; theoretical model and, 37–38; welfare and, 12
pay-as-you-go (PAYG) systems: credible government commitment to, 7; historical perspective on, 46–48, 53–58, 64, 67; market-mediated funded systems and, 201; private markets and, 96; redistribution and, 16, 18, 32, 53, 64, 67; subsidies and, 18, 67; time-inconsistency and, 16, 31–35, 47, 56, 96, 191, 193; transfers and, 16, 47, 55, 191; voters and, 193; welfare and, 16, 18, 33, 48, 53, 193; younger generation and, 16, 18, 31, 33, 47–48, 56, 64, 67, 96, 193
pay-how-you-drive (PHYD), 3
pensions: credit-based insurance and, 64–65; credit markets and, 64–65, 114, 131n14, 135n20, 141; funded systems and, 7, 17, 33, 53, 55, 58, 64, 193, 201; historical perspective on, 51, 53–60, 64–65; information and, 64–65; market-mediated funded systems and, 201; PAYG and, 31 (see also pay-as-you-go (PAYG) systems); private markets and, 18, 36, 70, 82; taxes and, 19, 31
"piggy bank", 12, 24
Placebo outcomes, 126–127, 148, 156–157
"Politics of Medicaid, The: Most Americans Are Connected to the Program, Support Its Expansion, and Do Not View It as Stigmatizing" (Grogan and Park), 99
Ponzi schemes, 48
poor people: attitudinal gap and, 176; becoming, 7; cost of insurance and, 30; credit markets and, 115, 133–140, 196;

labor markets and, 160, 176; Medicaid and, 8, 10, 60, 68, 96–99, 193; Medicare and, 2, 7, 9, 17, 59–60, 96–99, 193; private markets and, 96, 98, 100; support of by rich people, 4; transfers and, 7–8, 55, 115, 200; welfare and, 68 (*see also* welfare)

Portugal, 90, 102, 147

Potential Years of Life Lost (PYLL), 86–87, 101–102, 104

poverty: credit markets and, 115; destitution, 45, 67; elderly and, 46–47; fear of, 7–8; historical perspective on, 46–47, 55, 67–68; insurance against, 7–9, 193; private markets and, 71, 96, 99; transfers and, 13

Precision Medicine Initiative, 81

preferences: bifurcation of, 30, 163; constrained, 9, 59, 199; divergence in, 192; first-best, 9, 95; formation of, 35–37; increased information and, 18–19, 35–37; labor markets and, 14, 66, 160, 163, 165–177; market feasibility and, 18–19, 35–37; mass, 18; middle class, 59, 196, 200; partisan, 12, 19, 59, 200; polarization of, 2, 9, 12, 14, 16, 20, 37, 39, 66–67, 163, 169, 172, 176, 184; policy, 11–12, 14, 19, 26, 37, 67, 172, 184; political, 160, 163–177, 184, 186; private markets and, 95, 96n24, 99; public spending and, 18, 37, 59, 95, 192; redistribution, 12, 16, 18, 21n4, 35, 172, 174, 200, 203; risk and, 2, 12, 14, 16, 18, 21, 26, 30, 35, 37, 39, 57, 59, 66–67, 160, 163–176, 184, 192, 199–200, 203; shaping, 19, 59, 66, 160, 200; uncertainty and, 16, 26, 66, 199; welfare and, 2, 9, 12, 18, 21, 30, 37, 39, 68, 203

prescription databases, 75, 77

Preston, Ian, 93

price discrimination, 38

price nondiscrimination, 39

privacy, 10, 26–29, 40–42, 63, 78, 94, 202

private markets: actuarial approach and, 72, 81, 83, 89, 99–100; adverse selection and, 72, 82n17, 83, 88; Big Data and, 13, 63, 191; democracy and, 13, 70, 73, 89, 100; education and, 84, 92–95, 96n24; elderly and, 18, 96–97; Germany and, 80, 89n23, 90, 91, 96n25, 102; health insurance and, 70–102, 104, 201; homeownership and,

93; inequality and, 70–71, 82, 92, 100; life expectancy and, 72, 83–87; life insurance and, 70–94, 100–102, 103–104; market failure and, 94; middle class and, 69, 71, 92, 97, 200; mortality and, 72, 75–76, 79, 81, 84, 86, 101–102; mortgages and, 198; opting out and, 25; partisanship and, 71, 92, 94, 97, 101–102, 103–104, 195; pay-as-you-go (PAYG) systems and, 96; pensions and, 18, 36, 70, 82; poor people and, 96, 98, 100; poverty and, 71, 96, 99; preferences and, 95, 96n24, 99; public system and, 71, 82, 91–97, 100; reform and, 89–92; regression analysis and, 83; regulation and, 19, 37–38, 70, 73, 80–81, 87–94, 97, 100, 102; risk and, 70–100; segmentation and, 2, 5, 8, 11, 13–14, 18, 40, 53, 58–59, 63, 67, 70, 89, 94, 165, 180, 196; social insurance and, 70, 96; subsidies and, 94; taxes and, 89, 92, 100; time-inconsistency and, 71, 89, 96–99; top-up plans and, 9, 89, 179–182, 195; transfers and, 80n15, 81, 96; uncertainty and, 101; unemployment and, 4; United States and, 8, 18, 44, 51, 70, 74, 77–84, 89n23, 90, 91–99, 102–103, 195; voters and, 101; wealth and, 70, 97, 100; welfare and, 19, 37–38, 70; younger generation and, 84–86, 92, 96–97, 101

professional associations, 49, 66, 159, 161, 164, 179

Profeta, Paola, 53

Prudential, 80

Prussia, 44

Przeworski, Adam, 19

public spending, 29n13, 37, 68, 139, 145, 192, 199

public system: historical perspective on, 54, 57, 59, 63–64; information and, 8–9; labor markets and, 165, 177, 182–183; left's support for, 19, 37–38; opting out and, 8–9, 15, 19, 24–25, 30, 37, 54, 57, 59, 64, 71, 89n23, 94–96; private markets and, 71, 82, 91–97, 100; taxes and, 9, 15, 19, 25, 31, 37, 39, 54, 60, 195, 200; theoretical model and, 15–20, 24–25, 28–30, 35, 37–40; top-up plans and, 9, 36, 89, 179–182, 195; uncertainty and, 8, 15–16, 30, 61, 67

Putnam, Robert, 203

Qualcomm, 80

Rawls, John, 8, 15n1, 54, 67
recessions, 46, 189
reciprocity, 46, 203
Recovery Act, 76
redistribution: credit markets and, 109, 115, 124, 128, 144; division of insurance pools and, 5; historical perspective on, 46, 53, 58, 60, 64, 67; intergenerational, 32, 67; labor markets and, 172, 174–176, 183, *186–187*; literature on, 21n4, 189; lump-sum benefits and, 36; market failure and, 6, 12, 67, 191, 200; pay-as-you-go (PAYG) systems, 16, 18, 32, 53, 64, 67; preferences and, 12, 16, 18, 21n4, 35, 172, 174, 200, 203; risk, 5, 17, 30, 38, 53, 58, 60, 172, 174–176, 183, *186–187*, 197, 200; time-inconsistency and, 30; transfers and, 16, 30, 64, 109, 144, 188–189, 200; welfare and, 6, 12, 16, 18, 21, 36, 38, 53, 56, 58, 68, 115, 188, 191, 197, 203; younger generation and, 16, 30, 64
redlining, 11, 116, 202
reform, 201; credit markets and, 116–117, 120, 131–137, 140; Hartz IV, 14, 65, 131–137, 140, 198; historical perspective on, 65, 67; labor markets and, 165, 177–182, 198; private markets and, 89–92; regulation and, 14, 18, 65, 89, 117; Scottish Reformation, 44; unemployment, 14, 29, 65, 67, 131–137, 165, 177–182, 198; voters and, 18, 29
regression analysis: credit markets and, 125–126, *127*, 130, 146, *147–158*; discontinuity results and, 148; labor markets and, 166, 172, *173*, *185–186*; private markets and, 83
regulation: adverse selection and, 37–38; constraints from, 2, 63, 68, 94, 111; credit markets and, 14, 109–111, 115–131, 138, 140; historical perspective on, 50, 60–65, 68; inequality and, 119–131; of information, 2, 14, 18, 38, 63–65, 70, 73, 81, 87–89, 93–94, 100, 110, 117–131, 140, 199, 202; labor markets and, 159; loans and, 115–131; mortgage markets and, 14, 65, 109, 115, 117–131, 138, 140, 197; partisanship and, 37–38;

private markets and, 19, 37–38, 70, 73, 80–81, 87–94, 97, 100, 102; redistribution and, 172, 174–176, 183, *186–187*; reform and, 14, 18, 65, 89, 117; risk and, 2, 14, 18–19, 33, 42, 50, 60–61, 64–65, 70, 73, 81, 89, 94, 109, 115–120, 130–131, 138, 140, 159, 195, 197, 199, 202; role of, 37–38, 115–118; segmentation and, 2, 6, 11–14, 16, 18, 40, 50, 52–53, 58–67, 70, 89, 94, 159, 162, 165, 177, 180, 188–189, 192–193, 196, 198; tax, 19, 50, 63, 115, 195, 199; trackers and, 80–81; welfare and, 37–38
Reinfeldt, Fredrick, 92, 177
Republican Party, 94
retirement: adverse selection and, 45; Employee Retirement Income Security Act and, 50n2, 60–61; funded systems and, 16, 33, 45, 64, 96; individual retirement accounts (IRAs), 47, 64, 193; pensions and, 64–65 (*see also* pensions); Social Security, 47, 67
rich people: attitudinal gap and, 176; credit markets and, 133–137, 140, 196; democracy and, 2, 73, 183; education and, 9, 40, 60, 92, 95; health and, 2, 4, 8–9, 58, 60, 91, 95, 193; self-insurance and, 11–12, 20–22, 50n2, 51, *57*, 60, 67, 73, 93, 190; self-insuring by, 12, 22; support of poor by, 4
risk: adverse selection and, 1–2, 4, 6, 13, 30, 34, 45–46, 49–50, 54, 65, 67, 72, 82, 112, 199, 202; Akerlof model and, 6, 12, 19, 23–25, 27, 29, 190, 196; argument synopsis on, 189–192; average, 16, 22–23, 24n7, 25n8, 28, 38, 54–55, *57*, 59, 163n2; aversion to, 20, 22n6, 29n14, 36–37, 41–42, 54, 56, 105, 108–120, 128–146; default, 144–146 (*see also* default); discretionary income and, 100, 105, 108–115, 138, 196; distribution of, 5, 16–17, 29–30, 38, 53–60, 108, 112, 128n13, 132, 140, 183, 189, 191, 197–200; education and, 7, 11, 17, 33, 40, 60, 66, 69, 84, 93, 115, 138, 141, 159, 161–162, 165, 174, 179, 183–184, 192, 197n3, 198; flat-rate benefits and, 144–146; historical perspective on, 44–69; inequality and, 2, 7, 12, 14, 19, 33, 59–61, 65, 82, 92, 100, 108, 111–114,

130, 138, 144, 188–189, 196–198, 201; information and, 1–15, 18–30, 35–37, 160–165; labor markets and, 159–185; Lexis Nexis Risk Classifier and, 76; life expectancy and, 34; loans and, 65, 105, 108–109, 111–112, 115–117, 130, 132, 141–142, 202; market failure and, 184 (*see also* market failure); medical data and, 75; moral hazard and, 10, 45, 48, 184, 198; mortgages and, 14, 65, 109, 115–117, 120, 128, 132, 134–138, 197, 202; pooling of, 1–16, 19, 22–29, 38–42, 50–51, 54–55, 58–68, 72, 128, 159–160, 171, 177, 179–180, 184–185, 188, 191, 200–203; preferences and, 2, 12, 14, 16, 18, 21, 26, 30, 35, 37, 39, 57, 59, 66–67, 160, 163–176, 184, 192, 199–200, 203; private markets and, 70–100; redistribution and, 5, 17, 30, 38, 53, 58, 60, 197, 200; regulation and, 2, 14, 18–19, 33, 42, 50, 60–61, 64–65, 70, 73, 81, 89, 94, 109, 115–120, 130–131, 138, 140, 159, 195, 197, 199, 202; segmentation and, 189; subsidies and, 1, 4, 11, 17–18, 23, 25, 28, 30, 54, 61, 67, 109, 116, 118, 185, 192, 197, 199; theoretical model and, 15–43; time-inconsistency and, 7, 30–35, 45, 47, 54, 56, 89, 96, 191, 199; traditional classification of, 3; uncertainty and, 8, 13, 16, 26, 30, 36, 56, 61, 66–67, 160, 163, 191, 196, 199; unemployment and, 5, 8–14, 18, 20, 26, 29, 35, 44, 46, 51, 60, 65–67, 108–109, 131–132, 136–138, 159–166, 169, 171–174, 177–180, 183–184, 188, 191–192, 197–198; voters and, 18, 25, 29, 61, 64, 163, 184, 188–191, 197n3, 199; welfare and, 2, 6–30, 33, 36–39, 48, 51–58, 68–69, 105, 108–109, 115, 138, 140, 188, 191, 193, 197, 201, 203
Rogers, Will, 108
Rothschild, Michael, 19, 25, 41
Rothstein, Bo, 52
Rueda, David, 162

Sample Survey of Income and Expenditure (EVS), 134–135, 137
SAP government, 182–183
savings: credit markets and, 114, 116–117, 133, 157; health savings plans and, 7, 17,

33, 96; private markets and, 96–97; wealth and, 1, 7–8, 17, 20–21, 29, 33–34, 36, 46–47, 51, 66, 96–97, 114, 116–117, 133, 136, 141, 160, 180, 190, 193
savings and loans (S&Ls), 116–117
Scottish Mutual, 55
Scottish Presbyterian Widows Fund, 44–46, 49, 83, 193
Scottish Reformation, 44
segmentation: choice and, 8; concept of, 6; credit markets and, 40, 159, 192; health insurance and, 70; historical perspective on, 50, 52–53, 58–59, 61, 63, 66–67; inequality and, 59, 61, 188–189, 196; information and, 2, 5–8, 11–18, 58–59, 66–67, 70, 89, 94, 159, 162, 165, 177, 180, 188–189, 192, 196; information levels and, 2, 5; integration and, 2, 5; interest rates and, 52, 58, 70; labor markets and, 14, 50, 67, 159, 162, 165, 177, 180, 182, 188, 192, 198; opting out and, 8; private markets and, 2, 5, 8, 11, 13–14, 18, 40, 53, 58–59, 63, 67, 70, 89, 94, 165, 180, 196; regulation and, 2, 70, 89, 94; risk and, 2, 6, 11, 13–14, 16, 18, 40, 50, 52–53, 58–59, 61, 63, 66–67, 70, 89, 94, 159, 162, 165, 177, 180, 188–189, 192–193, 196, 198; state programs and, 11, 18, 50, 52–53, 159, 188; theoretical model and, 16, 18, 40; unemployment insurance and, 177–183; welfare and, 8, 18, 52–53, 188
self-insurance, 11–12, 20–22, 50n2, 51, 57, 60, 67, 73, 93, 190
self-interest, 19, 29, 52, 191
Shapley decomposition, 169, *170*, 170
sickness pay, 44, 48
Single Family Loan Level Dataset, 121
social capital, 51–52, 203
social insurance: future politics of, 199–201; historical perspective on, 44, 51–52, 54, 56–60, 65, 67; information and, 2–13, 189–190, 193, 198; labor markets and, 159–160, 163, 177; private markets and, 70, 96; theoretical model and, 15, 19, 21n4, 30, 35, 37, 39
social media, 80–81
social networks, 11–12, 14, 18, 25, 66–67, 164, 183–184, 196
Social Security, 47, 67

solidarity: COVID-19 pandemic and, 61; cross-class, 8, 14, 18, 203; emergence of, 53–58; fragmentation of, 58–67; information revolution and, 58–67, 71, 201; mutual aid societies (MASs) and, 46, 53–58; reciprocity and, 203; uncertainty and, 66, 160, 196; unemployment insurance and, 183, 192; welfare and, 8, 18, 40n21, 201, 203

Spain, *90*, 102, *147*

Stiglitz, Joseph, 19, 25

Stolle, Dietlind, 52

Study Watch, 62

subsidies: credit markets and, 109, 116, 118, 131n14, 138, *139*, 144; historical perspective on, 54, 61, 67; homeownership, 131, 138–139, 197; labor markets and, 182, 185; pay-as-you-go (PAYG) systems and, 18, 67; private markets and, 94, 192; risk and, 1, 4, 11, 17–18, 23, 25, 28, 30, 54, 61, 67, 109, 116, 118, 185, 192, 197, 199; tax, 4, 37, 54, 199

supplementary health insurance, 88–94

Swaan, Abram de, 50–51

Sweden, 11, 38, 66, *90*, 102; "Alliance for Sweden" campaign, 184; Bildt and, 11, 177; credit markets and, *107*, *147*; Democrats, 182–183; Ghent system and, 177, 179–180, 182, 184, 198; Job Pact and, 182; Law on Employment Protection and, 180; Left Party, 182; politics of private markets and, 180; Reinfeldt and, 92, 177; SAP government and, 182–183; unemployment insurance funds (UIFs) and, 180–184; unions and, 182

Swedish Confederation of Professional Associations (SACO), 179–180, 182

Swedish Confederation of Professional Employees (TCO), 180, 182

symmetric information, 20, 25–29, *39*, *55*, 82n17

taxes: coercive, 12; credit markets and, 114–115, *139*, 144; credits, 9, 195, 199; deductions, 50, 92, 115, 199; flat-rate, 37, 114–115, 132, 144–146; historical perspective on, 47, 50, 54–56, 60, 63, 66; inequality and, 19, 60, 100, 188–189; labor markets and, 159, 177, 180, *181*; mutual aid societies (MASs) and, 47;

paying for social protection by, 4, 8, 15, 19, 25, 31, 198–200; pensions and, 19, 31; power to, 54, 191; preference formation and, 35–37; price nondiscrimination and, 39; private markets and, 89, 92, 100; public system and, 9, 15, 19, 25, 31, 37, 39, 54, 60, 195, 200; regulation and, 19, 50, 63, 115, 195, 199; subsidies and, 4, 37, 54, 199; transfers and, 8, 114–115, 144, 188–191, 200; voters and, 25, 31, 188–191

time-inconsistency: adverse selection and, 30, 34; asymmetric information and, 56, 190, 199; elderly and, 7, 16–18, 30–35, 47, 56, 89, 96, 193; historical perspective on, 45, 47–48, 54, 56; intergenerational bargains and, 47, 191, 193; market feasibility and, 16–18, 30–35; mutual aid societies (MASs) and, 6–7, 16, 45, 47–48, 54, 56, 199; overlapping generations models and, 32; pay-as-you-go (PAYG) systems and, 16, 31–35, 47, 56, 96, 191, 193; persistence of, 7; private markets and, 71, 89, 96–99; redistribution and, 30; risk and, 7, 30–35, 45, 47, 54, 56, 89, 96, 191, 199; theoretical model and, 30–35; voters and, 32, 191, 193, 199; younger generation and, 6–7, 16–18, 30–35, 47–48, 56, 96, 190, 194

top-up plans, 9, 36, 89, 179–182, 195

trackers, 3–4, 29, 76, 79–81, 100, 191

transfers: credit markets and, 109, 114–115, 144; democracy and, 16, 30, 67, 190; funded systems and, 7, 16, 47, 64, 96; intergenerational, 6–7, 13, *55*, 56, 190; mutual aid societies (MASs), 6, 48, 57–58; pay-as-you-go (PAYG) systems, 16, 47, *55*, 191; poor people and, 7–8, *55*, 115, 200; poverty and, 13; private markets and, 80n15, 81, 96; redistribution and, 16, 30, 64, 109, 144, 188–189, 200; taxes and, 8, 114–115, 144, 188–191, 200; theoretical model and, 16, 20, 30, 47–48, *55*, 56–57, 64–65, 67; younger generation and, 6–7, 13, 16, 30, 47–48, 56, 67, 96, 190

uncertainty: democracy and, 8; incomplete information and, 8, 66–67; industrialization and, 189; labor markets and, 160, 163n2; preferences and, 16, 26,

66, 199; private markets and, 101; public
system and, 8, 15–16, 30, 61, 67; risk and,
8, 13, 16, 26, 30, 36, 56, 61,
66–67, 160, 163, 191, 196, 199;
solidarity and, 66, 160, 196; voters and,
31, 61, 101, 163, 199; welfare and, 8, 13,
36, 56, 189, 191
underwriting: actuarial science and, 49;
artificial intelligence (AI) and, 81–82;
COVID-19 pandemic and, 74, 77; current
practices of, 73–76; Department of Motor
Vehicles and, 75; diagnostics and, 10, 27,
49, 62, 81,
83–88, 94, 100, 193; digitalization and,
76–79; electronic health records (EHRs)
and, 76–79; health insurance and, 17, 92–
94, 100; innovations in, 76–82;
laboratories and, 81, 83, 87; Lexis Nexis
Risk Classifier and, 76; life insurance and,
71, 73–82, 87–88, 100–101; Medical
Information Bureau (MIB) and, 72n4, 75,
78–79; mortgages, 120–121, 207–208;
prescription databases and, 75, 77;
trackers and, 3–4, 29, 76, 79–81, 100,
191; unemployment insurance funds
(UIFs) and, 180
unemployment: benefits during, 14, 65, 109,
131–133, 136n24, 137–138,
169–172, *173*, 182–184, *185*, 198, 200;
credit markets and, 108–109, 131–138;
disability and, 44, 139, 197; education
and, 11, 60, 66, 159, 161–162, 165, 174,
179, 183–184, 192, 197n3, 198;
Germany and, 14, 65, 165, 168–173,
185–186, 198; high levels of, 180, 182,
184; historical perspective on, 44, 46, 51,
55, 60, 65–67; homeownership and, 134–
137; information and, 8–14; insurance
for, 4, 11, 14, *34*, 35, 46, *55*, 65–67, 159–
160, 163, 165, 177–184, 192, 198; lost
income and, 109, 188; occupational
unemployment rates (OURs), 174n0;
private markets and, 4; reform and, 14,
29, 65, 67, 131–137, 165, 177–182, 198;
risk and, 5, 8–11, 13–14, 18, 20, 26, 29,
35, 44, 46, 51, 60, 65–67, 108–109, 131–
132, 136–138, 159–166, 169, 171–174,
177–180, 183–184, 188, 191–192, 197–
198; theoretical model and, 16, 18, 20,
25, 26n10, 29–30, 35; United States and,
198

unemployment insurance funds (UIFs), 11,
14, 66, 177–184, 192, 198–199
unemployment protection, 46, 159, 164,
197n3
unions: fall of, 12, 188; historical
perspective on, 58, 66; Job Pact and, 182;
labor markets and, 159, 161, 164, 174,
177–184, 200; rise of, 12; Sweden and,
182; unemployment insurance funds
(UIFs) and, 11, 14, 66, 177–184, 192,
198–199
UnitedHealth, 80
United Kingdom, 80, *90*, 93, *147*
United States: 401(k) plans, 33, 64; Bush
and, 17; Clinton and, 116; credit markets
and, *106–107*, 109, 117, 121, 124, 131,
139–140; employer-based coverage, 58;
Fair Housing Act and, 12; Fannie Mae,
65, 109, 116–117, 121; financial crisis of,
14; fraternal societies and, 47, 52; Freddie
Mac, 65, 109, 116–117,
119–130, 140n25, 197; Great
Depression, 30, 46, 117, 189; guaranty
associations and, 33; healthcare costs in,
29n13, 62; health savings accounts
(HSAs), 17, 195; individual retirement
accounts (IRAs), 193; information
revolution and, 58–60; labor markets
and, 66; Medicaid, 8, 10, 60, 68, 96–99,
133; Medicare, 2, 7, 9, 17, 59–60, 96–99,
193; mutual aid societies (MASs) and, 44,
46, 49, 55; Obama and, 76, 81, *90*;
private markets and, 8, 18, 44, 51, 70, 74,
77–84, 89n23, *90*, 91–99, 102–103, 195;
Republican Party and, 94; self-insurance
and, 11; Social Security, 47, 67; as stingy
welfare state, 197; unemployment and,
198
universal public system, 18, 30, 91
University of Edinburgh, 45
urbanization, 6, 30, 51, 189
US Genetic Information Nondiscrimination
Act (GINA), 38, 63, 93, 94

Verily Life Sciences, 62, 81
Vitality Health, 79–80
voluntary private health insurance (VPHI),
63, 89–93
voters: Comparative Study of Electoral
Systems (CSES), 176; labor markets and,
163–164, 184; median, 25, 32, 64;

middle-class, 1; pay-as-you-go (PAYG) systems and, 193; private markets and, 101; reform and, 18, 29; risk and, 18, 25, 29, 61, 64, 163, 184, 188–191, 197n3, 199; self-interested, 29; taxes and, 25, 31, 188–191; time inconsistency and, 32, 191, 193, 199; uncertainty and, 31, 61, 101, 163, 199

wage protection, 159
Wallace, Robert, 45
wealth: credit markets and, 108, 110, 111n2, 133, 140; discretionary income and, 100, 105, 108–115, 118, 138, 140, 142, 196; historical perspective on, 56; mobility and, 49, 66, 68, 189, 191–192, 200; private markets and, 70, 97, 100; public system and, 15; savings and, 1, 7–8, 17, 20–21, 29, 33–36, 46–47, 51, 66, 96–97, 114–117, 133, 136, 141, 160, 180, 190, 193; self-insurance and, 11–12, 20–22, 50n2, 51, 57, 60, 67, 73, 93, 190, 192
Webster, Alexander, 45
welfare: Bismarckian, 52–53, 58, 67, 191, 199–201; credit markets and, 105, 108–115, 131–138, 140; democracy and, 8; destitution and, 45, 67; discretionary income and, 110–111; elderly and, 4, 7–8, 13–14, 18, 33, 53–54, 58, 105, 188, 193, 199; Golden Age of, 54; historical perspective on, 44–58, 68–69; homeownership and, 131–138; information and, 2–14; loans and, 110–111, 113–115, 131–138; middle class and, 6, 8, 13, 15, 54, 68–69, 193–195, 199; mutual aid societies (MASs) and, 6, 8, 10, 12–13, 15–16, 25, 48, 51–

52, 54, 56; partisanship and, 12; pay-as-you-go (PAYG) systems and, 16, 18, 33, 48, 53, 193; preferences and, 2, 9, 12, 18, 21, 30, 37, 39, 68, 203; private markets and, 19, 37–38, 70; public system and, 19; redistribution and, 6, 12, 16, 18, 21, 36, 38, 53, 56, 58, 68, 115, 188, 191, 197, 203; regulation and, 37–38; risk and, 2, 6–30, 33, 36–39, 48, 51–58, 68–69, 105, 108–109, 115, 138, 140, 188, 191, 193, 197, 201, 203; role of, 188; segmentation and, 8, 18, 52–53, 188; solidarity and, 8, 18, 40n21, 201, 203; theoretical model and, 15–25, 30–33, 36–40; uncertainty and, 8, 13, 36, 56, 189, 191
Westcott, Edward Noyes, 108
Wiedemann, Andreas, 109
Wienk, Ron, 116n7
Willen, Paul, 120–121
World Health Organization (WHO), 86, 93
World War II era, 4, 30, 36, 51, 189

younger generation: deductibles and, 17; health and, 4, 6–7, 13, 17–18, 30–31, 48, 56, 67, 86, 92, 96, 101, 193–195; health savings plans and, 7, 17, 33, 96; market feasibility and, 16–18, 30–35; pay-as-you-go (PAYG) systems and, 16, 18, 31, 33, 47–48, 56, 64, 67, 96, 193; private markets and, 84–86, 92, 96–97, 101; redistribution and, 16, 30, 64; support of elderly by, 4; time-inconsistency and, 6–7, 16–18, 30–35, 47–48, 56, 96, 190, 193; transfers and, 6–7, 13, 16, 30, 47–48, 56, 67, 96, 190

CAMBRIDGE STUDIES IN COMPARATIVE POLITICS

Other Books in the Series (continued from page ii)

Laia Balcells, *Rivalry and Revenge: The Politics of Violence during Civil War*

Lisa Baldez, *Why Women Protest? Women's Movements in Chile*

Kate Baldwin, *The Paradox of Traditional Chiefs in Democratic Africa*

Stefano Bartolini, *The Political Mobilization of the European Left, 1860–1980: The Class Cleavage*

Robert H. Bates, *The Political Economy of Development: A Game Theoretic Approach*

Robert H. Bates, *When Things Fell Apart: State Failure in Late-Century Africa*

Mark Beissinger, *Nationalist Mobilization and the Collapse of the Soviet State*

Pablo Beramendi, *The Political Geography of Inequality: Regions and Redistribution*

Nancy Bermeo, ed., *Unemployment in the New Europe*

Carles Boix, *Democracy and Redistribution*

Carles Boix, *Political Order and Inequality: Their Foundations and their Consequences for Human Welfare*

Carles Boix, *Political Parties, Growth, and Equality: Conservative and Social Democratic Economic Strategies in the World Economy*

Catherine Boone, *Merchant Capital and the Roots of State Power in Senegal, 1930–1985*

Catherine Boone, *Political Topographies of the African State: Territorial Authority and Institutional Change*

Catherine Boone, *Property and Political Order in Africa: Land Rights and the Structure of Politics*

Michael Bratton and Nicolas van de Walle, *Democratic Experiments in Africa: Regime Transitions in Comparative Perspective*

Michael Bratton, Robert Mattes, and E. Gyimah-Boadi, *Public Opinion, Democracy, and Market Reform in Africa*

Valerie Bunce, *Leaving Socialism and Leaving the State: The End of Yugoslavia, the Soviet Union, and Czechoslovakia*

Daniele Caramani, *The Nationalization of Politics: The Formation of National Electorates and Party Systems in Europe*

John M. Carey, *Legislative Voting and Accountability*

Kanchan Chandra, *Why Ethnic Parties Succeed: Patronage and Ethnic Headcounts in India*

Eric C. C. Chang, Mark Andreas Kayser, Drew A. Linzer, and Ronald Rogowski, *Electoral Systems and the Balance of Consumer-Producer Power*

José Antonio Cheibub, *Presidentialism, Parliamentarism, and Democracy*

Ruth Berins Collier, *Paths toward Democracy: The Working Class and Elites in Western Europe and South America*

Daniel Corstange, *The Price of a Vote in the Middle East: Clientelism and Communal Politics in Lebanon and Yemen*

Pepper D. Culpepper, *Quiet Politics and Business Power: Corporate Control in Europe and Japan*

Sarah Zukerman Daly, *Organized Violence after Civil War: The Geography of Recruitment in Latin America*

Christian Davenport, *State Repression and the Domestic Democratic Peace*

Donatella della Porta, *Social Movements, Political Violence, and the State*

Alberto Diaz-Cayeros, *Federalism, Fiscal Authority, and Centralization in Latin America*

Alberto Diaz-Cayeros, Federico Estévez, Beatriz Magaloni, *The Political Logic of Poverty Relief: Electoral Strategies and Social Policy in Mexico*

Jesse Driscoll, *Warlords and Coalition Politics in Post-Soviet States*

Thad Dunning, *Crude Democracy: Natural Resource Wealth and Political Regimes*

Thad Dunning et al., *Information, Accountability, and Cumulative Learning: Lessons from Metaketa I*

Gerald Easter, *Reconstructing the State: Personal Networks and Elite Identity*

Antje Ellerman, *The Comparative Politics of Immigration: Policy Choices in Germany, Canada, Switzerland, and the United States*

Margarita Estevez-Abe, *Welfare and Capitalism in Postwar Japan: Party, Bureaucracy, and Business*

Henry Farrell, *The Political Economy of Trust: Institutions, Interests, and Inter-Firm Cooperation in Italy and Germany*

Karen E. Ferree, *Framing the Race in South Africa: The Political Origins of Racial Census Elections*

M. Steven Fish, *Democracy Derailed in Russia: The Failure of Open Politics*

Robert F. Franzese, *Macroeconomic Policies of Developed Democracies*

Roberto Franzosi, *The Puzzle of Strikes: Class and State Strategies in Postwar Italy*

Timothy Frye, *Building States and Markets After Communism: The Perils of Polarized Democracy*

Mary E. Gallagher, *Authoritarian Legality in China: Law, Workers, and the State*

Geoffrey Garrett, *Partisan Politics in the Global Economy*

Scott Gehlbach, *Representation through Taxation: Revenue, Politics, and Development in Postcommunist States*

Edward L. Gibson, *Boundary Control: Subnational Authoritarianism in Federal Democracies*

Jane R. Gingrich, *Making Markets in the Welfare State: The Politics of Varying Market Reforms*

Miriam Golden, *Heroic Defeats: The Politics of Job Loss*

Yanilda María González, *Authoritarian Police in Democracy: Contested Security in Latin America*

Jeff Goodwin, *No Other Way Out: States and Revolutionary Movements*

Merilee Serrill Grindle, *Changing the State*

Anna Grzymala-Busse, *Rebuilding Leviathan: Party Competition and State Exploitation in Post-Communist Democracies*

Anna Grzymala-Busse, *Redeeming the Communist Past: The Regeneration of Communist Parties in East Central Europe*

Frances Hagopian, *Traditional Politics and Regime Change in Brazil*

Mark Hallerberg, Rolf Ranier Strauch, Jürgen von Hagen, *Fiscal Governance in Europe*

Henry E. Hale, *The Foundations of Ethnic Politics: Separatism of States and Nations in Eurasia and the World*

Stephen E. Hanson, *Post-Imperial Democracies: Ideology and Party Formation in Third Republic France, Weimar Germany, and Post-Soviet Russia*

Mai Hassan, *Regime Threats and State Solutions: Bureaucratic Loyalty and Embeddedness in Kenya*

Michael Hechter, *Alien Rule*

Timothy Hellwig, *Globalization and Mass Politics: Retaining the Room to Maneuver*

Gretchen Helmke, *Institutions on the Edge: The Origins and Consequences of Inter-Branch Crises in Latin America*

Gretchen Helmke, *Courts Under Constraints: Judges, Generals, and Presidents in Argentina*

Yoshiko Herrera, *Imagined Economies: The Sources of Russian Regionalism*

Alisha C. Holland, *Forbearance as Redistribution: The Politics of Informal Welfare in Latin America*

J. Rogers Hollingsworth and Robert Boyer, eds., *Contemporary Capitalism: The Embeddedness of Institutions*

Yue Hou, *The Private Sector in Public Office: Selective Property Rights in China*

John D. Huber, *Exclusion by Elections: Inequality, Ethnic Identity, and Democracy*

John D. Huber and Charles R. Shipan, *Deliberate Discretion? The Institutional Foundations of Bureaucratic Autonomy*

Ellen Immergut, *Health Politics: Interests and Institutions in Western Europe*

Torben Iversen, *Capitalism, Democracy, and Welfare*

Torben Iversen, *Contested Economic Institutions*

Torben Iversen, Jonas Pontussen, and David Soskice, eds., *Unions, Employers, and Central Banks: Macroeconomic Coordination and Institutional Change in Social Market Economics*

Thomas Janoski and Alexander M. Hicks, eds., *The Comparative Political Economy of the Welfare State*

Joseph Jupille, *Procedural Politics: Issues, Influence, and Institutional Choice in the European Union*

Karen Jusko, *Who Speaks for the Poor? Electoral Geography, Party Entry, and Representation*

Stathis Kalyvas, *The Logic of Violence in Civil War*

Stephen B. Kaplan, *Globalization and Austerity Politics in Latin America*

David C. Kang, *Crony Capitalism: Corruption and Capitalism in South Korea and the Philippines*

Junko Kato, *Regressive Taxation and the Welfare State*

Orit Kedar, *Voting for Policy, Not Parties: How Voters Compensate for Power Sharing*

Robert O. Keohane and Helen B. Milner, eds., *Internationalization and Domestic Politics*

Herbert Kitschelt, *The Transformation of European Social Democracy*

Herbert Kitschelt, Kirk A. Hawkins, Juan Pablo Luna, Guillermo Rosas, and Elizabeth J. Zechmeister, *Latin American Party Systems*

Herbert Kitschelt, Peter Lange, Gary Marks, and John D. Stephens, eds., *Continuity and Change in Contemporary Capitalism*

Herbert Kitschelt, Zdenka Mansfeldova, Radek Markowski, and Gabor Toka, *Post-Communist Party Systems*

David Knoke, Franz Urban Pappi, Jeffrey Broadbent, and Yutaka Tsujinaka, eds., *Comparing Policy Networks*

Ken Kollman, *Perils of Centralization: Lessons from Church, State, and Corporation*

Allan Kornberg and Harold D. Clarke, *Citizens and Community: Political Support in a Representative Democracy*

Amie Kreppel, *The European Parliament and the Supranational Party System*

David D. Laitin, *Language Repertoires and State Construction in Africa*

Fabrice E. Lehoucq and Ivan Molina, *Stuffing the Ballot Box: Fraud, Electoral Reform, and Democratization in Costa Rica*

Benjamin Lessing, *Making Peace in Drug Wars: Crackdowns and Cartels in Latin America*

Janet I. Lewis, *How Insurgency Begins: Rebel Group Formation in Uganda and Beyond*

Mark Irving Lichbach and Alan S. Zuckerman, eds., *Comparative Politics: Rationality, Culture, and Structure, 2nd edition*

Evan Lieberman, *Race and Regionalism in the Politics of Taxation in Brazil and South Africa*

Richard M. Locke, *The Promise and Limits of Private Power: Promoting Labor Standards in a Global Economy*

Julia Lynch, *Age in the Welfare State: The Origins of Social Spending on Pensioners, Workers, and Children*

Pauline Jones Luong, *Institutional Change and Political Continuity in Post-Soviet Central Asia*

Pauline Jones Luong and Erika Weinthal, *Oil is Not a Curse: Ownership Structure and Institutions in Soviet Successor States*

Doug McAdam, John McCarthy, and Mayer Zald, eds., *Comparative Perspectives on Social Movements*

Gwyneth H. McClendon and Rachel Beatty Riedl, *From Pews to Politics in Africa: Religious Sermons and Political Behavior*

Lauren M. MacLean, *Informal Institutions and Citizenship in Rural Africa: Risk and Reciprocity in Ghana and Côte d'Ivoire*

Beatriz Magaloni, *Voting for Autocracy: Hegemonic Party Survival and its Demise in Mexico*

James Mahoney, *Colonialism and Postcolonial Development: Spanish America in Comparative Perspective*

James Mahoney and Dietrich Rueschemeyer, eds., *Historical Analysis and the Social Sciences*

Scott Mainwaring and Matthew Soberg Shugart, eds., *Presidentialism and Democracy in Latin America*

Melanie Manion, *Information for Autocrats: Representation in Chinese Local Congresses*

Isabela Mares, *From Open Secrets to Secret Voting: Democratic Electoral Reforms and Voter Autonomy*

Isabela Mares, *The Politics of Social Risk: Business and Welfare State Development*

Isabela Mares, *Taxation, Wage Bargaining, and Unemployment*

Cathie Jo Martin and Duane Swank, *The Political Construction of Business Interests: Coordination, Growth, and Equality*

Anthony W. Marx, *Making Race, Making Nations: A Comparison of South Africa, the United States, and Brazil*

Daniel C. Mattingly, *The Art of Political Control in China*

Kevin Mazur, *Revolution in Syria: Identity, Networks, and Repression*

Bonnie M. Meguid, *Party Competition between Unequals: Strategies and Electoral Fortunes in Western Europe*

Joel S. Migdal, *State in Society: Studying How States and Societies Constitute One Another*

Joel S. Migdal, Atul Kohli, and Vivienne Shue, eds., *State Power and Social Forces: Domination and Transformation in the Third World*

Eduardo Moncada, *Resisting Extortion: Victims, Criminals and States in Latin America*

Scott Morgenstern and Benito Nacif, eds., *Legislative Politics in Latin America*

Kevin M. Morrison, *Nontaxation and Representation: The Fiscal Foundations of Political Stability*

Layna Mosley, *Global Capital and National Governments*

Layna Mosley, *Labor Rights and Multinational Production*

Wolfgang C. Müller and Kaare Strøm, *Policy, Office, or Votes?*

Maria Victoria Murillo, *Political Competition, Partisanship, and Policy Making in Latin American Public Utilities*

Maria Victoria Murillo, *Labor Unions, Partisan Coalitions, and Market Reforms in Latin America*

Monika Nalepa, *Skeletons in the Closet: Transitional Justice in Post-Communist Europe*

Noah L. Nathan, *Electoral Politics and Africa's Urban Transition: Class and Ethnicity in Ghana*

Ton Notermans, *Money, Markets, and the State: Social Democratic Economic Policies since 1918*

Simeon Nichter, *Votes for Survival: Relational Clientelism in Latin America*

Richard A. Nielsen, *Deadly Clerics: Blocked Ambition and the Paths to Jihad*

Aníbal Pérez-Liñán, *Presidential Impeachment and the New Political Instability in Latin America*

Roger D. Petersen, *Understanding Ethnic Violence: Fear, Hatred, and Resentment in Twentieth-Century Eastern Europe*

Roger D. Petersen, *Western Intervention in the Balkans: The Strategic Use of Emotion in Conflict*

Simona Piattoni, ed., *Clientelism, Interests, and Democratic Representation*

Paul Pierson, *Dismantling the Welfare State? Reagan, Thatcher, and the Politics of Retrenchment*

Marino Regini, *Uncertain Boundaries: The Social and Political Construction of European Economies*

Philipp Rehm, *Risk Inequality and Welfare States: Social Policy Preferences, Development, and Dynamics*

Kenneth M. Roberts, *Changing Course in Latin America: Party Systems in the Neoliberal Era*

Marc Howard Ross, *Cultural Contestation in Ethnic Conflict*

David Rueda and Daniel Stegmueller, *Who Wants What? Redistribution Preferences in Comparative Perspective*

Ignacio Sánchez-Cuenca, *The Historical Roots of Political Violence: Revolutionary Terrorism in Affluent Countries*

Ben Ross Schneider, *Hierarchical Capitalism in Latin America: Business, Labor, and the Challenges of Equitable Development*

Roger Schoenman, *Networks and Institutions in Europe's Emerging Markets*

Lyle Scruggs, *Sustaining Abundance: Environmental Performance in Industrial Democracies*

Jefferey M. Sellers, *Governing from Below: Urban Regions and the Global Economy*

Yossi Shain and Juan Linz, eds., *Interim Governments and Democratic Transitions*

Beverly Silver, *Forces of Labor: Workers' Movements and Globalization since 1870*

Prerna Singh, *How Solidarity Works for Welfare: Subnationalism and Social Development in India*

Theda Skocpol, *Social Revolutions in the Modern World*

Dan Slater, *Ordering Power: Contentious Politics and Authoritarian Leviathans in Southeast Asia*

Austin Smith et al., *Selected Works of Michael Wallerstein*

Regina Smyth, *Candidate Strategies and Electoral Competition in the Russian Federation: Democracy Without Foundation*

Richard Snyder, *Politics after Neoliberalism: Reregulation in Mexico*

David Stark and László Bruszt, *Postsocialist Pathways: Transforming Politics and Property in East Central Europe*

Sven Steinmo, *The Evolution of Modern States: Sweden, Japan, and the United States*

Sven Steinmo, Kathleen Thelen, and Frank Longstreth, eds., *Structuring Politics: Historical Institutionalism in Comparative Analysis*

Susan C. Stokes, *Mandates and Democracy: Neoliberalism by Surprise in Latin America*

Susan C. Stokes, ed., *Public Support for Market Reforms in New Democracies*

Susan C. Stokes, Thad Dunning, Marcelo Nazareno, and Valeria Brusco, *Brokers, Voters, and Clientelism: The Puzzle of Distributive Politics*

Milan W. Svolik, *The Politics of Authoritarian Rule*

Duane Swank, *Global Capital, Political Institutions, and Policy Change in Developed Welfare States*

David Szakonyi *Politics for Profit: Business, Elections, and Policymaking in Russia*

Sidney Tarrow, *Power in Movement: Social Movements and Contentious Politics*

Sidney Tarrow, *Power in Movement: Social Movements and Contentious Politics, Revised and Updated Third Edition*

Tariq Thachil, *Elite Parties, Poor Voters: How Social Services Win Votes in India*

Kathleen Thelen, *How Institutions Evolve: The Political Economy of Skills in Germany, Britain, the United States, and Japan*

Kathleen Thelen, *Varieties of Liberalization and the New Politics of Social Solidarity*

Charles Tilly, *Trust and Rule*

Daniel Treisman, *The Architecture of Government: Rethinking Political Decentralization*

Guillermo Trejo, *Popular Movements in Autocracies: Religion, Repression, and Indigenous Collective Action in Mexico*

Guillermo Trejo and Sandra Ley, *Votes, Drugs, and Violence: The Political Logic of Criminal Wars in Mexico*

Rory Truex, *Making Autocracy Work: Representation and Responsiveness in Modern China*

Lily L. Tsai, *Accountability without Democracy: How Solidary Groups Provide Public Goods in Rural China*

Lily L. Tsai, *When People Want Punishment: Retributive Justice and the Puzzle of Authoritarian Popularity*

Joshua Tucker, *Regional Economic Voting: Russia, Poland, Hungary, Slovakia and the Czech Republic, 1990–1999*

Ashutosh Varshney, *Democracy, Development, and the Countryside*

Yuhua Wang, *Tying the Autocrat's Hand: The Rise of The Rule of Law in China*

Jeremy M. Weinstein, *Inside Rebellion: The Politics of Insurgent Violence*

Andreas Wiedemann, *Indebted Societies: Credit and Welfare in Rich Democracies*

Martha Wilfahrt, *Precolonial Legacies in Postcolonial Politics: Representation and Redistribution in Decentralized West Africa*

Stephen I. Wilkinson, *Votes and Violence: Electoral Competition and Ethnic Riots in India*

Andreas Wimmer, *Waves of War: Nationalism, State Formation, and Ethnic Exclusion in the Modern World*

Jason Wittenberg, *Crucibles of Political Loyalty: Church Institutions and Electoral Continuity in Hungary*

Elisabeth J. Wood, *Forging Democracy from Below: Insurgent Transitions in South Africa and El Salvador*

Elisabeth J. Wood, *Insurgent Collective Action and Civil War in El Salvador*

Deborah J. Yashar, *Homicidal Ecologies: Illicit Economies and Complicit States in Latin America*

Daniel Ziblatt, *Conservative Parties and the Birth of Democracy*

David Austen-Smith, Jeffry A. Frieden, Miriam A. Golden, Karl Ove Moene, and
  Adam Przeworski, eds.,*Selected Works of Michael Wallerstein: The Political
  Economy of Inequality, Unions, and Social Democracy*
S. Erdem Aytaç and Susan C. Stokes, *Why Bother? Rethinking Participation in
  Elections and Protests*
Andy Baker, *The Market and the Masses in Latin America: Policy Reform and
  Consumption in Liberalizing Economies*

CPSIA information can be obtained
at www.ICGtesting.com
Printed in the USA
BVHW041809110522
636808BV00001B/17